Advertising
in Contemporary Society

Advertising in Contemporary Society

Perspectives toward Understanding

Third Edition

Kim B. Rotzoll and James E. Haefner

with Steven R. Hall

University of Illinois Press

Urbana and Chicago

© 1996 by the Board of Trustees of the University of Illinois
Manufactured in the United States of America
1 2 3 4 5 C P 5 4 3 2 1

This book is printed on acid-free paper.

Library of Congress Cataloging-in-Publication Data
Rotzoll, Kim B.
Advertising in contemporary society : perspectives toward
understand / Kim B. Rotzoll and James E. Haefner with
Steven R. Hall. — 3rd ed.
p. cm.
Includes bibliographical references and index.
   ISBN 0-252-02212-2 (acid-free paper). —
   ISBN 0-252-06542-5 (pbk. : acid-free paper)
   1. Advertising. I. Haefner, James E. II. Hall,
Steven R. III. Title.
HF5821.R67   1996
659.1'042—dc20   95-41806
                                               CIP

Teresa Mastin
Fall '94

Contents

Preface

"It appears to me," William Dean Howells said in 1893, "that our enterprising American advertising has about reached its limit."[1] About advertising at least, Howells is clearly not one of our better prophets.

Advertising is a paradox. It is with us constantly, sometimes sought out, but generally unloved. It may be tolerated, but it is rarely championed. It is the giver of jokes and the target of them. It displays more about our more selfish, grasping natures than we find comforting to address as often as it relentlessly assures we must. The public's judgments of its ethical standards place it at or near the bottom of virtually any occupational array, while leading academics savage its social and cultural role. There is also no real shelter under the cloak of expertise, for many of us may realize that we couldn't (or shouldn't) prescribe a drug, examine an optical system, design a house or bridge, or prepare a legal brief, but we're pretty certain *we* could come up with one of those catchy slogans, clever headlines, or arresting jingles.

All of this, of course, sometimes makes it difficult to take advertising seriously. Yet, an article in the *Chronicle of Higher Education* carried the headline "Scholars Sold on the Importance of Studying Advertising's History and Role in Society" in which the author discussed six book-length treatments of advertising from communication scholars, historians, and a sociologist.[2] The *New York Times* devoted a half page to "The Big Pitch for Old Ads," with the subheading "More Scholars Mine Madison Avenue's Past for Clues on How the Culture Has Changed."[3] Advertising may be unloved, but it seems to be at least intriguing.

On a somewhat less lofty plane, T-shirts and everyday discourse attest to the advertising-spawned influences in our popular culture, advertisers scramble for the somewhat dubious honor of paying in excess of $1,000,000 for thirty seconds of television time during the Super Bowl and eagerly explore the commercial potentials of the Internet-cyberspace-interactive future, all the while critics are viewing with alarm what the *Washington Post* has referred to as "The Commercialization of Almost Everything."[4]

•   •   •

Almost two decades have passed since the first edition of this work was published. And, as the brief sampling of diversities above suggests, advertising in contemporary society is still a crossroad where many interests meet and, not infrequently, collide. Then, as now, we attempt to offer readers

1. A basically *deductive approach* to the subject matter
2. A source that attempts to raise provocative questions in a context that may provide some overall *understanding* of their implications
3. A basic *format* for the organization of a college-level or university-level course in the subject area

When approaching the frequently highly charged subject area of advertising and society, there is a temptation to fill academic hours with yeasty discussions of timely topics likely to spur immediate student interest. Such potentially provocative subjects might include children and advertising; cigarettes, beer, sex, and advertising (perennial favorites); and the elusive advertising and the "quality of life."

For better or worse, we have avoided this ad hoc avenue of study. We first offer basic perspectives (part 1), which may be fruitfully brought to bear in an attempt to understand advertising, and only then turn our attention to issues of consequence (part 2), which seem likely to endure as long as the institution itself.

If there is a prevailing theme to the book, it is simply that how we as individuals think about things has a great deal to do with how we perceive them, how we act toward them, the kinds of "problems" that we define, and what we may consider appropriate "solutions."

Our former colleague Richard Nielsen once offered the tale of the three scholars shipwrecked on a desolate island with but a single can of beans. The chemist suggested, "We can build a fire, place the can in it, and the ensuing molecular activity will cause the can to rupture, thus freeing the contents." The engineer added, "If we construct an enclosure from indigenous materials, we can contain the contents of the ruptured vessel." Their eyes turned to the economist, who said, "Assume we have a can opener . . ."

Basically, the "assumptions" we make about what advertising *is* doing in society, as well as what it *ought* to be doing, are, we believe, crucial to understanding much about the defenses raised, charges aired, and practices endorsed or condemned.

This new edition maintains the thrust of its predecessors but is, we feel, conceptually richer and more ambitious in its sweep. Every word has been examined anew. We have, of course, updated with fresh examples to ground the basic perspectives in contemporary realities. Both academic concepts and professional concerns are interwoven throughout. In short, we hope the reader of this edition will emerge with both a clear sense of the landscape of advertising thought and practice in the last decade of this century and, of greatest lasting importance, an understanding of perspectives to help make sense of it all.

We are, of course, indebted to many. Vince Norris first exposed Rotzoll to advertising's larger picture during provocative years at Penn State and has continued to serve as both mentor and gadfly. Arnold Barban, now of Alabama, suggested the idea of a book based on the structure of the University of Illinois course by the same name.

Our colleague Charles Sandage has been elected to the Advertising Hall of Fame, the only modern-day educator so honored. It was clearly Sandy's farsighted principles-first approach to advertising education and his Socratic examinations during his prolific teaching years at Illinois that provided the true inspiration for this work. Still youthful in intellect and demeanor in his early nineties, he continues to enlighten us.

And a word of appreciation to countless colleagues who have, over the years, offered us their insights through their conversations, letters, and general probings in these interesting waters. Particular thanks go to Richard Pollay of the University of British Columbia and Gordon Miracle of Michigan State. Both offered valuable suggestions on the second edition that, we hope, they will find reflected here. Thanks also go to numerous colleagues throughout the country who have indicated their appreciation for the book's perspectives by using it in their own teaching and scholarship.

Finally, Rotzoll has had the pleasure of teaching the course Advertising in Contemporary Society at Illinois for the last twenty-five years. To all the students from whom I have learned so much, my thanks. The torch is passed.

Notes

1. William Dean Howells quoted in Stephen Fox, *The Mirror Makers* (New York: William Morrow, 1984), 39.

2. "Scholars Sold on the Importance of Studying Advertising's History and Role in Society," *Chronicle of Higher Education,* Oct. 3, 1984, 5–6.

3. Randall Rothenberg, "The Big New Pitch for Old Ads," *New York Times,* Oct. 9, 1988, sect. 4, p. 3.

4. Peter Carlson, "It's an Ad, Ad, Ad, Ad World," *Washington Post Magazine,* Nov. 3, 1992.

Introduction:
Tools to "Clear the Deadwood"

The late Howard Gossage, a member of the Copywriters Hall of Fame and resident critic of the business, once served a stint as a visiting professor of advertising at Penn State. Reflecting on the experience, he observed: "In my lecturing I find I must spend about half my time clearing away the deadwood before I can begin to talk constructively about advertising and what it can do and occasionally does do."[1]

Students and teachers of advertising can probably be sympathetic to this. Simply, advertising in America comes with a great deal of baggage that often gets in the way of any reasonably dispassionate attempt to understand the subject. As we will attempt to make clear, some of this baggage comes with each of us—i.e., we "see with our ideas as well as our eyes," to borrow Walton Hamilton's wonderful phrase[2]—while some is simply inherent in the complexity of the business and its processes.

We all feel we know advertising very well—often *too* well—in part because we are exposed to so much of it and also because its often simpleminded content makes it easy to understand (and sometimes hard to forget). As a result, we find it easy to generalize and offer sweeping assertions that begin with "Advertising does . . ." and "All ads are . . ." By way of example, a critic observed with seeming omnipotence that "our system of advertising purposefully promotes envy, creates anxiety, and fosters insecurity,"[3] and seasoned advertising executives have often defended advertising practice with simpleminded phrases such as "Advertising follows, it doesn't lead." So much for caution in murky waters. Such lack of needed qualification deadens analysis, cheapening the subject and the observer alike.

The purpose of this introduction, then, is to share with you four premises that we have found quite useful in preparing the fascinating topic of advertising and society for meaningful discussion—for "clearing away the deadwood." We believe that if we keep these four ideas in mind from the outset, the subject is more likely to be clarified through analysis rather than through argument.

1. Advertising must be considered in light of cultural expectations.
2. The advertising process has varied intents and effects.
3. Advertising's actual effects are usually not clearly known.
4. Because of its cultural boundness, its complexity of forms and functions, and the difficulty in ascertaining its outcome, advertising is highly prone to disparate interpretations.

Let's examine each.

Advertising Must Be Considered in Light of Cultural Expectations

It has been reported that the United States spends more money on advertising than sixty-six other nations combined, including Japan, the United Kingdom, Germany, Canada, and France.[4] One might pause to wonder why our relatively young nation should assume such leadership and why first-time visitors to this country are often stunned by the sheer presence of advertising in virtually every facet of our lives—a presence many of us simply take for granted.

Two authors of important books on American advertising—one a historian, the other a sociologist—offer us insights about the wellsprings of advertising in America.

Stephen Fox:

> One may build a compelling case that American culture is—beyond redemption—money mad, hedonistic, superficial, rushing heedlessly down a railroad track called Progress. De Tocqueville and other observers of the young republic describe America in these terms in the early 1800s, decades before the development of national advertising.[5]

And Michael Schudson:

> We live and shall live, barring nuclear or other disaster, in what has been called a "promotional culture." America has long been a nation of salesmen and the "shoeshine and a smile" that were Willy Loman's stock-in-

trade are now the tools of politicians and religious evangelists and hospital administrators as much as of advertising agents and public-relations directors. The promotional culture has worked its way into what we read, what we care about, the ways we raise our children, our ideas of right and wrong conduct, our attribution of significance to "image" in both public and private life. The promotional culture has been celebrated and indulged in. It has been ridiculed and reviled. It still needs to be understood.[6]

Given how deeply rooted it is in our society, it is not difficult to understand why advertising seems so "natural" to us. It follows, then, that an important first step in coming to grips with advertising in contemporary society is grasping what, generally, the society expects of it—how advertising might fit into what Walton Hamilton has called the dominant institution in a society, "that body of ideas taken for granted which is called common sense."[7]

In this society, these "ideas" have generally included at least a toleration (and sometimes admiration) of *persuasion* (Schudson's "promotional culture"), based on such well-worn assumptions as self-interest as a driving force of human action, the ability of a person to be "deliberate and calculating" in pursuit of that self-interest, and the implicit expectation that the self-interested actions of individuals will ultimately work themselves out for the good of the whole.

Now, most Americans feel quite at home with these notions, which can have a strong influence on our perceptions of the world around us, often without our awareness of them. Consider, for example, how easily we accept not only the enormous presence of advertising in our mass media but also in/around/above our athletic stadiums, on our clothing, beside our roadways, in our motion picture theaters, and so forth. Somehow, it all seems "natural," and it is important that we keep this in mind from the outset.

For much of advertising in contemporary society can be understood with greater clarity if we realize that, as James W. Carey expressed it, "institutions are the embodiment of *ideas*."[8] And from the beginning, we need to understand what these ideas, these expectations, are to fully understand our society's institutions—including advertising.

Now, what else do we need to keep in mind to "clear the deadwood"?

⎯⎯⎯ The Advertising Process Has Varied Intents and Effects

In addition to understanding the ideas with which we "see" advertising, we have to keep in mind that the advertising each of us is normally exposed to is only a fraction of all the advertising activity underway—and, all too frequently, we tend to generalize from that relatively limited experience to the whole. Consider, for example, that while you read these pages, *at least* the following advertising functions are under way:

- *Producers* (singly or in association, national or regional) of consumer goods and services are advertising to reach prospective consumers through radio, television, magazines, newspapers, billboards, direct mail, transit, and other media to encourage sales of a branded product or service. (An ad for a soft drink on network television is an example.)
- *Producers* (singly or in association, national or regional) of consumer goods and services for *resale* are advertising to reach retailers and wholesalers through trade magazines, newsletters, and direct mail to encourage retailers and wholesalers to stock and promote the product or service to *their* customers. (An ad for a brand of flea collar in *Pet Store Owner* is an example.)
- *Producers* (singly or in association, national or regional) of consumer and business goods and services are advertising to reach prospective consumers, government, groups, and their own employees through consumer and business print and broadcast media to influence favorable thinking and possible action among key groups concerning *public relations*. (An oil company advertising in the *New York Times* to boast of its conservation efforts is an example.)
- *Producers* (singly or in association) of consumer and business goods and services are advertising to reach other producers, retailers and wholesalers, government, social institutions, and groups through business magazines and newsletters, direct mail, and some consumer media to encourage sales for a particular *business* product or service for use or recommendation. (A manufacturer of oil drilling bits advertising in *Oil and Gas Journal* is an example.)
- *Producers* (singly or in association) of consumer and business goods and services in *international* distribution are advertising to reach individual consumers, retailers, other businesses, governments, social institutions, and groups through consumer and business media in other countries to encourage specific purchases, to influence key groups, and to foster retail distribution. (An American fast-food franchise advertising in German newspapers and a producer advertising Russian vodka in American magazines are examples.)

- *Retailers* (singly or in association) of goods and services are advertising to reach potential consumers through local newspapers, radio, television, magazines, billboards, transit, and direct mail to encourage purchases of particular items and/or services. (A supermarket ad is an example.)
- *Individual citizens* are advertising to reach other citizens, primarily through local newspapers (classified), posters, electronic bulletin boards, etc. to encourage purchases of a particular item or service. (A student advertising to sell a bike in the campus newspaper is an example.)
- *Governments, organizations, and groups* are advertising to reach persons, government bodies, groups, and associations through consumer and specialized media to encourage belief in particular practices, to alter behavior in socially desirable ways, and to seek political ends, as well as to "sell." (The Save the Children Foundation seeking donations in a magazine ad is an example.)

Now, there is much to be learned from these varied advertising activities, particularly in the clearing-the-deadwood sense.

For starters, when we begin to discuss advertising with others we'd better be certain we know what parts of advertising we're talking about. For example, are critics distinguishing between the advertising of the Great Book Series in the *New Yorker* and the thirty-second minidrama concerning sanitary napkins in late prime time when they assert that advertising is irritating? And are supporters being appropriately selective between (say) a simpleminded jingle for toothpaste and a supermarket ad when they assert baldly that "Advertising provides consumers with useful product information"? Simply, these are different forms with different *intents*, not easily compared.

And do all advertisers use advertising with identical *expectations?* Most, of course, are *ultimately* interested in altering behavior in some way—for instance, getting people to switch to their product—but advertisers may have many different strategies to achieve that end—such as establishing awareness *or* communicating new selling information *or* reinforcing existing brand loyalty *or* attempting to alter attitudes, etc.

Then there is advertising's interdependency with other tools of marketing. Clearly, for example, the advertising of a firm relying primarily on personal selling (e.g., Avon) is expected to achieve far different ends than that of a company using advertising to attempt to establish brand name preference in expectation of future purchases in retail outlets (e.g., Revlon). A business-to-business advertiser might be interested in using the company's advertising to secure direct orders *or* developing leads for the sales force. Sales promotion contests and the like can be advertised either to retailers *or* to potential customers *or* both. And so on.

Not infrequently, there are also intents that are anything but obvious to the outside observer. For example, a marketing manager of a large urban hospital confided, "I'm certain that at least two important groups read our ads—our employees and our competitors. If the ads do nothing more than influence them they'll have paid their way." Yet, if each of us were asked to assess whether this hospital's advertisements were "effective," we would probably have assumed they were directed to potential patients and make our judgments with that "target audience" in mind.

Thus, to evaluate an advertisement, it would seem prudent to at least attempt to understand the *type of advertising* as well as the *advertiser's intent*. Due to the presence of myriad agendas—some more apparent than others—even that may not be as simple as we might expect.

Nor, of course, is the *individual's response*. A headline for an advertisement from the American Association of Advertising Agencies suggested our sometimes unpredictable selectivity: "Isn't it Funny How Stereo Ads are Boring until You Want a Stereo?" We do, of course, selectively perceive advertisements, as we do other items in our environment. (Former practitioner Howard Gossage often commented, "Nobody reads ads *per se*. People read what interests them, and sometimes it's an ad."[9]) Now, one could, then, assume that as media become more specialized—and the "fit" between media vehicle and audience interests more precise—the irritation factor of advertising will diminish. Thus, a person watching a cable sports channel, one seeking out commercial information on the Internet, or another reading *Modern Maturity* magazine, may be more likely to find advertisements of interest than the same persons watching the unpredictable advertising mix on prime-time network television.

Of course the advertising encounters may be involuntary as well, since much of the time advertising seeks *us* rather than the other way around, with our responses ranging from surprise, amusement, or interest to irritation, disgust, or apathy.

There are, then, many different advertisers using advertising for many different purposes with many different possible reactions from those exposed, much less those missed. All of which would seem to reinforce the stupidity and unproductiveness of "Advertising does . . ." thinking.

———— Advertising's Actual Effects Are Usually Not Clearly Known

Commenting on advertising's presumed cultural influence, the historian Stephen Fox observed: "Outsiders see only the smooth, expertly contrived finished product, often better crafted than the programming and editorial material it interrupts. Insiders know the messy process of creating an ad, the false starts, rejected ideas, midnight despair, the failures and account losses and creative angst behind any ad that finally appears."[10]

If one were to harbor any illusions about the omnipotence of the advertising process in the hands of steely-eyed technicians of communication, Fox's observation should give us pause. And certainly the television critic Michael Arlen's engrossing account of the creative odyssey of a single AT&T advertisement[11] and John Pfeiffer's disbelieving description of the creation of two Rolaids commercials[12] should turn us into card-carrying skeptics.

Simply, trafficking in the uncertain realms of symbolic persuasion as they do, advertisers find it difficult to be as powerful as they might like—and as influential as critics assume. There are, we believe, two central reasons:

1. *It is difficult to determine advertising's effect in relation to other possible influences on the same outcome.*

    As we all know, most advertisers, most of the time, are interested in affecting behavior with their messages. But they are also interested in affecting behavior with their pricing strategy, sales promotional efforts, sales force deployment, packaging, and so on. (The currently in vogue term "integrated advertising/marketing communications" reconfirms the interdependence of advertising with other elements of the advertiser's "marketing mix.") So if behavior *does* occur (e.g., someone buys an advertised product) it's usually quite difficult to determine which part (if any) of the influencing process belongs to advertising and which to all of these other factors controlled by the advertiser and attempting to achieve the same end.

    Then there are those factors the advertiser *cannot* control. Start with the fickle fads and fancies of the public, currently embracing such socio-pop phenomena as wellness, cocooning, channel surfing, food grazing, "safe" sex, and a generalized assertion of more "traditional" values. Add the often vexing unknowns of the weather, for example, or the competition. Or consider the impact of the state of the economy, the regulatory/antiregulatory mood in Washington or in the state capitals, breakthroughs in technology, and on and on. These and many other such factors can strongly influence what people may or may not buy and are the "givens" that advertisers can rarely alter, but must inevitably accommodate. With the notable exception of direct-response advertising, and a few other forms with an extremely tight advertising-action loop, advertising's success (or lack of it) is, at best, one contribution among many.

2. *It is difficult to determine advertising's actual effects because of the quixotic nature of human thought and behavior.*

Human beings are, as one practitioner wryly commented, "no damned good" when it comes to always behaving according to marketers' expectations—e.g., a creative chief at a sophisticated advertising agency admitted with a shrug that a two-year multimillion-dollar campaign for a popular soft drink was simply "wrong," even though the agency had every reason to believe it was "right on target" when it was proposed and implemented.

Advertising's elusive target is, of course, the individual, and she or he is *quite* a challenge. Why? Well, if we conceive of the forces at work to influence an individual's observed behavior at any given moment as constituting a "frame of reference," we soon realize that the interaction of factors outside of ourselves (e.g., the presence or absence of other people, the physical environment) and those inside ourselves (e.g., our moods, past experiences, current knowledge, physiological state) *changes from moment to moment.*[13] To return to the earlier example, we may not be interested in that stereo ad at the moment, but tomorrow, or next week . . .

Given this backcloth of uncertainty, then, much can be understood about advertising thought and practice—some trivial, some of considerable consequence.

- *The longevity of the commission system of agency remuneration.* If there were any adequate measure of performance in the marketplace, advertisers would compensate their agencies on the basis of their proven successes on the advertiser's behalf. Lacking that, advertisers frequently rely on a hoary system that rewards the agency not for how well its products (ads) perform—which, as we have seen, they frequently don't know—but for how much of the advertiser's money it spends. ("You show me a business," Gossage commented, "where one's income is dependent on the amount of money spent rather than on the amount of money that comes in and I will show you a business that is doomed, even with the very best of intentions, to mutual distrust and enormous psychological barriers."[14])

- *The "me-too" nature of much advertising content.* If practitioners are frequently uncertain about what will "work" with their ads, they may be inclined to imitate those that presumably are certain. Just think of the countless imitators of the "MTV style" or the use of the hand-held camera with quick/jumpy cuts or computer-generated graphics or "morphing" special effects or celebrities (living or dead) or "spokesanimals" or . . . fill in your own examples.

- *The lack of true "professionalism" in the business.* Here someone scuttles an advertising campaign because he doesn't like the "look" of the female model. There an account executive is browbeaten by an advertising manager because her agency could not come up with some "new, creative ideas." (The J. Walter Thompson agency, having lost the giant Burger King account, ran a farewell ad in *Advertising Age* with a graph showing that Burger King's sales had increased 145 percent since coming with the agency. *Sic transit gloria.*[15]) Or witness the countrywide "creative" award ceremonies, often requiring no proof of marketplace performance, but focusing instead on the "likability" or "overall impression" of thirty-second commercials, momentarily transformed from uncertain exercises in persuasive communication to spotlighted art forms.

If we are to begin to understand advertising in contemporary society, then, it is essential that we constantly keep in mind the frequent uncertainty of the process—and the far-reaching consequences of that reality.

Because of Its Cultural Boundness, Its Complexity of Forms and Functions, and the Difficulty in Ascertaining Its Outcome, Advertising Is Highly Prone to Disparate Interpretations

Psychologists tell us that ongoing psychological activity tends toward *patterning* of experience—i.e., looking for order rather than being satisfied with randomness. Now, sometimes order is inherent in the experience—e.g., we see a picture of a cube and recognize it as such—and little additional structuring from our own experiences, or interpretation, is required. But when the experience is fluid, ambiguous, lacking in clear definition—e.g., we see an inkblot—each of us "makes sense" of it by supplying our own patterning, by interpreting. Ask people to interpret an abstract painting and there will probably be as many different interpretations as there are people; ask the same people to interpret a realistic photograph and there will be general agreement.

Now, given the variance in the cultural expectations for advertising, the variety of advertising forms and functions, and the difficulty in assessing advertising's "effects," it can be contended that advertising in contemporary society is highly susceptible to differing interpretations because of its complexity, fluidity, and lack of clear outcome. That is, it's much more like an inkblot than a cube. To follow this reasoning, then, *much of what is seen in advertising depends on who's looking and where.*

In relation to the *who*, to note the obvious, critics "see" advertising very differently than do supporters. For them, the reality is very clearly patterned as exploitation of a frequently helpless public by advertisements that intrude, debase the language and our symbolic life, and appeal to our worst rather than best characteristics. Supporters, observing the *same* spectrum, "see" advertising joining the self-interests of sellers with the self-interests of savvy customers to their mutual satisfactions with advertisements that faithfully mirror the totality (rational *and* emotional) of the human condition. These strikingly different perceptions can be explained in part by the past experiences, values, and current aspirations of the observers. Argue though they may, they're simply not likely to "see" advertising the same way.

In relation to the *where*, there is also the very real possibility that discussants may simply be observing *different parts of the whole.* As we know, business-to-business advertising, for example, is quite different in purpose, content, and media form than most "consumer" advertising directed to individuals. Even *within* a type (say, retail advertising), one can come to quite different conclusions because all retailers do not have similar intents with their advertising, nor are they likely to have similar effects. So if we are using a particular type of advertising as our (often implicit) reference point, we may come to very different conclusions, regardless of our predispositions, than if we were looking elsewhere.

So, to begin to "clear away the deadwood" in any discussion of advertising, it would seem prudent to *at least* determine what the culture expects of advertising and to recognize that advertising presents itself in many different forms for many different purposes. Further, we need to recognize that the determination of the success of those efforts is, under the best of conditions, obscure; and finally, because of all these conditions, we need to be clear about who's looking (what the assumptions are) and where (at what form or forms).

_____ Summary

"Advertisements" are bits and pieces of reality. "Advertising" is an abstraction from these elements, and much more. At the outset of our approach to advertising in contemporary society we suggest four premises to begin a serious look at advertising:

1. *Advertising must be considered in light of cultural expectations.* Advertising can play different roles in different societies, depending on the set of assumptions held about such fundamental matters as the relationship between individual and societal interests.
2. *The advertising process has varied intents and effects.* There are many different types of advertisers using advertising for a variety of different purposes, arguing against the common tendency to generalize to the "All advertising . . ." level.
3. *Advertising's actual effects are usually not clearly known.* Most advertisers are interested in affecting behavior—usually sales. But because advertising is affected by societal forces and is only one factor in the firm's marketing options, and because individuals' reactions to advertisements are inherently complex and unpredictable, simple cause-and-effect conclusions are elusive.
4. *Because of its cultural boundness, its complexity of forms and functions, and the difficulty in ascertaining its outcome, advertising is highly prone to disparate interpretations.* Advertising can be loosely compared to the inkblot, with patterning through perceptions affected by who is doing the observing and where in its complex overall structure one chooses to look.

These are, we feel, necessary reference points as we begin to probe this fascinating subject—advertising and advertisements—which Daniel Boorstin has called "the characteristic rhetoric of democracy."[16]

Notes

1. Howard Luck Gossage, *Is There Any Hope for Advertising?* ed. Kim Rotzoll, Jarlath Graham, and Barrows Mussey (Urbana: University of Illinois Press, 1986), 18.
2. Walton Hamilton, "Institution," *The Encyclopedia of the Social Sciences* (New York: Macmillan, 1932), 8:88.
3. Ronald K. L. Collins and Michael F. Jacobson, "Commercialism versus Culture," *Christian Science Monitor,* Sept. 19, 1990, 19.

4. Lena Vanier, "U.S. Ad Spending Double All Other Nations Combined," *Advertising Age*, May 16, 1988, 36.

5. Stephen Fox, *The Mirror Makers* (New York: William Morrow, 1984), 381.

6. Michael Schudson, *Advertising: The Uneasy Persuasion* (New York: Basic Books, 1984), 13.

7. Hamilton, "Institution," 85.

8. James W. Carey, "Advertising: An Institutional Approach," in *The Role of Advertising*, ed. C. H. Sandage and V. Fryburger (Homewood, Ill.: Richard D. Irwin, 1960), 4.

9. Gossage, *Is There Any Hope for Advertising?* 19.

10. Fox, *The Mirror Makers*, 380.

11. Michael G. Arlen, *Thirty Seconds* (New York: Penguin Books, 1980).

12. John Pfeiffer, "Six Months and Half a Million Dollars, All for Fifteen Seconds," *Smithsonian*, Oct. 1987, 134–45.

13. See chap. 8 in C. H. Sandage, Vernon Fryburger, and Kim Rotzoll, *Advertising Theory and Practice* (New York: Longman, 1989).

14. Gossage, *Is There Any Hope for Advertising?* 9.

15. *Advertising Age*, Oct. 12, 1987.

16. Daniel G. Boorstin, "Advertising and American Civilization," in *Advertising and Society*, ed. Yale Brozen (New York: New York University Press, 1974), 11–12.

1

Basic Perspectives

1

Idea Systems ⟷ Institutions: Advertising and Classical Liberalism

In the introduction, we suggested that it's important to keep in mind that advertising can be better understood by examining it in light of cultural expectations. And since the sets of assumptions that cultures hold are commonly expressed as (and reinforced as) institutions, it would seem appropriate to begin with an attempt to explore the relationship between ideas and institutions. For, as Carey contends: "An understanding of advertising rests on an understanding of the nature of ideas and institutions in which advertising found a fertile seedbed to grow. Consequently, much of the modern controversy surrounding advertising is meaningless unless the listener is aware of the implicit assumptions carried by the protagonists about the nature of man, of society, of the economic and political order."[1]

Institutions, Hamilton informs us, "fix the confines of and impose form upon the activities of human beings"[2] or, as Vincent P. Norris puts it, institutions "are the 'rules' according to which social life is carried on."[3] Let's begin, then, with the *ideas*, the "implicit assumptions" as Carey calls them, that are shared in some fundamental way by the members of a society and, hence, shape its institutions—including advertising.

Three Powerful Idea Systems

Any attempt to classify the incredible diversity of human societies risks ridicule. Yet a great deal can, we feel, be illuminated by asserting with Robert L. Heilbroner[4] that at least three powerful idea systems (or "worldviews" or *Weltanschauungen*) have characterized many of our societies and, consequently, have helped shape the institutions that arise to deal with ongoing societal problems: (1) Tradition, (2) Authority, and (3) Classical Liberalism. Some, as we shall see, are far more likely to produce Carey's "fertile seedbed" for advertising than others.

Tradition

Briefly, a society embracing ideas of tradition places a heavy investment in the status quo, often for religious reasons. Events and customs are thought to be as they are for a reason, perhaps known only to a higher power or fate. It is frequently assumed that individuals are performing roles in a drama staged by a strong-willed higher power or, at least, stern ancestors. Thus, economic tasks are handed down from father to son, mother to daughter, with "life chances" virtually set at birth. Any deviation would be considered an affront to those keepers of the tradition, both seen and unseen.

Now, *all* societies have traditional *elements* (e.g., our own family "traditions" surrounding holidays and birthdays), and given the spread of worldwide communications, current examples of entire *societies* based solely on idea systems of tradition do not readily leap to mind. But we need to expand our vision; for this idea system, along with authority, has dominated the activities of hundreds of millions throughout history.

To get a better grasp of the trappings of a traditional society, remember the musical *Fiddler on the Roof*. From the opening song ("You ask me why we do these things, and I'll tell you . . . I don't know. It's *tradition!*") and throughout the play, Tevye, the milkman, confronts the pain of the shattering of tradition as his daughters break from the institution of the matchmaker and his village and its population are uprooted, along with the heavy investment in the past they embody. You may be familiar with the film *Witness*, in which actor Harrison Ford's detective character intervenes in the tradition-rich subculture of the Amish, producing a predictable clash of values and actions ("It's not *our way!*"). On a grander scale, virtually every facet of life in the Middle Ages can be illuminated by understanding the implicit assumptions of the traditional worldview, with the ensuing dominance of the medieval church.

Now, if Idea Systems ⟷ Institutions, would we expect advertising to arise as an institution under an idea system based on tradition? It would seem unlikely. Certainly, a compelling case can be made that one of advertising's primal messages is a call for *change*. Change your hair, your toothpaste, your lifestyle. Aspire to be more. Indulge yourself. Be "all that you can be." These and other siren calls are familiar to us, but they would seem both alien and threatening when perceived from a worldview of tradition.

This is not to say that the modern world cannot produce some striking accommodations of presumably conflicting idea systems. In a trip to Bahrain, a Middle Eastern country with a predominantly traditional society much in the news during the Persian Gulf War, one of the authors led a seminar on advertising practices during which one of the participants used the coffee break to face Mecca and pray. At a nearby shopping center, Arabic women in traditional dress could be seen wearing fashionable footwear and shopping with apparent ease among a plethora of stores offering modern Western products.

Still, a society dominated by ideas of tradition generally would not seem likely to view advertising as a "natural" practice.

Authority

If the idea system of tradition relies on direction from the past, the idea system of authority provides direction in the present and from the top. Basically, the makers of an authoritarian system contend that actions in a society are better determined by a few rather than by many. These few may be presumed to have special connections to a higher power, be proven in combat, hold particular expertise, have been blessed with a high level of intelligence, or possess that elusive element, wisdom. They may be anointed, elected, or affirmed by raw power; and they may be one, a few, or a body. Whatever the rationale and structure for authority, it is assumed that some will direct while others will follow.

Throughout history more civilizations have shared this idea system than any other, with variations ranging from the iron rule of the dictator to the enlightened leadership of a popular revolutionary leader. Here, we find the seedbeds for institutions as diverse as planning boards, concentration camps, five-year plans, and "cultural revolutions."

And what of advertising's presence? On the surface, it would seem that a society choosing, to one degree or another, to have many decisions made from the top down would have no compelling reason to call on such a pervasive form of paid persuasion to attempt to influence the decision making of individuals. Certainly, Hitler had little need for advertising as we know it. Yet even in highly authoritarian societies there are reasons to attempt to reinforce individual thinking and action, if not change it, and advertising has been called on to play a role. Thus, we saw advertising in what we used to call the USSR—to inspire the pursuit of national goals, to encourage particular consumption patterns (e.g., buy margarine rather than butter). Now of course we are likely to see more advertising there directed at personal consumption as the various economies of the new Commonwealth of Independent States (much of the former Soviet Union) begin to develop more "market" characteristics. For, as planning and decision making become more decentralized, advertising is seen as more compatible—e.g., with the reference point of 1979, the People's Republic of China is far more decentralized economically with, predictably, a growing presence of advertising.

Basically, then, societies relying heavily on an idea system of authority make many of the decisions *for* (or "on behalf of") the citizens. Yet, advertising may still be a presence to reinforce decisions that have already been made—e.g., practice family planning in line with government policy—or, as decentralization of authority allows, to offer individuals real alternatives—e.g., government brands competing against imported brands.

Now, as it becomes clear that advertising is more likely to flourish where decision making is decentralized rather than concentrated, we logically move to the most fertile of advertising seedbeds.

Classical Liberalism

It is important from the outset to make clear that we write here of *classical* liberalism, not its modern-day variant. Indeed, those individuals most closely embodying "classical" liberal ideas today would be considered political libertarians, at the far right of the ideological spectrum.

Now, classical liberalism, Harry K. Girvetz informs us, was crucial to the "epic transition of the Western world from an agrarian, handicraft society to the urban mechanized civilization of the present century."[5] Classical liberalism's ascendance in the seventeenth and eighteenth centuries was made possible, in part, by such enormous social convulsions as the Protestant Reformation, the Scientific Revolution, and the Renaissance. Based on these and other major societal forces, this startling idea system presented both an attack on the feudal order and an assertion of basic concepts about people and society that we still find engraved on public buildings, enshrined in the Constitution and Declaration of Independence, and falling easily off the tongues of politicians from many points on the political continuum. It is simply impossible to overstate the significance of this body of related ideas about human nature and the relationship of the individual to the whole in a quest for understanding virtually every facet of American society.

These ideas, breaking with the sway of tradition and authority that had dominated Europe for centuries, centered on the *sovereign individual*. The starting point was *egoism*. Apparently the ideas of Thomas Hobbes (psychological egoism) and Jeremy Bentham (psychological hedonism) found the time (roughly the seventeenth and eighteenth centuries) a fertile one. Basically, the egoistic interpretations of "human nature" held that the individual was, "by nature," self-seeking. In this thinking, *all* of an individual's actions—even compassion—could be interpreted as being motivated by self-interest. It is important to realize that there was *no moral judgment* to be applied to the actions. In this context, Girvetz suggests an interpretation of particular relevance to activities of the economic system: "Passion is no less noble than compassion. And, more significantly in the rough youth of capitalism, the callousness and venality of the most aggressive businessman are morally indistinguishable from the humanity and generosity of the dedicated idealist: each has exercised his preference and, while anyone may err in what best satisfies his preference, here error halts."[6]

Even by today's decidedly selfish standards, these sentiments may seem shockingly stark. Yet, consider how frequently we ascribe the motives of others to naked self-interest—e.g., "She's (or he's) only out for number one." Or how regrettably common it is to see the misdeeds of public officials attributed to unvarnished greed. And who would expect to find a text on advertising copywriting without the directive of appeal to the consumer's self-interest woven throughout its chapters?

Individuals, the classical liberal philosophers held, are self-interested animals. But there were other dimensions of the classical liberal idea system that broke down feudal society.

The most important of these was *intellectualism*. It held that the individual was "rational," to use that much abused word. Unlike instinct-driven animals, an individual's behavior was thought to be deliberate and calculating. "Reason looks to the consequences, carefully balances one promised pleasure or pain against another, and then, solely by reference to the quantity of pleasure or pain involved, delivers the verdict. The verdict having been rendered, conduct follows automatically. If the verdict should prove to be wrong, this will be because of imperfect education or inadequate information."[7]

Herein, we find the skeletal structure of the concept of "economic man," the basic rationale for public education, and certainly one of the more persistent arguments behind the call for more "informative" advertising content, more consumer-friendly package labeling, and so forth.

Dwell on this. After centuries of individuals being controlled by the weight of custom or the pressure of authority, the individual was now being seen as capable of discovering the laws of the world (the Scientific Revolution), of communing directly with God (the Protestant Reformation), and of being celebrated in art, architecture, and literature (the Renaissance). As John Stuart Mill professed in his classic essay *On Liberty,* "Over himself, over his own mind and body, the individual is sovereign."[8] And lest you think this has little bearing on a subject like advertising in *contemporary* society, think of the defenses that cigarette advertisers are, *at this moment,* using to fend off proposed government regulation of their advertising activities. "Let the individual," they assert, "make up his or her own mind." Intellectualism—a powerful idea—is embraced, as we shall see, by both supporters and critics of advertising thought and practice.

It is the proposition of *quietism* that adds a necessary dimension to the idea of a self-seeking, calculating individual. For if, as was assumed, effort is painful, it must follow that a person will expend energy only when there is some definite promise of reward, so the effort is worthwhile. The implication, then, is that an individual pursues various activities—hiking, surfing the Internet, reading—not because the activity is desired for itself, but rather in pursuit of self-interest. Thus, in the absence of an acceptable stimulus, the individual will remain "quiet," apathetic, disinterested.

Certainly the recruiters who visit college campuses still operate—in addition to the more ambiguous flirtations with the "quality of the work experience"—under the assumption that work itself is not sufficiently appealing that blandishments of salary, bonuses, and employee benefit programs are not required. The importance of the assumption of quietism to advertising is perhaps best captured in these oft-quoted lines of Winston Churchill: "Advertising nourishes the consuming power of men. It creates wants for a better standard of living. It sets up before a man the goal of a better home, better clothing, better food for himself and his family. It spurs individual exertion and greater production. It brings together in fertile union those things which otherwise would never have met."[9]

Today, it is still an article of faith among many advertising practitioners that without the strong and continuing presence of advertising, the economy would falter. They thus express their implicit assumption that individuals are in need of constant stimulation to enter the market as buyers. Without that belief, one of the stronger rationales for the existence of advertising would be removed.

Now, thus far in the classical liberal vision we have self-seeking individuals pursuing their self-interests in deliberate and calculating manners after concluding that the reward is worth the effort. But what prevents this clash of self-interests from resulting in chaos? That is the province of *atomism*.

The idea of atomism was taken from the "natural laws" as formulated by Newton and other scientists and philosophers of the time. If the atom was the fundamental building block of all matter, then by analogy the individual could be assumed to be the essential element in society. The whole (society) was thus perceived as nothing more than the sum of its parts (sovereign individuals) in the same manner that a chair was nothing more than the sum of its individual atoms.

Now, from this perspective, it would be simply absurd to believe that persons could be "manipulated" by institutions of any form—e.g., government, the mass media, religion, advertising. For, as Girvetz observed, "social institutions are created by the fiat of self-contained individuals, they are instruments, even expedients, which the individual can employ or discard without fundamentally altering his own nature."[10]

So the picture completes itself. *The sovereign self-seeking individual is the key.* She or he acts in a calculating manner to obtain self-interest after it has been aroused by a sufficient promise of reward. He or she creates institutions to further reasoned self-interests and can discard them as they prove unproductive to achieving that end.

Egoism, Intellectualism, Quietism, Atomism: The Psychological Crucible of the Classical Liberal Idea System

As Girvetz summarizes, "One emerges with a pattern of ideas which, even though no individual nor generation has entertained in its entirety, still profoundly influences the intellectual climate of this country."[11] It is, we believe, simply impossible to understand the American society and its institutions without first understanding the power of classical liberal thought. For from this body of ideas emerges our institutions of religion, speech, press, justice, government, and countless others. Commenting on one of these, a writer for Time magazine observed: "Trial by jury realizes an essential democratic ideal: that the citizen's security is best protected not by any institutional or intellectual elite, but by the common sense of his fellow citizens; and that the jury system was quite properly designed, not to be efficient, but to be just."[12]

Thus, the institution of the jury system is a "natural" outgrowth of classical liberal roots, as is the dominant economic institution where we will find the most fertile of seedbeds for our subject. For, to understand advertising in contemporary society we must *first* understand classical liberalism, and *then* come to understand one of its most important institutional progeny: the remarkable market system.

The Classical Liberal Market

Markets, as exchanges between buyers and sellers occurring at particular times in particular places, have existed through much of recorded history (today's farmer's market or flea market are examples of these exchanges). But the *market system,* as a means of allocating resources of an entire society, is really quite new, a creature of classical liberalism scarcely more than two to three hundred years old.

The market system has been so much a part of this country that it is difficult to realize what a revolutionary idea it was. Ask the typical college student about the market system, and he or she will probably offer something about the interplay of supply and demand, but little more. Yet, here was a system that, as classical liberalism itself, "staked it all" on the *individual.* What an astounding contrast to the institutions based on tradition and authority that preceded it and that coexist to this day.

Consider that under an economic system whose institutions manifest idea systems based on *tradition,* economic roles established by custom are perpetuated from generation to generation. The goods of the society that are not provided within the self-sustaining household are usually distributed in accordance with status hierarchies—more for the feudal lord, less for the serfs, and so on.

Under *authority,* on the other hand, economic priorities and the life chances of the workers in the society can change dramatically, depending on the whim of the authority structure—planning board, dictator, etc. If military expenditures or the space program are considered more important than consumer goods, human and natural resources will be channeled accordingly.

But consider the *market*. As an institution arising from the classical liberal worldview, it holds that the priorities of the society should be determined not by the weight of custom or the directives of the few, but rather by the aggregate of *individual decisions—all* individuals, not simply the elect or the select.

The market emerged in part *inductively*, with pressures from the growing activities of the practitioners of commerce in seventeenth- and eighteenth-century Europe. These aspiring entrepreneurs sought change and agitated government to permit their profit-seeking activities to be carried on without undue restraint. And, as we have seen, the market as an articulated system also emerged *deductively*—with the supporting ideas of egoism, intellectualism, quietism, and atomism that culminated in the "worldview" of classical liberalism.

If the writings of John Locke still influence our governmental system, there can be little doubt that Adam Smith and his masterpiece *An Inquiry into the Nature and Causes of the Wealth of Nations* (first published in the auspicious year of 1776) still shape the ideology of much of our economic system. (There are no value judgments intended here—merely the observation that the rationale for the classical liberal market remains very much a part of the "conventional wisdom" of much of American economic life in spite of often glaring discrepancies between idea and reality.)

Smith, Heilbroner informs us,[13] was living in a time (the eighteenth century) and place (Great Britain) in which the division of labor was becoming a dominant economic fact. Thus, the decline of self-sufficiency was a major current in his work, as, apparently, was the thinking of seventeenth- and eighteenth-century British clergymen, particularly the Puritans, who believed in a rational, mechanistic universe.[14] But how was this supposed to relate to a system of resource allocation with the sovereign individual as its master?

First, Smith assumed that individuals were self-seeking by nature (egoism). "It is not from the benevolence of the butcher, the brewer or the baker that we expect our dinner," he reminded us, "but from their regard to their own interest."[15] Likewise, someone buying goods would attempt to acquire those that brought the greatest pleasure at the *lowest* price and, while in the labor market, would strive to perform as *little* work as possible for as *much* money as she or he could secure. The producer, of course, would attempt to sell the *lowest* quality merchandise at the *highest* possible price, and hire the *cheapest* labor to perform as *much* work as possible. It seemed a sure formula for chaos.

But, it was reasoned, the self-seeking individual would inevitably collide with others (atomism) seeking the same end. What then? Violence? Not if it is also assumed that the individual is by nature deliberate and calculating (intellectualism). For the self-seeking individual, stimulated from apathy (quietism) by an appeal to gain (egoism), will quickly realize that the reward for which he has exerted effort will not be achieved unless his behavior is modified to some minimal degree. Thus, the producer who wishes to sell poor quality products at high prices will have to face the realization that the deliberate and calculating individuals will not purchase them if more "rational" choices are available. And the individual entering the labor market may shortly find herself without work if she encounters others willing to toil slightly longer for the same wages.

But all of this hinges on the assumption that economic power will be fragmented among *many* buyers and sellers (atomism). With many suppliers, it is assumed that some will attempt to seek their self-interests by offering a better economic and/or qualitative value than their competitors. With many potential self-seeking laborers, it is certain that some will work longer hours for less money, and so on. If this fragmentation did not exist, it is easy to predict (according to the classical liberal worldview) that those with some degree of power would pursue their self-interests through the exploitation of others.

Thus, in order for the market mechanism to perform its task of resource allocation with greatest efficiency, individuals *must* be stimulated to put forth effort in the pursuit of self-interest, they *must* be deliberate and calculating in that pursuit, and there *must* be a sufficient number of buyers and sellers so that no one or few can influence the process. (In reviewing the 1990 book *The Competitive Advantage of Nations,* Robert Samuelson observed, "the basic secret of nations' economic success [competition] hasn't changed since the days of Adam Smith."[16])

And on whom does the market shower its favors? On the *efficient.* It is the efficient individual who stretches her or his earnings by buying the best quality at the lowest price. It is the efficient wage earner who expends appropriate effort to maximize his or her return. And it is the efficient producer who can offer the highest-quality goods at the lowest possible cost, and hence be rewarded with the patronage of the efficient consumer.

With this background, let us examine the three pressing economic questions common to *all* societies, which, until the evolution of the market, had been answered only by economic institutions based on tradition or authority.

What Will Be Produced?

What will be produced will, simply, be determined by what sovereign individuals, in their self-interests, wish to buy. Thus, as Heilbroner observes, the market "has no goal orientation, save to existing demand."[17] If there is a considerable demand for shoes, the fact that shoe supply lags behind existing demand means that shoe prices will rise, along with the profits of the current producers. But the abnormally high profits will soon attract producers of other goods (say, hats) who have fallen upon hard times with potential supply exceeding existing demand, thus leading to subnormal return. As hat producers become shoe producers, shoe supply increases until demand is met. Thus, in the long run, aggregate demand determines the types and qualities of what is to be produced. (To use a contemporary example, a demand for pornographic films, particularly for the home video market, has led to a sizable allocation of human and material resources to meet that demand. It was not decreed by authority that this should be so, nor was it determined by custom—at least not in this country—but rather it was the result of a sufficient number of individuals willing to part with a certain portion of their earnings for the opportunity to view these epics. If demand slackens, many of the current participants will presumably seek other opportunities for profit and employment.)

To Whom Will It Be Distributed?

The output of the market system will be distributed to whomever has money to pay for its offerings. There is no welfare built into the pure ideology or its mechanism. Social Darwinism is a reasonable approximation of the humanitarian dimension of the market in its pure classical liberal form. Those having "marketable" skills who are willing to sell their services in the labor market will be compensated. They may then, in turn, partake of the output of the production sector that is theoretically responding to their demands and those of other sovereign individuals like them. Yet, if the lure of gain is not sufficient to overcome their quietistic nature, the market will offer no rewards. (Certainly the still-heard call that disenfranchised individuals should "pull themselves up by their bootstraps" comes from this credo, as does the resistance some still express to the idea of "welfare.")

How Will the Work of Society Get Done?

Since the market visionaries assumed a geographically mobile labor force (a crucial condition), self-interested individuals would seek employment wherever wages were highest. As we have already seen, it is in production areas of high demand and short supply (to use our earlier example—shoes) where wages are likely to rise. Thus, workers would presumably be attracted to those areas of production that are high on the economy's list of priorities. Always assuming the lure of gain and the deliberate and calculating path to self-interest, it is assured that, at least in the long run, those tasks that society deems important will be undertaken. (Today, we see reference to "pockets of poverty," while other sections of the country may be experiencing solid economic growth and good job markets. Classical market theorists would assume that rational individuals would go where the jobs are. Obviously, today, we know the matter is more complex.)

Now, it is important to keep in mind that the market was seen as a system harmonious with the *natural laws* of society as articulated by the classical liberals. If supply should fall short of demand, the "laws" of the market would naturally be set into motion to correct the deficiency. Being in tune with "natural" order, it was, of course, self-correcting. It follows that the market, as a self-contained, self-repairing, complex mechanism, must be left alone (laissez-faire) to follow its natural course. Its greatest enemy, then, was, predictably, *any* concentration of power that could disrupt the atomistic nature of the market and, hence, the natural processes of the system. (It is often assumed that government was considered the greatest potential villain in the saga. Not so. Equally calamitous effects could be expected to result from any concentration of undue—i.e., "unnatural"—power by big business, big labor or, even, consumer co-ops. *Any form of action that superseded individual decision making was considered a threat to the system.*)

The self-corrective powers of the market could thus be impaired by any deviation from its fundamental assumptions. For example, the development of a producer monopoly (affecting atomism) would enable the supplier to withhold output, leading to higher prices. Thus, wages and prices would be distorted, and the deliberating and calculating consumer would be thwarted.

"The great flaw in the market," one may hear from some sectors, "is that it provides no incentive for social responsibility on the part of the participants." Precisely so. In the pure atomistic market, it was assumed that participants would follow only one overriding law—do what is best for their own monetary interests. The atomistic force of competition (producers, laborers, buyers) would take care of the rest. For, in the process of "naturally" seeking his or her own self-interest, the individual contributes to the good of the whole (society) "as if by an invisible hand."[18] Indeed, always assuming that the other factors are operative, *the individual who did not seek monetarily selfish ends would be doing a disservice to herself or himself, and society.*

There is yet another point deserving of emphasis. The ghost of Adam Smith is far more likely to be called forth by defenders of the market than its critics. Yet, Smith must certainly be considered a "Consumerist," who regarded the end of all production as consumption and held no lofty illusions about the motives of the business community. As he stated: "People of the same trade seldom meet together, even for merriment and diversion, but the conversation ends in a conspiracy against the public, or in some contrivance to raise prices."[19]

To counter this, Smith looked to the fragmentation of power through competition and relied upon the individual's presumed deliberate and calculating nature, as well as self-control through "discipline and parsimony."[20]

So the *sovereign individual*—particularly the industrious and efficient— would be the beneficiary in the market. As production increased, so would the division of labor and the varieties of goods and services offered in response to aggregate demand. All who would diligently and intelligently participate would benefit. The lure of gain, the directive of reason, and the discipline of competition . . .

"The market thus determines how society shall invest its resources, human and material. It decrees when, where, and how men shall labor. It determines the disposition of capital. The market becomes the regulator of what shall be produced, its quality, quantity, and price. The market is truly called sovereign."[21]

A remarkable vision, and an essential reference point for understanding advertising in contemporary society.

____ A "Fertile Seedbed" for Advertising

After examining the relationships between idea systems and institutions, it seems clear that the perspective of *tradition* provides the least compatible environment for advertising. The idea system centered around assumptions that *authority* should rule could provide the grounds for the rise of advertising, depending upon the degree of individual decision making allowed. But it is clearly in the ideas of *classical liberalism* that we find the most enabling philosophy for the emergence and proliferation of advertising as a natural part of society.

Understanding Advertising's Classical Liberal Roots

During the latter years of the Reagan administration, Federal Trade Commission chairman Dan Oliver asserted:

> Advertising is one of the basic mechanisms through which the marketplace acts to ensure consumer sovereignty. It contributes to the achievement of an efficient allocation of resources and benefits consumers in several different ways. . . . First, advertising provides information about product characteristics and enables consumers to make informed choices among competing goods. . . . Second, economic theory and empirical studies indicate that advertising generally increases new entry and price competition and hence reduces market power and prices.[22]

Note the classical liberal cues: "consumer sovereignty," "efficient allocation of resources," "informed choices," "new entry," "price competition." The roots are clear. From egoism comes the assumption that advertisers can feel free to seek their self-interests through various forms of business activities, including advertising. And potential buyers are also presumably seeking *their* self-interests, assuming they are aroused from their natural quietistic states, perhaps through advertising messages. Advertisers can, of course, attempt to persuade as robustly as they wish, safe in the assumption that the deliberate and calculating individual will not be manipulated. Potential buyers can, of course, sort through the wealth of competing messages caused by the atomism of the competitive structure and arrive at a reasoned choice. And, who, presumably, is in charge of this directionless, self-correcting system? With this set of assumptions at least, the *individual,* who can accept, reject, or ignore, directs the flow of societal resources through the full meaning of *consumer sovereignty.*

The seeds of conflict should also be apparent. As William Leiss, Stephen Kline, and Sut Jhally observe in *Social Communication in Advertising*, the starting point of advertising supporters

> is not the "bewildered" but the "rational" consumer who uses the goods of the capitalist marketplace and the information provided by advertising to satisfy his or her needs. This concept of how things *should* work, rooted in classical liberal economic theory, is something many defenders and critics of advertising share, but while the defenders claim that with the help of advertising, the market actually operates in this way to match people's needs with suitable products, many of the critics think that advertising actually destroys the competitive and rational nature of the free market.[23]

An interesting insight into this clash of visions was provided by a series of print advertisements prepared by the American Association of Advertising Agencies to attempt to counter some of the common criticisms of advertising. They hoped to raise advertising's standing in public opinion polls, while attempting to make advertising's case among such key groups as government officials, academics, and so forth. Here are some of the headlines from the series:

- "Isn't It Funny How Stereo Ads Are Boring Until You Want a Stereo?" (Advertising is a guide for the rational consumer.)
- "Without Advertising Even the Best Ideas Take Ages to Catch On" (Advertising quickly joins the self-interest of sellers and buyers for the benefit of both.)
- "Is Advertising a Reflection of Society or Is Society a Reflection of Advertising?" (Advertising is a mirror, not a shaper.)

You get the idea. A particularly telling example of the ideas behind this ideological posture of advertising supporters is found in another ad in the series with the headline "This Ad Is Full of Lies." At this point in our discussion, the reasoning behind the refutation of each of the "lies" should be predictable:

- "Advertising makes you buy things you don't want." (No one, short of actual force, can do that. You're too smart, and there are too many other choices open to you.)
- "Advertising makes things cost more." (Competition, spurred by advertising, makes possible the efficiencies of mass production as advertising introduces individuals to products suited to their self-interests.)

- "Advertising helps bad products sell." (Once consumers have tried a product, they decide, in some self-interested manner, whether it is of value to them. If it isn't, future advertising efforts are wasted.)
- "Advertising is a waste of money." (Advertising is a friend of the market because it provides information and fosters competition. We *all* benefit.)

And finally the slogan for the entire campaign, encompassing strong classical liberal themes—"Advertising. Another word for freedom of choice."

(There are some interesting asides. For example, the copy asserts that it is a "lie" that advertising *makes* you buy things you don't want. Yet advertising is also given credit for "creating" a mass market for calculators. One might wonder: If a market needed to be "created," was the product needed in the first place?)

In a similar mode, Jerry Kirkpatrick provides a "Philosophical Defense of Advertising," relying heavily on the thinking of the widely read author Ayn Rand. Confronting several of the common criticisms of advertising's social role (e.g., "Advertising Changes Tastes," "Advertising Offends Tastes") he asserts: "The moral justification of advertising is that it represents the implementation of an ethics of egoism—the communication of one rational being to another rational being for the egoistic benefit of both." He summarizes: "The relationship between advertisers and consumers is strictly voluntary."[24]

If we return to the working premise Idea Systems ⟷ Institutions, it seems apparent that advertising's philosophical roots (its fertile seedbed), as well as much of its current rationale and defense, can be found in the idea system of classical liberalism and its major economic institution, the market system.

To begin to understand advertising in contemporary society then, we must start here. For, as suggested in the introduction, much about the controversies of advertising can be illuminated by realizing "who's looking and where." And those asserting advertising's case generally believe "advertising is part and parcel of a highly industrialized, market-oriented society. Information and persuasion from uncounted sources swirl around all the individuals who live, work, and shop in this setting. Both informative and persuasive communications are vital and indeed necessary ingredients of decision-making processes in politics, in social relations, and in the marketplace."[25]

Now, in the next chapter we continue to explore this Idea Systems ←→ Institutions relationship by examining how well the classical liberal assumptions have fared in the last years of the twentieth century. For, if our idea systems differ, so, logically, will our perceptions and expectations of the resulting institutions.

_____ Summary

In examining the relationship between fundamental societal idea systems and institutions, we began a search for the fertile seedbed of ideas that could provide an appropriate growth medium for advertising as an institution.

It is clearly not in *tradition,* the set of assumptions placing heavy emphasis on the status quo, based on a well-understood societal plan provided by a higher power, ancestors, or both.

It may, in part, be in *authority,* with its assumptions of the wisdom of the few directing the many. But much depends upon the degree of individual decision making allowed.

The fit seems tightest with *classical liberalism,* with its assumptions of self-interest (egoism), rationality (intellectualism), apathy (quietism), and the whole being no greater than the sum of the parts (atomism).

Still more understanding is added by examining the *market* as a resource allocation mechanism. Based on classical liberalism, it is assumed to be self-perpetuating and self-correcting, with the good of the whole ensuing from self-centered actions of individuals—"as if by an invisible hand."

Much assertion and defense of advertising's thought and action can be seen in these ideas. Shopworn and controversial as they may be in the last years of the twentieth century, they still provide much comfort for supporters of advertising in contemporary society and useful analytic perspectives for those seeking to understand its dimensions.

Notes

1. James W. Carey, "Advertising: An Institutional Approach," in *The Role of Advertising,* ed. C. H. Sandage and V. Fryburger (Homewood, Ill.: Richard D. Irwin, 1960), 3.

2. Walton Hamilton, "Institution," *The Encyclopedia of the Social Sciences* (New York: Macmillan, 1932), 8:84.

3. Vincent P. Norris, "Toward the Institutional Study of Advertising," *Occasional Papers in Advertising* (University of Illinois Department of Advertising) 1, no. 1 (Jan. 1966): 60–61.

4. See, in general, Robert L. Heilbroner, "The Economic Revolution," *The Worldly Philosophers* (New York: Time, 1961), 7–33.

5. Harry K. Girvetz, *From Wealth to Welfare* (Stanford: Stanford University Press, 1950), 23. Used by permission.

6. Ibid., 10.

7. Ibid., 15.

8. John Stuart Mill quoted in Otto Friedrich, "The Individual Is Sovereign," *Time*, July 21, 1986, 80.

9. Winston Churchill quoted in S. Watson Dunn and Arnold M. Barban, *Advertising: Its Role in Modern Marketing* (Hinsdale, Ill.: Dryden Press, 1974), 5.

10. Girvetz, *From Wealth to Welfare*, 23.

11. Ibid., 11.

12. "Idealism on Trial," promotional ad, *Time, Inc.*, 1982.

13. Heilbroner, *The Worldly Philosophers*. The authors acknowledge their debt to the ideas expressed throughout chaps. 1–3 in this excellent work.

14. Thoughts attributed to Sabin Rashid, professor of economics at the University of Illinois. See Tom Day, "Author of 'Wealth of Nations' 'Borrowed' Many of His Ideas," *IlliniWeek*, Apr. 19, 1984, 1.

15. Adam Smith quoted in "Revolution of Self-Love," *Time*, Apr. 21, 1980, 45.

16. Robert J. Samuelson, "Competition: Tried and True," *Newsweek*, June 11, 1990, 47.

17. Robert L. Heilbroner, *The Economic Problem*, 2d ed. (Englewood Cliffs, N.J.: Prentice-Hall, 1970), 547.

18. Paul A. Samuelson, "Adam Smith," *Newsweek*, Mar. 15, 1976, 86.

19. Adam Smith quoted in Heilbroner, *The Worldly Philosophers*, 65.

20. Charles L. Griswold Jr., "Adam Smith: Conscience of Capitalism," *Wilson Quarterly* 15 (Summer 1991): 53–61.

21. Girvetz, *From Wealth to Welfare*, 117.

22. Dan Oliver quoted in "The New FTC: Steady as She Goes," *American Advertising*, Jan. 1987, 9.

23. William Leiss, Stephen Kline, and Sut Ghally, *Social Communication in Advertising: Persons, Products, and Images of Well-Being* (New York: Methuen, 1986), 31.

24. Jerry Kirkpatrick, "A Philosophical Defense of Advertising," *Journal of Advertising* 15, no. 2 (1986): 44, 48.

25. Leiss, Kline, and Ghally, *Social Communication in Advertising*, 42.

2

Idea Systems ⟷ Institutions: Advertising and Neo-Liberalism

We begin with Walton Hamilton's perceptive observation on the linkage between ideas and institutions: "In the continuous process of the adaption of usage and arrangement to intellectual environment, an active role is assumed by that body of ideas taken for granted which is called *common sense*. Because it determines the climate within which all others must live, it is the dominant institution in a society."[1]

In the last chapter, we explored the relationship between a particular idea system—classical liberalism—and the types of institutions that would seem to be a "natural" outgrowth of that system—e.g., freedom of the press/speech/religion, representative government, and the market system. Of course, the reason for this emphasis was to make clear the extremely supportive role these classical liberal assumptions (about egoism, intellectualism, quietism, atomism) played (and play) in the development and maintenance of advertising thought and practice.

Now, if Idea Systems ⟷ Institutions, and the idea systems (or "common sense") change, how will this affect the expectations we have for our institutions?

Our purpose in this chapter, then, is to hold up several of the key assumptions of the classical liberal idea system—spawned more than two hundred years ago—to the light of some of the prevailing thoughts and practices of America in the last decades of the twentieth century. We will attempt to determine what is retained, and what altered, and to draw out conclusions about the effects of our contemporary idea system on our institutions, particularly advertising.

We will, of course, be operating on a high level of generalization, attempting not to be exhaustive, but insightful, pointing to events, trends, and prevailing modes of thought that seem modal. First, we'll explore where we may stand today with such critical classical liberal assumptions as those dealing with self-interest, the individual's presumed rationality, the division of power in society, the role of the market economy, and the place of government. Then we'll narrow the focus to advertising.

It is, we feel, an important undertaking. For, as we suggested in the introduction, it would seem that much about advertising in contemporary society can be understood as a clash of different perceptual realities, caused in part by individuals operating from differing sets of assumptions about the world around them.

———— A Reexamination of Classical Liberal Concepts

Egoism

Certainly a case can be made that the classical liberal assumption about the driving force of self-interest is alive and well in contemporary America. Author Thomas Wolfe dubbed the 1970s the "Me Decade," and the 1980s were described by at least one observer as "greed run rampant." The much-publicized "Yuppie" (young urban professional) lifestyle has proven strong on pursuits of the ego—through narcissistic physical fitness, throw-away romance, and self-above-all career moves. And the contemporary world of professional sports may represent the zenith in the naked self-interest business. We are not, then, in short supply of examples of ego-driven behavior.

Yet we also know that much of the past, present, and pending local, state, and federal legislation dealing with the modern agenda of societal concerns assumes that these matters will *not* be dealt with effectively *unless a check on self-interest is instituted.* As the scholar Charles L. Griswold Jr. observed in a reexamination of Adam Smith: "The challenges posed by great inequality of wealth, by individualism, by social and moral decay, and by supposedly rampant greed—in sum the problems of liberal society—are now prominent on the national agenda."[2]

Now, keep in mind that classical liberalism assumed that individuals pursuing their self-interests in single-minded ways would *naturally* result in the good of the whole. Theodore Levitt put it in blunt economic terms in his classic 1958 article, "The Dangers of Social Responsibility": "The governing rule in industry should be that *something is good only if it pays.* Otherwise it is alien and impermissible."[3] But clearly today there are other currents at work as well. As the columnist Robert G. Samuelson has observed: "Twenty years ago, the vague concepts of 'social responsibility' and 'consumerism' barely existed; now diluted to be sure, they are the conventional wisdom, even in business. . . . [Ralph] Nader's social regulation—of everything from auto safety to pollution—has triumphed. The boundaries of the market have been redrawn."[4]

The 1980s and early 1990s were dominated by conservative Republican administrations with oft-expressed views of faith in the market system and preferences to "deregulate" the marketplace, and the 1994 elections provided Republican control of both houses of Congress, reaffirming this bias as government-as-part-of-the-problem. But even in this relatively supportive climate, businesses have apparently been sufficiently institutionalized in a "responsibility" ethic to support company activities that seem to have no directly self-interested "bottom line"—e.g., to underwrite programs to hire and maintain minorities and contribute to various local, regional, and national charities and special projects.

Some of this is, of course, clearly enlightened self-interest—e.g., "If we don't help make the downtown area a more attractive place, we'll have difficulty getting employees"—and a former Federal Trade Commission activist has observed: "Americans are under no illusion about business practices. . . . One does not have to be a cynic to conclude that those areas where business is perceived as socially progressive have a striking tendency to coincide with its economic self-interest, while those areas where business is given low marks for moral and civic virtue happen to be those areas where there is little or no (apparent) advantage to be gained."[5]

We can imagine, then, a continuum, polarized by acts of pure self-interest in its narrowest sense and acts of pure altruism at their most selfless. Realistically, the stark egoism position is no longer as easily defensible, in public life at least. Today, as we move into what some have termed a "post-yuppie" era, we *may* be more inclined to expect a certain "pulling of the punch" by individuals, groups, and organizations as we become more sensitive, more "politically correct," or, simply, more understanding of the needs of others as well as ourselves. (An interesting stream of scholarship by feminist economists challenges the basic concepts of self-interest underlying the classical liberal construct "economic man" with assertions such as, "What happens if you begin your thinking with a mother and a small infant?"[6]) *To the extent we perceive the need for more "responsibility," we are assuming that the automatic adjusting mechanisms of the classical liberal worldview (e.g., the invisible hand) cannot consistently be relied upon to produce societal good from self-interested acts.* Thus, as our ideas change, so do our expectations from our institutions.

The implications for advertising are significant.

Intellectualism

For better or for worse, we are a nation that has, in important ways, "staked it all" on the individual. Thus, many of our contemporary institutions reflect that belief, even while others manifest grave reservations:

Item: The American jury system rests on the premise that ordinary men and women, not the elect or the elite, can make reasonable judgments on matters of justice ranging from the trivial to those of life or death. But these same individuals may be fined if they are not securely buckled into their *own* cars—hardly a ringing endorsement of their abilities to make sound decisions concerning their *own* well-being.

Item: Enough faith is placed in the rationality of individuals that we are encouraged to vote for a person (presumed rational as well) who may ultimately have to make a decision that could destroy life as we know it on this planet. Yet, in many states these same individuals are discouraged from pursuing the private satisfaction of smoking by increasingly restrictive laws and regulations.

Item: High school graduates throughout the land hear speakers congratulate them on their citizenship in a land of freedom and opportunity where all doors are open to inquiring minds. Yet these same students may not have been able to find certain books in their school libraries because groups offering their standards as the norm agitated to remove books they deemed "unfit."

Item: Consumer Reports testing revealed that food store brands in seven out of ten common categories were equal to or superior to their more costly national brand counterparts. Yet a survey of the magazine's own consumption-savvy readers revealed that "80 percent or more preferred a national brand."[7]

As this minuscule sample may suggest, we as a society are frequently uncertain about exactly what to make of our current version of "human nature." Clearly we have based countless of our institutional systems (e.g., government, justice, communication, religion) firmly on our classical liberal beliefs in the fundamental intelligence of individuals, particularly in pursuit of their self-interests. Yet common sense has obviously caused us to question how well this is all working out.

James W. Carey, referring to Ernst Cassirer's distinction between *animal rationale* and *animal symbolicum*, observes, "Economic man [*animal rationale*], buying and selling, and equating cost and utility at the margin, has been replaced by psychological or symbolic man [*animal symbolicum*] who makes economic decisions on the basis of economic and also noneconomic but equally potent psychological need-want stimuli."[8] This is not to suggest that this modern perception is superior, only that it is different. Thus, at least by ideological contrast, individuals can be seen as less predictable, more complex, and, to some, more vulnerable.

Now, recall that in our earlier discussions of classical liberalism it was contended that, in absence of any conscious social responsibility, the two principal forces that would channel the individual's inherent self-interest (egoism) into socially beneficial channels were assumed to be intellectualism and atomism. If today we are apparently uncertain about the first of these—the individual's inherent rationality—then we can feel less comfortable with the likelihood that the invisible hand will turn self-interested acts into socially beneficial consequences. Now, what of the second force, the presumed diffusion of power (atomism)?

Atomism

The sum and substance of much of sociology and social psychology is that the individual is, to a considerable degree, molded by society. In contrast to the classical liberal conception of a society composed solely of sovereign individuals who control by their self-interested actions, today we accept a certain level of powerlessness as institutions impose form upon us through their sets of norms or expected behaviors. Of course, this sense of being controlled by societal forces is simply not a psychological state with which classical liberals could feel comfortable. Remember that, with classical liberalism, individuals—not institutions—were the masters. They were the "atoms" that constituted the whole.

Now, if societal power is *not* diffused among all participants (e.g., "the people"), where *does* it reside? Some would assert: big government; big labor; big business; the mass media. Clearly, seeds of conflict are abundant.

A useful perspective on this issue in the economic sphere is found in the Justice Department's Antitrust Division, originally established to keep economic competition at least reasonably "atomistic" by preventing mergers ("trusts," etc.) that could presumably nullify competition and pave the way for exploitation. Yet, the head of this division during the Reagan administration was highly critical of the "populist bigness-is-badness notion." William Baxter was apparently willing to assume that companies "got big because they were successful at pleasing customers, not successful at ripping off customers."[9]

By contrast, the consumer advocate Ralph Nader sees the functioning of "big business" quite differently:

> The contemporary challenge to giant business . . . is almost primitive in its simplicity. It is a call for corporations to stop stealing, stop deceiving, stop corrupting politicians with money, stop monopolizing, stop poisoning the earth, air and water, stop selling dangerous products, stop exposing workers to cruel hazards, stop tyrannizing people of conscience within the company and start respecting long-range survival needs and rights of present and future generations.[10]

An interesting parallel is found with the subject of media diversity in our mass communications system. Assuming that more is better than few, some contend that diversity (i.e., atomism) in the mass media can be best achieved by letting the *market* decide. "Underlying this approach is the premise of a fluid, competitive marketplace and a fairly broad distribution of economic power that will permit all sectors to enter the marketplace and provide needed information-communication services."[11] But another position calls for *government* to assume an active role to assure a truly "democratic social structure"—a greater degree of atomism. For, the argument goes, "in this era of giant national and transnational corporate dominance it is absurd to presuppose that there is sufficient equitable distribution of economic power to allow market forces alone to ensure equitable distribution of services. . . . Information should not be considered simply a marketable commodity distributed only to those with the capacity to pay."[12]

There is no question that economic power is becoming more concentrated than diffused, and often, as the media scholar Leo Bogart informs us, with intriguing international dimensions:

> Most Americans couldn't care less that the two biggest advertising agency organizations are now owned by British companies. It doesn't matter to them that magazines like *Scientific American* and *Parents* are owned by a German firm or that the largest U.S. newspaper chain—in number of daily newspapers—is Thomson, a Canadian company. There was no great furor when UPI was sold to a Mexican publisher. And, except in Akron, it doesn't bother anyone that Firestone, our third biggest tire manufac-

turer, is being bought by the Japanese. New Yorkers are oblivious to the fact that Saks Fifth Avenue is owned by the British.[13]

But a critical question concerns the *effects* of that concentration. Does big overcome small to the benefit of the few? Or do we exist in a society (and, increasingly, a global marketplace) of enormous countervailing power blocks, where big business is countered by big labor, held in check by big government and big press, so that a hybrid competition is maintained that ultimately serves all in an acceptable fashion? Or is there collusion among the titans and, if so, between whom, and to whose benefit?

Does advertising, then, flow with these currents or, in fact, help channel them? The answers result in strikingly different perceptions of advertising in contemporary society.

The Economy

Now, depending on the assumptions one makes about the states of egoism, intellectualism, and atomism, an individual can arrive at very different conclusions about how our economy works and what role (if any) government should play in its maintenance and/or direction.

Remember that the market system, as seen by the classical liberals, was a self-contained, self-correcting system, driven by competition and in harmony with the "natural laws" of human nature and the relationship of the individual to society. And certainly these assumptions have staying power, as suggested by Michael Porter's study of ten nations "to determine the secrets of economic success." The secret of the successful nations? Competition.[14]

At the time of this writing, the American economy is generally considered to be robust by many standards, although there are ongoing concerns about the national debt, the imbalance in the balance of payments, the future funding of the Social Security System, etc. The Reagan administration of the eighties took credit for sustained growth, new job creation, and relatively low inflation and unemployment. Yet critics argued that much of this benefited the few rather than the many, that the new jobs created were predominantly in the relatively low-paying service sector, and that the national debt became an "economic time bomb" as the United States assumed the mantle of the world's premier debtor nation. In addition, at least one economist argued that the *"environmental* deficit" was (and is) of even greater concern: "A pervasive thought underlying . . . policy is the notion that the environment is somehow less important than marketable goods and services, that producing things that individual people buy—such as Cadillacs and cosmetics—is more valuable than protecting things that are consumed collectively, such as air and water."[15]

Notice the distinction here between the individual and the collective (i.e., assumptions about atomism) and the implicit assumption that individuals pursuing their own self-interests (i.e., assumptions about egoism) will *not* necessarily result in the good of the whole.

Today, then, we continue in an economy of contradictions, attempting a balancing act of relatively uncontrolled economic activity by individuals and momentous actions by mammoth corporations, labor unions, and governmental bodies. It is important to note that the Reagan government, the most conservative administration of modern times, was unwilling (and/or unable) to make any significant changes in the "Welfare State" programs and mentality that have characterized much of our economic activity since the New Deal of the thirties, and the midnineties conservatives are still meeting popular resistance when it comes to implementing any fundamental reforms in spite of their expressed desire to "give government back to the people."

"The market," Robert L. Heilbroner observed, "has no goal orientation other than to existing demand."[16] The ongoing challenge of our economy, then, may be seen as when—if at all—to *force* the direction, to put governmental hands on the economic rudder. There are profound philosophical differences here, ranging from those (often Republicans) who see an unfettered economy unleashing the self-seeking energies of individuals and firms for the eventual good of all to those (often Democrats) who see short-run gains turning into long-run tragedies as resources are misallocated to the advantage of the haves and the disenfranchisement of the have-nots.

Advertising, predictably, can be seen as friend or enemy of this mixed system, as mirror or shaper of fundamental economic and social tides.

Government

Laissez-faire was a term introduced in France in the eighteenth century and used in the writings of Adam Smith "to argue against the theory of mercantilism and governmental restrictions and regulations of economic activity characteristic of his day."[17] Today, the idea that government should not interfere in any way with economic or social activity can commonly be found only among members of the Libertarian party, "reactionary" politicians, and such fringe groups as "survivalists" and their ilk. Yet there is *ample* room for divergence on the matter of how much "assistance or control" should be offered, where, and for what ends.

A reasonable approximation of a middle-range position on the role of government in social and economic matters has been provided by the economist Irving Kristol.[18] A "neo-conservative," Kristol contended, would generally hold views such as these:

- In general there would be approval for those social reforms that, "while providing needed security and comfort to the individual in our dynamic, urbanized society [e.g., social security, unemployment insurance, some kind of national health insurance and family assistance plan] do so with a minimum of bureaucratic intrusion in the individual's affairs."
- There would be great respect for the market "to respond efficiently to economic realities while preserving the maximum degree of individual freedom." There is a willingness to interfere with the market for "overriding social purposes," but this, ideally, should be done by "rigging" the market to take advantage of its own dynamics—e.g., housing vouchers for the poor rather than government-built low-income housing.
- There would be belief in the traditional American value of equality, but not egalitarianism, "as a proper goal for government to pursue." A favoring of equality of *opportunity* (e.g., Affirmative Action) rather than equality of *outcome* (e.g., "quota" programs).

Now, keep in mind that Kristol's points represent a relatively conservative position. Yet, they still recognize and, indeed, encourage a significant role for government, as both *regulator* and *planner.*

The regulating dimension essentially involves government tinkering with what is already present. Often government works in this role to attempt to achieve classical liberal *ends*—e.g., more competition—even while using decidedly nonclassical liberal *means*—e.g., government antitrust activity. Yet we remain ambivalent concerning the "proper" limits, as the results of the 1994 congressional elections were interpreted by many as a widespread dissatisfaction with some government regulatory programs and initiatives.

Of course government has also played the role of *planner*—to attempt to chart the course of the economy and the society. For example, income tax programs rest on assumptions of future as well as present states—that is, how income should be redistributed in society, what activities are to be encouraged and which discouraged, etc. And there are those who feel that government needs to play a far more active role in order to avert what they consider to be likely ecological or social disorder on a planetary scale—e.g., to attempt to save the rain forests, curb the spread of AIDS, and protect endangered species. If the world is going to be a reasonably habitable place for our children and their children, the arguments go, government—perhaps world government—must direct resources toward a sane and just future. From this position, the market, and its narrowly self-interested premises, can no longer suffice in a world that may be poisoning itself ecologically and socially.

But the answer to this dilemma, a more conservative perspective offers, is not governmental planning with all its ineptitude and strangling bureaucracy, but a vigorous world market, where the benefits will accrue to all through the creation of new economic opportunities.

There is, then, no shortage of positions for government as regulator or planner—locally, regionally, nationally, or even on a planetary scale. What is evident is an acceptance (sometimes grudging) of government's role in significant dimensions of the lives of every citizen of this country. The significant role of government is certainly the most obvious deviation from the classical liberal worldview. And that, as we have seen, can only be assessed properly against the backdrop of changing perceptions of self-interest, the individual's rationality, and the presumed buffering force of competition.

• • •

We can, then, call this series of compromises and uncertainties "neo-liberalism," as they represent grafts on the classical liberal trunk rather than a radically different philosophical species. We have, after all, trusted much to the individual, with all that implies, and we are reluctant to abandon our ideological roots, no matter how ambiguous the resulting idea system.

———— The Implications of Neo-Liberalism for Advertising

Recall that we started with the premise that Idea Systems $\longleftrightarrow$ Institutions.

Then, moving to the idea system with the greatest explanatory power for the institution of advertising, we investigated the relationship of Classical Liberalism $\longleftrightarrow$ Advertising in the previous chapter.

Now, as the classical liberal idea system represents a theoretical base and not a current perceptual reality, we turn to Neo-Liberalism ←—→ Advertising. Based on the reexamination of several of the key elements of the classical liberal worldview (i.e., egoism, intellectualism, atomism, the economy, and the role of government), we could expect that advertising as an institution would be regarded with some suspicion. For if advertisers are presumed to be self-interested, and the expected counterforces of the individual's rationality and the purifying effect of atomistic competition are qualified, then the potential for exploitation—economically and psychologically/socially—exists. Thus, presumably, the need for regulation—internally (within the advertising business) based on social responsibility and externally (from government bodies)—exists.

But obviously there are disagreements about this perception of advertising in contemporary society. Those associated with the advertising business, for example, feel quite differently about the practice and effects of their craft. They are troubled that advertising is viewed as shaper rather than mirror, sovereign rather than servant of the individual, and they are concerned about their generally low standing in public opinion polls concerning their business (advertising), its products (advertisements), and themselves as responsible professionals.

One perspective for seeing these different visions of advertising in contemporary society with greater clarity is offered in figure 2-1.

Note that the range of individual positions encompassing what we call neo-liberalism is represented on continuums, with those positions toward the top being far closer to the theoretical set of classical liberal assumptions we explored in the preceding chapter than those further down the continuums. Basically, then, we suggest: *That in order to understand different perspectives on advertising in contemporary society, it is useful to examine the implicit or explicit assumptions about intellectualism, atomism, and egoism. These will likely lead to compatible views of the economy and the role of regulation. Depending, then, upon where one falls in these dimensions, he or she will "see" advertising very differently.*

Now, in order to deepen our understanding, let's examine each of these dimensions separately, offering some notion of the possible implications for advertising.

Depending upon One's Assumptions about "Intellectualism". . .

In their focus on modern advertising as "privileged discourse through and about objects," William Leiss, Stephen Kline, and Sut Ghally comment

Figure 2-1. The Neo-Liberal Continuum

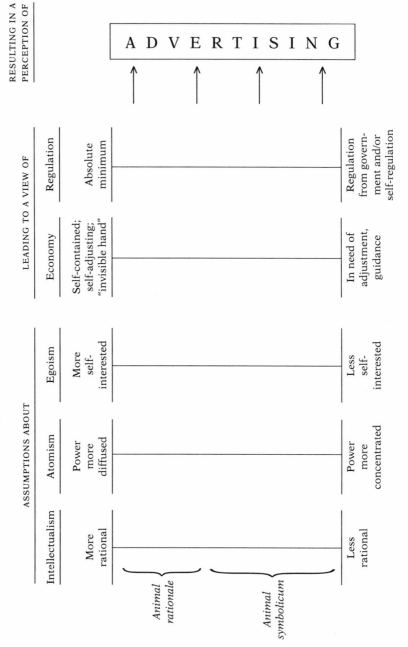

on the critics of advertising, who commonly assert: "Advertisers . . . manipulate people by subtly mixing reality and fantasy, by creating a 'magic show' that makes it hard to tell what one's 'real needs' are or where to draw the line between sensible behaviour and careless overindulgence."[19]

Note the deviation from the ideal of the deliberate and calculating individual with the assertions about manipulation based on the assumption that one's "real needs" can be redefined by the powerful force of advertising. This is clearly a position on the intellectualism continuum destined to lead to perceptions of advertising quite different from a defense for advertising, which could assert: "Information and persuasion from uncounted sources swirl around all individuals who live, work, and shop. . . . Both informative and persuasive communications are vital and indeed necessary ingredients of decision making processes in politics, in social relations, and in the marketplace."[20]

Here we are clearly closer to classical liberal turf, with the implicit assumption of consumer sovereignty and the capable consumer directing the system by the expression of her or his self-interest.

Note how different positions on the neo-liberal continuums enable critics and defenders to "see" advertising quite differently, a phenomenon made possible by the ambiguity of advertising's effects.

The defenders are clearly closer to the classical liberal vision of *animal rationale,* the individual as a sovereign, calculating decision maker, reasonably comfortable in an arena of commercial pleading, and able to extract from the babble whatever information will be of help in his or her pursuit of self-interest.

By contrast, the critics see the individual operating as *animal symbolicum,* responding to a host of psychological/social/cultural stimuli in addition to the more narrowly defined economic dimensions of the classical liberal system.

To deepen our understanding in this pivotal area, we must further address two questions central to the concept of "information."

What Is Meant by "Information"?

In a major study assessing the information content of television advertising, Preben Sepstrup evaluated a large sample of television commercials on twenty-four criteria, including considerations such as:

- Does the commercial carry a brand name?
- Does the commercial show/describe the product?

- Does the commercial mention the name of the company behind the brand?
- Does the commercial quote the price?
- Does the commercial mention varieties of the product?

Sepstrup concluded, "From a general consumer point of view, TV advertising has limited value, since information relevant for purchasing decisions is not communicated to a degree that would seem to have any practical significance to consumers."[21]

It should not surprise us that, based on these and nineteen other demanding criteria, television advertisements were found wanting, in the same manner that most consumer goods advertisements in *all* media seem inadequate sources of "information" when compared to the exhaustive evaluations of, say, *Consumer Reports*.

Yet, television advertising thrives because advertisers find it in their self-interests to use it because, presumably, individuals frequently find it in *their* self-interests to respond to it.

What we seem to have, then, are two competing definitions of "information." The *first* revolves around criteria that "information" should be product-centered, functional in a mechanistic sense, and relatively objective. Thus an advertisement could be assumed to have adequate information if it contained facts about, say, price, durability, and performance in a relatively narrowly defined sense.

The *second* definition moves more to the symbolic dimension, suggesting that a host of psychological/sociological cues serve as "information" as well. For, as Leiss, Kline, and Ghally observe, advertising also routinely communicates about such matters as "interpersonal and family relations, the sense of happiness and contentment, sex role and stereotyping, the uses of affluence, the fading away of older cultural tradition, influence of younger generations, the role of business in society, persuasion and personal autonomy, and many others."[22] This, they could contend, certainly represents "information" as well, for products and services are frequently not perceived as narrowly functional by consumers. Hence, it is argued, individuals respond to market information, including advertising, that matches their own decision-making criteria. ("Jeans," clothing design guru Calvin Kline has said, "are about sssexx. . . . People love it."[23])

Clearly, differing positions on this essential element in the assessment of the individual's "deliberate and calculating" nature will lead to dramatically different visions of advertising at work in contemporary society. But we also must be concerned with the second question.

How Much "Information" Is Enough?

Reviewing several contemporary books on advertising, including works by the important advertising figures David Ogilvy, John O'Toole, and Jane Maas, Roger Draper of the *New York Times* observed:

> Advertising cannot consistently tell the truth, the whole truth, and nothing but the truth. If we are to settle for something less than the whole truth, so far as it can be known to us, what shall we settle for? "Some of the truth" would be the answer [from] Ogilvy, O'Toole, and Maas. . . . By this they mean not the amount of truth that can reasonably be compressed into a reasonable amount of space, but the product of efforts to suppress an important fact: *the similarity among competing brands*. If "some of the truth" in this sense is an acceptable alternative to all of it, the value of truth itself becomes puzzling. It is easier, and perhaps necessary, for the advertising industry to dethrone truth as a value, much as it is often necessary to distort the truth in advertising.[24]

Yet, there are those who would contend that—no matter how biased the individual messages—the "clash of ideas" in the marketplace will inevitably lead to the *recognition* of truth, since the individual is assumed deliberate and calculating. But what, others argue, if that information *doesn't* emerge? Will not the individual's rationality be thwarted?

These are muddy waters indeed. Consider, for example, that a study by the advertising agency BBDO Worldwide revealed that *two-thirds* of consumers surveyed in twenty-eight countries considered brands in thirteen major product categories to be *at parity*—i.e., virtually identical.[25] Yet, in many countries, including the United States, more expensive, generally highly advertised brands tend to dominate sales. For example, after warning readers "not to count on mouthwash to freshen your breath very long," *Consumer Reports* noted several that "did well in the short run," including well-known Listerine at thirteen cents an ounce and Kmart antiseptic at less than half that price.[26] This and similar findings could be interpreted to suggest that individuals *are* generally aware of "the similarity among competing brands" but still choose to pay a premium for the often more symbolic rewards offered in manufacturers' brand advertising.

Thus, advertising can be savaged, or praised, from virtually any point on the intellectualism continuum. What seems clear, however, is that, generally, the more the assumption is made that the individual represents *animal symbolicum* rather than *animal rationale,* the more likely it is that the individual will be seen as vulnerable—to advertiser and critic alike. And yet, when advertising practitioners defend their practice, they are more likely to evoke the model of the steely-eyed, deliberate and calculating, maddeningly fickle consumer, even as their advertisements frequently imply that *animal symbolicum* is alive and well—and buying.

Depending upon One's Assumptions about "Atomism" . . .

Remember that the second major buffer to egoism-run-rampant was assumed to be diffused power, so that no single entity, or group of entities, could avoid being brought into line with the wishes of the sovereign consumer because of the relentless forces of competition offering the rational individual cheaper, better alternatives. And that *because* of this diffused power, individuals controlled institutions, not the other way around.

Referring back to our previous discussion on the neo-liberal dimensions of intellectualism, you can imagine the volatile combination of assumptions of a vulnerable individual subjected to concentrated power. You begin to catch the flavor of this mind-set when encountering articles such as *TV Guide's* "Why You Watch Commercials—Whether You Mean to or Not,"[27] clearly implying power "out there." Basically, it can be argued that as an individual's position falls toward the "concentrated power" end of the continuum, he or she is more likely to assume that institutions, rather than individuals, are sovereign and, hence, capable of perhaps undue influence. Those toward the "diffused power" dimension are, predictably, likely to place more faith in the individual being in charge of her or his destiny. Let's examine some representative controversies linked to the question of where power resides.

- Assessing the dimensions of the advertising agency field in the United States in the late eighties, Leo Bogart observed:

> The three billion-dollar U.S. advertisers, RJR-Nabisco, P&G, and Phillip Morris represent 11% of all network TV advertising and 10% of all national advertising in consumer media. . . .
>
> This concentration of power has tremendous social and cultural consequences. A recent trade press item reports that the Saatchi and

Saatchi agencies among them account for one out of every five dollars spent on network television. I would be very much surprised if at this time the brothers Saatchi *have* sought to impose any guiding hand of corporate philosophy upon the time-buying practices of all their individual agencies. But could any television network, in its programming decisions, be unresponsive to the prevailing philosophy of Saatchi and Saatchi, of J. Walter Thompson, of Omnicom—of all the other giants of the agency world?[28]

- Planned Parenthood counted more than twenty thousand sexual scenes on prime-time network television in a single year. Using a full-page advertisement, the organization urged readers to send prepared coupons to the major media power brokers, the presidents of NBC-TV, CBS-TV, and ABC-TV. The coupon read: "Hyping sex on television while censoring references to birth control is giving a dangerous double message to American teens. The U.S. suffers the highest rate of teen pregnancy in the industrialized world, causing school dropouts, family breakups, and massive welfare. TV industry censorship of birth control is making a bad problem worse. Please reverse your policy. Permit programs *and* advertising to discuss birth control."[29]
- "Omnipresent commercialism," states Ronald K. L. Collins and Michael F. Jacobson, "is wrecking America," which closely resembles Aldous Huxley's *Brave New World*, where "corporate entities feed us Soma tablets, and they don't have to open our mouths. We open them freely."[30]

Where does power reside? If we believe the individual is in charge, there can be little concern of exploitation. But if those in concentrated power set the agenda, warnings are raised. Even the deliberate and calculating individual, it may be argued, can be overmatched if he or she is not in the position to set some priorities of choice. And when it is assumed that the individual is often adrift in a symbolic universe as well . . . alarms become shrill indeed.

Now, One's Assumption about "Egoism" Is Likely to Be Influenced by Her or His Position on Intellectualism and Atomism

Glance back at figure 2-1 and imagine a position near the top of the egoism continuum and one near the bottom. Now, look at the atomism and intellectualism continuums. It would seem that if the individual is considered rational and free to exercise his or her sovereignty, self-interest will be seen as "natural" and beneficial rather than potentially exploitive. But if the individual is perceived as potentially vulnerable and at the mercy of concentrations of power, then calls for restraint on self-interest will be heard.

Thus, advertisers can be seen in pursuit of their self-interests, which must "naturally" take into account the self-interests of the potential customers; *or* advertisers can be called upon to exercise social responsibility to avoid the potential exploitation that could occur if it is assumed that (1) the individual is not always "rational," (2) power is concentrated and thus not channeled in positive ways by the atomistic forces of competition, or (3) both of the above.

To use a topical example, there is ongoing concern about alcohol abuse, particularly among young people. Senator Strom Thurmond and others have challenged the alcoholic beverage industry to put responsibility over profit, particularly with advertising reaching underage drinkers, either through generalized media scheduling—particularly sporting events—or message content—particularly the association of social drinking with the "good life." If Senator Thurmond were making assumptions about self-interest similar to those of the classical liberals, he would probably not have raised the issue at all. For it would be assumed only "natural" that firms would seek their self-interests in whatever manner most benefited their profit interests. Any "responsibility" would be handled by the give-and-take of market forces. If the beverage companies offended they would be punished where it *really* hurt—at the cash register.

There is a *New Yorker* cartoon depicting an executive from the fictional Frizzly Corporation reviewing potential advertising approaches with slogans such as "It's People We're All About" and "Our Concern is People." "I'm sick of this whole approach," the Frizzly executive finally tells the nonplussed advertising executive, "Just tell the public we're cold and aloof and we make a damn good carburetor." For better or for worse, most advertisers today are called upon to do more than just make good products or services. Because of doubts about intellectualism and atomism, there may also be concerns about how they act in all their business activities as responsible city, state, national, and international citizens.

It's not difficult to see that an individual's assumptions about such a basic matter as the outcome of self-interest can lead to starkly different views about advertising as an institution—for example, whether servant or exploiter. But there is, we know, other contested ground as well.

Based on the Assumptions about Intellectualism, Atomism, and Egoism, the Individual Is Likely to Have a Compatible View of Advertising's Role in . . .

The Economy

In a 1992 advertisement, the American Advertising Federation presented an open letter to the President of the United States. It read:

> As you and the Congress are hard at work on ways to improve our country's economy, we respectfully remind you of advertising's role as an engine of economic growth.
>
> - It raises capital, creates jobs and spurs production.
> - It launches new products, provides consumer information and furthers competition, thereby lowering consumer prices.
> - It increases government revenue since jobs produce taxable income, and greater sales increase taxes. Like you, Mr. President, we want to help get America's economy started again. Incentives to advertise are incentives to growth.[31]

Notice the familiar assumptions of classical liberal thinking—an efficient, self-adjusting economy, ultimately serving the self-interests of all sensible participants. But note also the somewhat jarring references to advertising's role as an "engine of economic growth." For, it can be reasoned, if the economy needs to be started and maintained—to continue the "engine" metaphor—perhaps it is not consumer sovereignty driving the economy, but rather the pervasiveness and seduction of advertisements.

Herein, then, lies the essence of two strikingly different visions of advertising and the economy—advertising as (1) friend or (2) foe of the market system. The arabesques will be explored in much greater detail in chapter 4, but let's at least acknowledge the positions here.

As a friend of the market, advertising, as the AAF message implies, is seen to serve as a lubricant for the efficient exchange of goods and services between eager seller and cautious buyer, with power presumably residing in consumer demand. Competition is stimulated by self-interest, with advertising serving as a readily available communication device to reach, and hopefully persuade, the multitudes regarding what Charles H. Sandage refers to as the "want satisfying qualities of products and services."[32] Self-interest is well represented on all sides, thus stimulating the energy so typical of the best market economies.

But to the extent advertising "creates" demand, the power balance begins to shift from the consumer to the producer/supplier, with presumably ever larger advertising budgets carrying ever greater clout. If the market has no direction other than toward existing demand, and that demand is in some way contrived by advertising, the scenario suggests that large firms have their way, relatively immune to the disciplines of rigorous competition as they joust on the level of brand name rather than price—the recurrent concern with cereal prices is a classic example. Clearly, *animal symbolicum* is afoot here, easily impressed by the promises of the advertiser and responding accordingly. Consequently, the market is distorted, with a perceived need for government to enter to restore balance and/or fashion direction.

Simply, if one's assumptions involve the self-interested, rational individual, directing the economy through her or his "dollar votes," advertising will generally be perceived as helpful or, at least, not likely to do great harm. But if it is believed that the individual can be unduly influenced, that the power to pursue that influence is not checked by social responsibility, the forces of individual rationality, or diffused power, then advertising can be seen as a worrisome tool of the power brokers.

All of this, in turn, sets the stage for . . .

Regulation

As we have noted, an acceptance of a major role for government in virtually every facet of our society represents the greatest departure from "pure" classical liberal thought. Predictably, then, those whose positions are likely to fall near the top of the intellectualism, atomism, and economy continuums are also likely to feel comfortable high on the regulation continuum—urging the smallest possible role for government as a regulator in the economy and society at large, with whatever minimum constraints deemed necessary supplied by self-regulation. But as we move down the continuums through *animal symbolicum*, concentrated power, and the subsequent perceived need for a tinkered economy, the role of government as regulator planner to "set things right" becomes equally paramount, as does the vigorous exercise of social responsibility on the part of the advertising community in the form of self-regulation at the advertiser, agency, media, and association level.

The consequences for advertising are enormous, as will be explored in greater depth in chapter 7. By way of small example:

- Consumers Union endorses a ban on all cigarette advertising:

> Given the hazards of tobacco, the addictive nature of nicotine, which makes tobacco use less than voluntary, the sophisticated manipulation of cigarette advertising, the violations of the spirit (if not the letter) of the tobacco industry's own code of advertising conduct, the indication of an inverse relationship between cigarette advertising and media discussions of smoking hazards, the reinforcement of smoking by advertising that portrays cigarettes as not only socially acceptable but desirable—given all these, Congressional action to ban cigarette advertising and promotion is fully justified, in CU's judgment.[33]

By contrast, John O'Toole, then president of the American Association of Advertising Agencies, remarked:

> The fear underlying the compulsion to censor is groundless. Consumers are protected against untruthful advertising by media and advertising industry self-regulation and, ultimately, by the Federal Trade Commission. Truthful advertising for legal products and services can hurt no one. Indeed, it is inconsistent, if not erratic, to believe that those citizens who can distill the truth from the welter of diverse opinion heaved up each day by a free press cannot be trusted to decide, on the basis of commercial messages, which brand of soap or beer or even cigarettes to purchase—or whether to make such a purchase at all.[34]

The reader is invited to dissect these dramatically different positions in terms of the implicit assumptions of intellectualism, atomism, and egoism.

- During the eighties the Reagan administration pursued as strong a *de*regulation program as had taken place in half a century. Not surprisingly, the relative regulation vacuum at the federal level was filled by the states. It is instructive to note the philosophical differences apparent there as well:

> When deception occurs that hurts the citizens of our states, the state attorneys general cannot turn a blind eye, as the federal agencies have done. As the chief law enforcement officers of our states, it is our duty to stop deception and we will do so.[35]
>
> James Mattox
> Texas Attorney General

National advertising guidelines administered by the states repudiate the wisdom of the founders and bestow upon state officials the mantles of both the legislative and executive branches of the federal government.[36]

Hal Stratton
New Mexico Attorney General

Increasingly, there seems little respite for attempts to restrain or reshape advertising. For even early in the decade of the nineties, with another Republican administration, an *Advertising Age* editor stated that there were "over 30 pending bills in Congress [and 391 pieces of state legislation] which would restrict advertising and commercial speech," causing a veteran advertising representative to comment, "I have never seen such a volume and intensity of troubles with advertising."[37] Now in middecade and with a Republican Congress, there should be every expectation that at least the federal regulatory hand will again be lightened, but the assumptions about the "proper" levels of advertising regulation continue to span the neo-liberal continuum.

• • •

In the introduction, we offered this premise: "Because of its cultural boundness, its complexity of forms and functions, and the difficulty in ascertaining its outcome, advertising is highly prone to disparate interpretations."

Given the range of positions we contend are possible under neo-liberalism, we hope the reader is now in a better position to understand that perceptions of advertising in contemporary society are based in no small part on varying interpretations of such essential concepts as human nature, the seat of power, and the proper relationship between the individual and the state. Simply, advertising is "seen" differently, depending on the degree of neo-liberalism embraced.

_____ Summary

If Idea Systems ⟷ Institutions, then it is appropriate to inquire into what passes for our contemporary idea system by examining how it may differ from its classical liberal predecessor discussed in chapter 1. *Intellectualism* has been called into some doubt because of ambiguity about the dimensions of *animal symbolicum;* and *atomism,* the other major counterforce to narrow self-interest, is confronted with an economic and social landscape dominated by enormous power blocs. Hence, the notion of *egoism* is now qualified to some extent by the philosophy of "social responsibility," with its inherent assumption that the workings of the invisible hand are no longer certain.

As a result, the *economy* is now commonly regarded as in need of regulation and, perhaps, direction, often through the role of *government* as regulator and/or planner.

Given this range of ideas under what we have called neo-liberalism, advertising in contemporary society can be regarded quite differently. As master . . . or servant. As friend of the market . . . or foe. As information dispenser . . . or symbol manipulator.

Much can be better understood through such a perspective.

Notes

1. Walton Hamilton, "Institution," *The Encyclopedia of the Social Sciences* (New York: Macmillan, 1932), 8:85.

2. Charles L. Griswold Jr., "Adam Smith: Conscience of Capitalism," *Wilson Quarterly* 15 (Summer 1991): 54.

3. Theodore Levitt, "The Dangers of Social Responsibility," *Harvard Business Review* 36 (Sept.–Oct. 1958): 48, emphasis in original.

4. Robert G. Samuelson, "The Aging of Ralph Nader," *Newsweek*, Dec. 16, 1985, 57.

5. Michael Perschuk, "The Press and Business: As Biased as a Scream from the Dentist's Chair!" remarks before the Society of Professional Journalists, San Francisco, Nov. 10, 1983.

6. Ellen K. Coughlin, "Feminist Economists vs. 'Economic Man': Questioning a Field's Bedrock Concepts," *Chronicle of Higher Education*, June 30, 1993, A-8.

7. "How to Save $2500 a Year in the Supermarket," *Consumer Reports*, Mar. 1988, 163.

8. James W. Carey, "Advertising: An Institutional Approach," in *The Role of Advertising*, ed. C. H. Sandage and V. Fryburger (Homewood, Ill.: Richard D. Irwin, 1960), 16.

9. "Rewriting Antitrust Rules," *Newsweek*, Aug. 29, 1983, 50.

10. Ralph Nader, "Corporate Power in America," *The Nation*, Mar. 29, 1980, 367.

11. "What Kind of Media Diversity?" *Communication Research Trends* 4, no. 1 (1983): 7.

12. Ibid.

13. Leo Bogart, "Advertising: Art, Science, or Business?" James Webb Young Fund Address, Department of Advertising, University of Illinois, Apr. 7, 1988, transcript, 8–9.

14. Robert J. Samuelson, "Competition: Tried and True," *Newsweek*, June 11, 1990, 47.

15. "Nation's 'Third Deficit' Widening—Dovring," *IlliniWeek*, Dec. 10, 1987, 5.

16. Robert L. Heilbroner, *The Worldly Philosophers* (New York: Time, 1961), 336–52.

17. George A. Theodorson and Achilles G. Theodorson, *Modern Dictionary of Sociology* (New York: Thomas Y. Crowell, 1969), 224.

18. Irving Kristol, "What Is a 'Neo-Conservative?'" *Newsweek*, Jan. 19, 1976, 17.

19. William Leiss, Stephen Kline, and Sut Ghally, *Social Communication in Advertising: Persons, Products, and Images of Well-Being* (New York: Methuen, 1990), 32.

20. Ibid.

21. Preben Sepstrup, "Information Content in TV Advertising: Consumer Policy Implications of the Growing Supply of TV Advertising in Europe," *Journal of Consumer Policy* 8 (Sept. 1985): 250.

22. Leiss, Kline, and Ghally, *Social Communication in Advertising*, 1.

23. "What's It All About, Calvin?" *Time*, Sept. 23, 1991, 44.

24. Roger Draper, "The Faithless Shepherd," *New York Review*, June 26, 1986, 18.

25. Nancy Giges, "World's Product Parity Perception High," *Advertising Age*, June 20, 1988, 66.

26. "Listings—Mouthwashes," *Consumer Reports*, Mar. 1984, 146.

27. "Why You Watch Commercials—Whether You Mean to or Not," *TV Guide*, Feb. 20, 1988, 5–7.

28. Bogart, "Advertising," 8–9.

29. "They Did It Twenty Thousand Times on Television Last Year: How Come Nobody Got Pregnant?" *News-Gazette* (Champaign-Urbana, Ill.), Dec. 7, 1986, A-15.

30. Ronald K. L. Collins and Michael F. Jacobson, "Commercialism vs. Culture," *Christian Science Monitor*, Sept. 19, 1990, 19.

31. American Federation of Advertising, "An Open Letter to President Bush," *New York Times*, Jan. 23, 1992, D-21.

32. See Charles H. Sandage, "Some Institutional Aspects of Advertising," *Journal of Advertising* 1, no. 1 (1973): 6–9, for the essence of his position.

33. "Ban Cigarette Advertising?" *Consumer Reports*, Sept. 1987, 568–69.

34. John O'Toole, "Advertising and Democracy: Is Advertising Second-Class Speech?" *Gannett Center Journal* 1 (Spring 1987): 107.

35. "Should States Regulate Ads?" *Advertising Age*, Aug. 8, 1988, 18.

36. Ibid.

37. Charles S. Clark, "Advertising under Attack," *CQ Researcher*, Sept. 13, 1991, 659.

3

Helpful Perspectives on Advertising as an Institution

In the two preceding chapters we have probed the left side of the Idea Systems ⟷ Institutions concept. Here, we turn our attention to the right, as seen through the lens of several individuals who have asked fundamental questions: What functions does advertising perform as an institution in our society? With what consequences and trade-offs? Their ruminations deepen our understanding of advertising in contemporary society.

It has been said that "We don't know who discovered water, but we're pretty sure it wasn't a fish." That's a useful idea to bring to the study of an institution. For it's very difficult to appreciate the larger dimensions of something of which we ourselves are a part. Thus, the true impact of the idea "Island Earth" did not hit us until the astronauts photographed it from afar—colorful, but very, very much alone.

And so it is with institutional analysis. We often find it extraordinarily difficult to understand the full configuration of an institution that guides our behavior. Indeed, as Hamilton observes, until the academic community began to grudgingly accept the idea that the behavior of individuals could not be adequately explained solely as as result of their own free will or as the behavior of cells in a well-integrated and predictable organism, institutional analysis was simply not considered at all.[1]

As we have previously noted, an institution may be seen as representing a convention, an arrangement, or an answer to a problem considered important by the society. It was also held that the different "answers" that various societies choose to deal with the same fundamental problems (e.g., what to produce) can, in part, be attributed to their differing idea systems. Thus, the institution of the market (with its emphasis on resource allocation through the action of many self-seeking individuals) was seen to be most compatible with the idea system of classical liberalism (with its emphasis on the sovereignty and rationality of each individual).

_____ Why Institutional Analysis?

Why bother considering a phenomenon in our society from an institutional perspective? At a minimum, it can give us some view of the forest even as the trees compel our attention. For example, a marriage certificate, a high-school athletic jacket, a jail cell make little sense in and of themselves unless we see them as parts of the larger institutional whole of marriage, organized amateur athletics, and a system that attempts to define crime and punishment.

Similarly, advertisements for a personal computer, a perfume, a breakfast cereal, a bowling alley, or an abortion clinic are not readily understood in any significant dimension unless we first understand why it is we consider an impersonal information and persuasion process like advertising an acceptable means to attempt to alter the thinking and behavior of individuals; what the generally accepted "rules of the road" between advertiser and receiver are, etc. Sandage has put it this way—institutional analysis lets us be architects as well as bricklayers, with our vision filled with the total structure as well as the roles assigned to its component parts.[2]

Institutional analysis may also aid us in understanding the "conventional wisdom" of advertising as an institution. Hamilton notes: "As it crystallizes into reputable usages, an institution creates in its defense vested interest, vested habit, and vested ideas and claims allegiance in its own right."[3]

And thus does every institution create its own apology. The origins of an institution may be very utilitarian—e.g., to tend the sick—but as it flourishes and draws to it individuals whose vested interests lie in its perpetuation and ennoblement, an ideology and apparatus emerge to support it—e.g., the American Medical Association. By way of further example, as the institution of "the family" is challenged, it is frequently defended by references to the Scriptures; similarly, organized athletics is often charged with no less a noble endeavor than "character building."

It would thus seem reasonable that this institutional perspective may be useful in helping us to better understand not only the defenses of but also the attacks on advertising. For example, some critics proclaim that advertising directed to children is likely to do serious harm to their psyches or that advertising contributes to a massive waste of human and natural resources or that advertising is offensive and demeaning to the role of women, the elderly, minorities, and others. In a similar mode, it is not uncommon to attend advertising conventions where advertising is described as the consumer's best friend, an indispensable source of relevant market information, and, depending on the severity of the critical salvo, the bulwark of the free enterprise system. As we hope we have made clear this far, *all* advertising is—objectively—none of these things, although critic and defender believe the contrary. This tendency to generalize about the activities and purposes of an institution is, apparently, quite natural. We should, then, be on our guard, realizing that the perception of an institution that emerges from its more dedicated critics, *and* ardent defenders, is far more likely to resemble an impressionistic painting than a realistic photograph. Institutional analysis, then, holds the promise to lead us to higher analytical ground, while reminding us not to overlook the variations in the terrain below. To see the whole while appreciating the parts is, then, not an unpromising quest.

The following insightful and enduring perspectives offer us the opportunity to see advertising as an institution through perceptive eyes. They encompass four decades and are rich in analytical tools and insights. Learn and enjoy.

_____ Carey—Advertising as Market Information

James W. Carey, a communications scholar, offered this intriguing interpretation—"the information provided in purely competitive markets and in primitive markets is *advertising*. We here define market information as advertising."[4] But there is much more that needs to be said.

Carey devoted his penetrating 1960 essay to the search for "the ideas and institutions which favor the development of an economic system in which advertising becomes a part of the very logic by which commerce is carried on."[5] He found the "ideas" in the liberalism of the eighteenth and nineteenth centuries and, particularly, in the influence of Newton (indirectly) and Locke and Smith (directly): "For our purposes the ideas that were of fundamental importance in justifying the new economic order [the market] were the notions that all was mechanistic, that natural law governed the physical and social world, that the world was characterized by fundamental harmony, that man possessed reason and conscience, that men were equal and endowed with certain fundamental rights—life, liberty, and property."[6]

Sound familiar? The resulting institutions are thus seen as the market system and, of particular importance, the idea of property rights was born.

As seen from this classical liberal perspective, then, an individual expresses the rights to "property"—anything with which he or she has mixed labor—in the free marketplace, where she or he encounters other individuals in the same pursuit. Harmony rather than discord results due to the essentially rational and moral nature of the individual and—crucially—the great safeguard of competition. And it is *within this system*, Carey argues, that the institutional importance of advertising becomes evident:

> One of the fundamental assumptions underlying theoretical analysis of competitive markets, and the whole concept of economic man, is that all entrants into the economic market shall have perfect knowledge; that is, each should be aware of all prices resulting from supply and demand relationships and should have perfect knowledge of alternative forms of satisfying demand. *Caveat emptor*—let the buyer beware—simply means that every individual, being rational, is assumed to possess the ability to exercise correct judgment by basing his decisions on available market information.[7]

Now, under *purely competitive* markets (i.e., with unlimited numbers of buyers and sellers, undifferentiated products, etc.), the task of supplying relevant information is carried out by the "market" itself (contemporary approximations can be found in the stock market, the grain market, and so on) based on myriad interpersonal transactions. Thus, this market supplied information concerning supply and demand represented the interactions of many buyers and sellers concerning their property rights and, presumably, led to the "natural" value of the goods offered. It is here, in the supplying of relevant information, Carey stated, that advertising's institutional birth can be found. It is not, of course, advertising as we generally know it today (it differs in *content* and *source*) but it does, he felt, correctly place advertising's origins as a supplier of relevant information in a market economy in proper institutional perspective.

Advertising in its *modern* form, Carey held, developed as markets began to lose their interpersonal nature. As production became more centralized, as branded merchandise developed, the function of supplying market information shifted from the market itself to the firms in the market, with "the old interpersonal relationships in the marketplace . . . displaced by relationships mediated by mass communication facilities."[8] Of course, the self-seeking firms were interested in "market information" for persuasive (rather than simply informational) purposes.

Now, *under the assumption that the individual is rational,* it is quite appropriate to attempt to persuade. For, it is assumed that the rational person will be able to detect truth in the clashing views of self-interested individuals in the economic marketplace in the same manner that her or his discerning nature would enable truth to arise in the political arena. Thus, advertising's basic institutional function of supplying information "to facilitate judgment and free choice on the part of the consumer"[9] remains intact, but the fact that the "information" is now supplied by interested parties (firms) has certain consequences: "There is no longer any guarantee that the self-righting process operates to yield the 'true value' of goods when individual firms possess a measure of control over the market. Because competition no longer provides the check on self-interest that it did under atomistic market organization, control in the market is increasingly being sought in human and corporate conscience—a conscience expressed through the notion of social responsibility."[10]

Modern advertising was seen by Carey as still performing the traditional function of disseminating market information "as a logical corollary of a market system,"[11] but also as acting "as an agency of social control providing norms of behavior appropriate to current economic conditions."[12] Thus, as marketing is conventionally concerned with the development of demand in an abundant society, advertising is called upon not merely to "sell" but also to "create and develop" demand for a host of products and services that are well beyond any traditional definition of "necessity." He concluded:

> Consequently, the nub of the "advertising problem" really rests on a controversy over who shall supply the necessary market information, what type of information it shall be, and to what ends it should be directed. The reader may then reflect upon the following two propositions: (1) That the source of advertising or market information is determined by the demands of technology and the location of economic power; and (2) that the specific form and nature of advertising messages is dependent on the particular economic problem which the society recognizes as most pressing and, more importantly, on the view that society takes toward the nature of man and to what it is that motivates "appropriate" market behavior.[13]

For Carey, then, the key was the source and type of information necessary for the functioning of a market system and, implicitly, the assumptions about "human nature" that lie behind these functions. Advertising's basic institutional function is thus linked to the provision of "market information," however that be interpreted by the society.

• • •

Now, it would seem that considerable understanding is offered by the concept of market information. If the information necessary for the functioning of a market system is provided by the sellers through mass communication, then the content and frequency of that information will be different from that provided by the "market" itself, either through interpersonal exchanges (e.g., a flea market) or a formalized system (e.g., the grain market or stock market). The comparison can perhaps be made clear with table 3-1.

Who supplies the information, it can be contended, is at the heart of a great deal of ongoing controversy about the proper role of advertising. For the content of modern advertising is directed primarily by the best interests of the seller and thus may or may not include *all* the market information that might be necessary for the rational consumer to make a proper decision. To risk oversimplification, critics generally argue that the informational content of much advertising is not adequate to achieve

Table 3-1.

Information Supplied by	Content	Medium/Frequency	Example
Market			
1. Formal	Prices, quantities, qualities	Mass or controlled As needed by participants	Winter wheat information
2. Interpersonal	Relevant information	Person-to-person As controlled by participants	Flea market
Seller	Biased—whatever is in the best interest of the seller	As desired by the seller	Cosmetics advertising

that purpose, while many advertisers contend that it is. And here the arguments become quite complex indeed.

The critic may, for example, argue either (1) that the informational content of the *existing* market information (e.g., advertisements) needs to be enriched, usually through regulation—e.g., the requirement that cigarette advertising include health warnings—or (2) that *additional* sources of market information be made more widely available—e.g., the product ratings of government agencies, the judgments of such sources as *Consumer Reports*, and "counter" advertising.

The call for *additional* sources seems to stem from a view of human nature similar to that held by the classical liberals, implying that an increase in message sources will better enable the truth-seeking individual to make a wise decision. Proposals for enriching *existing* sources, however, can be viewed as suggesting that the individual is *not* a "truth seeker" (or at least is a lazy one) and must be catered to by making present sources of market information (e.g., advertisements) more informative (i.e., less "imperfect") in content.

Predictably, advertisers generally argue that the individual is quite capable of making satisfying market decisions on the basis of the existing state of the market information as represented by the advertisements of competing enterprises. The key here is "satisfying" (remember our discussion of "information" in chapter 2). While critics often assume that relatively objective criteria can be applied that will make some products and services objectively "better buys" over others, advertisers frequently suggest that the *individual* should be the sole judge of what criteria she or he will apply in reaching a purchase decision. Thus, it is reasoned, if an individual *bought* it, he or she must have *wanted* it, for whatever reason. And if the advertisement led in any way to that decision, then it *must* have been satisfying "market information," at least for *that* individual. (Pushed to its limit, this reasoning suggests there is no such thing as an "irrational" decision.)

The matter of the frequency of advertising is, of course, a subject of some contention, particularly in the broadcast media. Carey's perspective enables us to see that the frequency of market information, when supplied by self-interested participants, will be whatever they feel is necessary to achieve their ends. Thus, we find the irritation factor emerging among those who complain of increasingly lengthy interruptions of broadcast programming, repetition of particular advertisements, and so on. By contrast, looking at the market from basically classical liberal premises, the deliberate and calculating *individual would seek out "market" supplied information.* With information supplied by self-seeking firms, however, the information frequently *seeks out the individual,* with all the ensuing trade-offs.

Carey's analysis, then, raises a central question for the analysis of advertising: *What should be the proper source, content, and frequency of market information in the United States?* The position an individual takes, as this brief analysis is meant to suggest, is heavily dependent upon such contentions as how "rational" the consumer is assumed to be.

_____ Norris—The Quest for Market Power

"Institutions," the communications scholar Vincent P. Norris reminded us, "are the 'rules' according to which social life is carried on, and consequently our understanding of the life of any society is limited by our understanding of those institutions."[14]

To understand advertising as an institution, Norris held, one must avoid the temptation to trace it back to Pompeii or medieval Europe. Such a practice, he contended, is "roughly analogous to tracing the history of man back to the paramecium."[15] Advertising, for Norris, was only "on its way" to becoming an institution "when some sizable segment of the population (namely, the business class) came to look upon advertising not as an emergency measure to be used sporadically, but as the routine manner of solving an omnipresent problem (let us say, the profitable conduct of business)."[16]

Unlike Carey, who assumes a broad historical sweep, Norris contended that it was not until the last thirty years of the nineteenth century in America that advertising emerged as a "full-fledged" institution. It was during this period that advertising's volume increased tenfold, but, of far greater importance, the increase was due largely to "an entirely new form of advertising"—the advertising of *producers,* not retailers. Yet, Norris claimed, when advertising text writers dealt with the subject of the emergence of "national" (producer) advertising, they often got it wrong. For example: "As the Industrial Revolution brought technological advances, the output of the factory increased. Soon it was turning out goods in quantities far too great to be consumed in its immediate area; consequently, the manufacturer began shipping his output to more and more distant markets. And of course, *he had to use advertising, because the people in those areas did not know of him or his products.*"[17]

This, he asserted, is a gross oversimplification ("to say it as charitably as possible") because: (1) centralized supply had existed for centuries (e.g., the Phoenicians were perhaps the greatest source of goods in their time) without advertising; (2) these nineteenth-century producers were essentially operating in a seller's market, so there was no *incentive* to advertise for reputational reasons; and (3) it ignores the role of the wholesaler—"somewhat akin to describing the plot of *Othello* without mentioning Iago."[18]

To follow Norris's thinking, as nineteenth-century producers began to satisfy the demand of their local markets, they faced the question of how to distribute their goods to other cities, towns, and villages. For most suppliers, wholesalers filled the vacuum by serving as the link between a limited number of producers and a much larger number of retailers. As goods were still largely undifferentiated (e.g., the "cracker barrel" full of unbranded crackers), the wholesaler was in a position to translate the retailer's wishes ("I need thirty pounds of crackers") to his or her own economic advantage by buying from the supplier who would offer the lowest possible price. And, *since the producers needed the wholesaler more than she or he needed each of them,* the wholesaler was able to play one against the other. This worked out well for the wholesaler. It was, Norris asserted, quite another story for the producer.

> As a result of this price competition, the revenue of the manufacturers during this period of wholesaler domination was driven down very close to the cost of production. It was to escape from this predicament, to gain bargaining power, that manufacturers toward the end of the 19th century resorted to branding their output and advertising it "over the heads of the wholesalers to the ultimate buyers, the consuming public." To the extent that consumers could be induced to request a particular manufacturer's brand from the retailer, the retailer would order it from the wholesaler ["I need thirty pounds of Uneeda Biscuit"], who in turn would be forced to buy it from that manufacturer and no other. Now the manufacturer, not the wholesaler, was dominant, and he could name his price.[19]

Thus, Norris contended, *the reasons for the growth of national advertising had little to do with problems of selling per se,* for the producer could commonly sell all she or he could produce, as long as there was a willingness to accept the wholesaler's price. "The sole purpose of national advertising, in its early days, was to avoid competing on a price basis."[20]

Now, this intended function, Norris contended, was of great institutional import, because it totally *"changed* the pattern of economic activity."[21] For with national advertising and branding, competition became much less "perfect." This, in turn, led to certain positive and negative consequences, including the availability of "pure" profits, which could be used for research and development, and the shift of control over packaging and product quality from the retailer/wholesaler to the producer, but it also led to a clear move to nonprice competition as a producer option, resulting in an "imperfect" distribution of resources to market entrants who were not necessarily the most economically efficient.

Basically then, for Norris, advertising became a major institution in the latter part of the nineteenth century. Producer ("national") advertising emerged as an attempt to acquire market power and avoid damaging price competition. The market, he contends, was never the same again.

• • •

Norris directed our attention to advertising's institutional functioning in terms of its economic consequences. First, he suggested, it is fruitful to consider advertising in terms of a dominant *type* of advertising—in this case, that of producers. This in itself has interesting implications. At the beginning of this chapter, we suggested that one facet of institutional behavior is a tendency to generalize—to see uniformity among often diverse and conflicting activities. This clearly has pitfalls as well as assets. It may well be that a cogent case can be made—even today—for advertising's role as a provider of relatively factual information if we examine only such forms as retail, business, professional, and classified ads. Such an argument would, however, seem somewhat dubious when we turn to much advertising from producers directed at consumers—e.g., ads for beer, cosmetics, and cigarettes. Thus, Norris suggested, there are advantages to adopting a somewhat narrow analytic field.

Norris left little doubt that he felt the market system in this country changed with the emergence of national advertising as the ongoing solution to the firms' problem of how to acquire market power. The major question raised is whether advertising's effects on the nature of the market system are, on balance, positive or negative.

Interestingly, he has forced us to examine the alteration of one form of a market system, where all entrants are essentially powerless to affect the overall allocation of resources, to a hybrid where producers can acquire market power through the differentiating of their products with national advertising. Who wins in this "imperfect" market resulting from the emergence of producer advertising? Some perspectives:

Supporter

- Advertising enables the producer to achieve "pure" profits that can, in turn, be plowed back into product improvement, research and development, etc.
- Advertising, as an expression of property rights, is an efficient form of communicating the advantages of the producer's product to a large number of people.

Critic

- Advertising enables a producer to manipulate the price of a good to his or her own advantage. Thus the price has little relationship to the "real" market value of the product.
- Advertising leads to a waste of resources by shifting the reward system away from the standard of pure efficiency and by enabling producers to operate at less than full capacity for their own advantage.

Norris made his position clear. "As advertising works better and better," he asserted in a purposefully ungrammatical but telling phrase, "the market works worse and worse."[22] Note that he was starting from the assumptions of the "perfect" market and was also assuming that the alterations presumably caused by advertising are, overall, dysfunctional. Herein, it can be contended, lies his position's primary analytical rigor.

For Norris was offering a critical economic perspective that explains much about the assumptions behind many of the more persistent economic criticisms of advertising. For example:

- "Advertising leads to higher prices"—based on *what standard?*
- "Advertising restricts competition"—compared to *what?*
- "Advertising leads to a waste of resources"—defined *how?*

Basically, it can be contended that these familiar critical assertions are all assuming that "as advertising works better and better, the [perfect] market works worse and worse." At a very minimum, then, Norris's perspective forces us to probe the implicit standard behind critical economic themes concerning advertising and the economy and compare that model with its contender.

Herein, then, is both a more historically precise explanation of the origins of national advertising *and* a critical matrix for examining advertising's economic performance in differing visions of a market system.

———— Potter—Social Control without Social Responsibility

It was really a historian who first dealt explicitly with the idea of advertising as an institution in the modern era. David Potter, in his 1954 book *People of Plenty*, explored the role of abundance in society. Abundance, he contended, must be considered "a major force" in American history. Yet, unlike other major forces such as democracy, religion, and science, abundance had apparently not been considered as having developed its own distinctive institution comparable to representative government, the clergy, and the apparatus of scholarship, for example. However, Potter felt that he had found the appropriate institution of an abundant society: "If we seek an institution that was brought into being by abundance, without previous existence in any form, and, moreover, an institution which is peculiarly identified with American abundance rather than abundance throughout Western civilization, we will find it, I believe, in modern American advertising."[23]

Advertising, he felt, had been woefully neglected by historians of public opinion, popular culture, and the mass media, even though "advertising created modern American radio and television, transformed the modern newspaper, evoked the modern slick-periodical, and remains the vital essence of them at the present time."[24]

Potter noted the considerable growth of advertising in the last quarter of the nineteenth century and particularly the rise of the advertising of producers (Norris's emphasis) in an attempt to "create a consumer demand for their brand and thus of exerting pressure upon the distributor to keep their products in stock."[25] Soon, Potter contended, producers were no longer using advertising merely "as a coupling device between existing market demand and their own supply," but rather were trying "to create a demand."[26] This, he felt, altered the nature of the advertising message from one emphasizing information to one focused "upon the desires of the consumer." (He noted the appearance, in 1903, of Walter Dill Scott's article "The Psychology of Advertising."[27])

What accounts for advertising's growth? Potter quoted Neil Borden's explanation of the widening gap between producer and consumer, but placed particular emphasis on Borden's claim that advertising flourished in part when "the quest for product differentiation became intensified as the industrial system became more mature, and as manufacturers had capacity to produce far beyond existing demand."[28]

Advertising begins to fill its essential function in the society then, Potter held, when potential supply exceeds existing demand—a condition of abundance. And what, beyond the aims of the individual producers, does advertising accomplish in this capacity?

> Consumer societies, like all other kinds, seem to fall short of their utopias, and we revert to the question how the citizen, in our mixed production-consumption society, can be educated to perform his role as a consumer, especially as a consumer of goods for which he feels no impulse of need. Clearly he must be educated, and the only institution which we have for instilling new needs, for training people to act as consumers, for altering men's values, and thus for hastening their adjustment to potential abundance is advertising. That is why it seems to me valid to regard advertising as distinctively the institution of abundance.[29]

Thus, Potter contended, advertising's influence is not merely economic. In fact, he asserted that it is one of a very few "instruments of social control" that serve to "guide the life of the individual by conceiving of him in a distinctive way and encouraging him to conform as far as possible to the concept." He sees these few "institutions of social control" as illustrated in table 3-2.[30]

The church, schools, and industry, Potter felt, "have tried to improve man and to develop in him qualities of social value."[31] Advertising, how-

Table 3-2.

Institution	Conceives of the Individual as	Appeals to
The church	An immortal soul	Salvation, through conscience, spirit
The schools	A being whose behavior is guided by reason	Reason, with the hope of a perfected society
Industry	A productive agent	Skill, personal satisfaction
Advertising	A consumer	Desires and wants—cultivated or natural

ever, attempts none of this. "It is this lack of institutional responsibility, this lack of inherent social purpose to balance social power which, I would argue, is a basic cause for concern about the role of advertising."[32]

Potter devoted the remainder of this chapter to developing what he considered to be the dimensions of advertising's "power." First, there is the sheer dollar weight—e.g., "Our national outlay for the education of citizens . . . amounted to substantially less than our expenditure for the education of consumers."[33] But of particular concern is advertising's "profound influence on the media" and "through them" on the public.[34]

He asserted that as advertising revenues became more and more attractive to publishers—and essential to broadcasters—their products (the magazines, newspapers, television and radio programs) became less and less *ends* in themselves and more *means* to the end of attracting large numbers of potential customers to be exposed to the advertising messages. This necessitated the watering down of the nonadvertising content of the media—the avoidance of controversial themes, the emphasis on the bland "common denominator" that would attract the largest numbers of readers or viewers, and other similar strategies. Thus, he contended, Americans are more frequently titillated by the mass media than educated, and the appeal is to the attention-getting rather than the substantive. The result of all this is thus "to enforce already existing attitudes, to diminish the range and variety of choices and, in terms of abundance, to exalt the materialistic values of consumption."[35] He summarized:

> Certainly it marks a profound social change that this new institution for shaping human standards should be directed, not as are the school and the church, to the inclination of beliefs or attitudes that are held to be of social value, but rather to the stimulation or even the exploitation of materialistic drives and emulative anxieties and then to the validation, the sanctioning, and the standardization of these drives as accepted criteria of social value. Such a transformation, brought about by the need to stimulate desire for the goods which an abundant economy has to offer and which a scarcity economy would never have produced, offers strong justification for the view that advertising should be recognized as an important social influence and as our newest major institution—an institution peculiarly identified with one of the most persuasive forces in American life, the force of economic abundance.[36]

For Potter then, advertising is an institution of abundance whose important effects are not merely upon the economy but rather "upon the values of our society,"[37] as an instrument of social control. Clearly, he did not view the outcome positively.

•   •   •

Potter linked advertising's institutional functioning to the transition from a "producer's culture" to a "consumer's culture." Advertising, he contended, teaches us to be consumers. In this capacity, advertising becomes one of a handful of institutions that exert social control. The problem, as Potter saw it, is that the other major sources of social control—the schools, the church, the business system—have a higher "social responsibility," a need to temper their social power. Potter contended that advertising does not have this need, and this lack of higher purpose is a cause of considerable concern to him.

Remember that under the classical liberal worldview there was *no* explicit expectation of responsibility beyond individual self-interest. Indeed, the "laws" of the market would operate in their self-correcting manner only if each participant pursued her or his self-interest in a single-minded manner. The forces of competition (and the individual's inherent moral sense) would—at least in the long run—assure that all would work out well for the whole due to the "universal harmony of interests," or, if you prefer, the invisible hand.

To the extent that Potter chided advertising for its lack of social responsibility, he operated from a set of assumptions about "human nature" that are certainly in the *animal symbolicum* range on the neo-liberal continuum (see figure 2-1). Thus, Potter, by implication, seemed to be arguing that the individual will not be able to resist the seductive appeals of advertising to his or her "wants and desires" *in spite of the competition offered by the other major institutions* he offered for comparison (i.e., the church, the schools, businesses) as well as those not explicitly discussed but clearly influential (e.g., the family). Under these assumptions, it is not surprising that he called for less self-interest and more "social" interest on the part of advertisers.

It can further be assumed that from this perspective many of the "natural laws" of the classical liberals are no longer considered operative. Primary among the apparent defections are the decline of people's rationality under the onslaught of high advertising expenditures and the assumption that a "clash of ideas" will emerge from the normal functioning of the media system. (In fact, Potter asserted that because the media depend on advertising, they serve only the status quo in a dollar-sensitive quest to offend no one and, thus, maximize the audience size they sell to advertisers.)

More explicitly, Potter's view raises intriguing questions in the very broadest realms of "social control." Are massive doses of advertising necessary to sustain a "consumer culture"? And if they are, what are their costs—in terms of the clichélike "leading us to buy things we don't need or want," in the watered-down, status-quo-oriented values that the advertising-dependent media must perpetuate in order to survive? (It is important to note that in today's era of increasing media fragmentation, Potter's assertions of media homogeneity and editorial timidity do not appear as persuasive as they might have in the early 1950s. Yet, as common sense observation will suggest, and chapter 6 will explicate, the advertising/media relations today are no less troubling—e.g., are magazines with heavy reliance on cigarette advertising revenue likely to sidestep the moral issues of providing space for the promotion of a dangerous product? In any event, this should not detract the serious student from careful consideration of Potter's primary contribution to understanding and examination—the idea of advertising's presumed institutional directive to train us "to act as consumers" with all that it implies.)

Now, if Carey offers us analytical perspectives on advertising's communication dimensions and Norris provides insights into critical economic themes, then Potter helps us to understand the assumptions behind the criticisms of advertising as a *social* force.

Consider contemporary issues such as:

- Does advertising adversely influence children?
- Does advertising adversely affect our self-images?
- Does advertising "cause us to buy things we don't want or need"?

The answers, from this perspective, would seem to be *yes*. Why? Because, all critics basically assume, as did Potter, that advertisers' self-interests are *not* channeled toward socially desirable ends by individual rationality or the forces of competition. Thus, in the absence of "social responsibility," exploitation reigns.

In essence, Potter offers us insights into the common occurrence of a perspective on the neo-liberal continuum interacting with an institution that is perceived as operating from another dimension of the same continuum—e.g., an individual doubting the individual's rationality "seeing" advertising exploiting that weakness. Small wonder, then, that Potter's exploration of advertising as an institution has endured, for it illuminates areas of bedrock ideological conflict.

_____ Sandage—To Inform and Persuade

Charles Sandage addressed a 1973 essay[38] to the climate of criticism that surrounded advertising in the sixties-seventies phase of "consumerism." He made it clear from the outset that an institutional perspective can enable the practitioner to *respond to criticism* by "understanding the true nature of advertising and concentrating on its positive values."[39]

Thus, he asserted, it is first necessary to distinguish between the institution (advertising) and the instruments (advertisements). Much criticism, and much heated defense, has been spent on individual parts of the larger whole. But what is the nature of the whole?

Advertising, Sandage held, has been assigned the function of "helping society to achieve abundance" by *informing* and *persuading* members of society about products, services, and ideals.[40] In addition, another responsibility "is that of education in consumerism—the development of judgment on the part of consumers in their purchase practices."[41] Once we understand these larger functions, he contended, we will also realize that a great deal of the criticism of advertising is in fact criticism of such basic concepts as abundance, persuasion, and freedom of choice. The classical liberal tone of his argument is perhaps best revealed in the matter of freedom of choice:

> In a free society the nature of consumption is determined primarily by consumers themselves. They decide, through their actions in the marketplace, how many people will be employed to supply them with tobacco, clothing, homes, automobiles, boats, golf balls, cosmetics, air conditioners, books and paintings to hang on their walls. They decide, too, how much of their purchasing power will be spent to support preachers, private schools, research foundations, art galleries and symphony orchestras. In a little different fashion but still basic, they determine through their votes at the polls how much they will buy in the form of defense hardware, public school buildings, teachers' services, public parks, highways, help for the less fortunate, and pollution control.[42]

To the extent that individuals do *not* seem to be making choices that, objectively, appear to be in their best interests, the solution rests, he contended, not in "substituting a commissar for the free consumer," but rather in "raising the level of education in consumerism."[43] Thus, Sandage argued, advertising should serve to "implement freedom of choice" by "supplying consumers with adequate and accurate information about all of the alternatives available to them."[44]

He suggested that this necessary flow of information will be accomplished through two processes:

1. The ongoing conflict of ideas in the marketplace—e.g., the overweight person is exposed not only to the tempting messages of the candy makers but also to the persuasive arguments of the products and services of weight reduction.

2. "Full and honest disclosure, with competition available to provide knowledge of alternatives." This suggests that each message "will provide full disclosure of product characteristics that are important in evaluating its ability to meet a need or want."[45]

By performing these two functions, Sandage asserted, those who attempt to "inform and persuade" in respect to "things, services, and ideas" are indeed involved in socially beneficial activities. For, "it is a proper and justifiable social goal to help consumers maximize their satisfactions."[46]

Stepping back to an institutional perspective, Sandage contended, offers the practitioner of advertising the opportunity to assess the function that society expects advertising to perform. That function, he asserted, is to help society achieve abundance by informing and persuading its sovereign citizens in relation to products, services, and ideas. Thus, he reasoned, "advertising practitioners who accept this concept are indeed consumer advocates."[47]

• • •

Animal rationale is clearly in charge in Sandage's view of the system. It is the individual's decisions that determine what will be produced, in what quantities, of what quality, and so on. In direct contention with Potter's "social control" interpretation, he asserted: "Advertising is criticized on the ground that it can manipulate consumers to follow the will of the advertiser. The weight of evidence denies this ability. Instead, evidence supports the position that advertising, to be successful, must understand or anticipate basic human needs and wants and interpret available goods and services in terms of their want-satisfying abilities."[48]

The institution is not master here, but servant. This is, in general, quite consistent with the strongly classical liberal perspective of the Sandage analysis.

It should be noted, however, that he also suggested that the quality of the information supplied by advertisers *is not always sufficient to enable the sovereign individual to function rationally.* Thus, he called for "full and honest disclosure" in advertising. Carried to its full interpretation, this could at times require the disclosure of information by advertisers that is not in their best interests—e.g., the advertisers of lotteries routinely publicizing the real odds of winning. Such practices would, of course, represent a not insignificant qualification of the pursuit of the advertisers' self-interests and thus a rather striking deviation from the classical liberal thrust of Sandage's perspective. On balance, however, it should not seriously dilute the dramatic contrast between the different philosophical assumptions held by Sandage and the other major theorist of advertising and abundance—David Potter. Sandage, it is clear, inevitably comes down on the side of the *sovereign individual*—the true litmus test for a person with a classical liberal orientation.

If Carey offers insights into advertising's dimensions as market information, Norris into economic criticisms, and Potter into social critiques, clearly the Sandage perspective illuminates advertising's defensive posture:

- Advertising *cannot* "cause us to buy things we don't want or need."
- Advertising *does not* lead to adverse consequences for the consumer.

Why? Because the *individual is capable*—capable of seeking, capable of evaluating, capable of finding satisfaction from the market. Advertising, then, can do no more than the individual finds meaningful.

These sentiments, as we have seen, are easily found in the advertising business. Their basically classical liberal orientation is, again, apparent.

_____ Schudson—Advertising as Capitalist Realism

Perhaps the central conceptual contribution from Michael Schudson's 1984 book, *Advertising, the Uneasy Persuasion,*[49] is the contention that advertising in America (at least the national consumer goods variety) can be seen as "capitalist realism."

Unlike efforts of personal selling, Schudson argued, advertising "is part of the establishment and reflection of a common symbolic culture" that "connects the buyer to an assemblage of buyers through words and pictures available to all of them and tailored to no one of them."[50] He then explored the dimensions and consequences of that culture.

In advertising, he contended, experience is "flattened" in the sense that advertisements depict life that is relatively timeless and placeless. Even models/actors in advertisements are meant to be regarded not as distinct individuals but as representations of a "social type or a demographic category" (e.g., the "career woman," the "senior citizen") with which the reader or viewer can identify as a member of the expressed category. These neither real nor totally fictional messages are then seen as linked "to the political economy whose values they celebrate and promote."[51] Hence, "capitalist realism."

Advertising as a form of symbolic value expression can be seen with greater clarity, Schudson stated, by comparing it to socialist realism and the guidelines for socialist realist art, with its emphasis on the collective over the individual:

1. Art should picture reality in simplified and typified ways so that it communicates effectively to the masses.
2. Art should picture life, but not as it is so much as life as it should become, life worth emulating.
3. Art should picture reality not in its individuality but only as it reveals larger social significance.
4. Art should picture reality as progress toward the future and so represent social struggles positively. It should carry an air of optimism.
5. Art should focus on contemporary life, creating pleasing images of new social phenomena, revealing and endorsing new features of society and thus aiding the masses in assimilating them.[52]

The parallels with advertising, Schudson continued, are striking:

American advertising, like socialist realist art, simplifies and typifies. It does not claim to picture reality as it is but reality as it should be—life and lives worth emulating. It is always photography or dramas or discourse with a message—rarely picturing individuals, it shows people only as incarnations of larger social categories. It always assumes that there is progress. It is thoroughly optimistic, providing for any troubles that it identifies a solution in a particular product or style of life. It focuses, of course, on the new, and if it shows some signs of respect for tradition, this is only to help in the assimilation of some new commercial creation.[53]

Of course socialist realism was "state art," intended to extol the virtues of the collective (the state) over those of individual action or achievement. Yet, Schudson contended, American advertising is similarly linked to a supporting culture, because "without a masterplan of purposes [advertising] glorifies the pleasures and freedoms of consumer choice in defense of the virtues of private life and material ambitions."[54] Thus, the satisfactions portrayed in this idealization of the consumer are "invariably private" as individuals are "encouraged to think of themselves and their private worlds, values entirely compatible with the self-interested spirit of capitalism."[55]

A particularly important quality of advertising as an art form, Schudson contended while citing Krugman and others, is that it need not necessarily command belief to be effective. Indeed, advertising "may shape our sense of values even under conditions where it does not greatly corrupt our buying habits."[56] Thus, since advertising is frequently not taken seriously by individuals, it may be received while our "perceptual defenses" are relatively open.[57]

This potential openness becomes even more plausible because advertising is essentially confronting us with values *with which we already basically agree.* Thus, advertising's institutional function can be seen as *materializing a way of experiencing a consumer way of life*—reinforcing the satisfactions of private consumption, with which we are already familiar and comfortable. "Making the implicit explicit is necessary to engage and renew a whole train of commitments, responsibilities, and possibilities. . . . In the same way that married couples continue to make the 'implicit explicit' by stating, 'I love you,' advertising," Schudson contended, "is capitalism's way of saying 'I love you' to itself."[58]

And what are the consequences of this reaffirmation of widely shared values? "Advertising does not make people believe in capitalist institutions or even in consumer values, but so long as alternative articulations of values are relatively hard to locate in the culture, capitalist realist art will have some power."[59]

Advertising, of course, has no monopoly in the symbolic marketplace, Schudson added, but "advertising has a special cultural power" since:

- No other cultural form is as accessible to children.
- No other form confronts visitors and immigrants to our society so forcefully.
- Only professional sports surpass advertising as a source of visual and verbal clichés, aphorisms, and proverbs.[60]

Advertising, Schudson concluded, is not a *shaper* of our values, but because the values that *are* relentlessly presented "are not the only ones people have or aspire to, . . . the pervasiveness of advertising makes us forget this. Advertising picks up some of the things people hold dear and re-presents them to people as *all* of what they value, assuring them that the sponsor is the patron of common ideals."[61]

• • •

There are some clear parallels between Schudson's perspective and that of at least two other theorists discussed here. First, like Norris, he limited his analysis to one form of advertising—that of national consumer goods—while recognizing the different functions of other types—e.g., retail. Second, with his concentration on advertising's relationship to values, his views are akin to Potter's. What, then, does his perspective assume, and what analytical tools does it offer?

Interestingly, there seem to be mixed signals in relation to atomism or the seat of societal power. Schudson made it clear that the individualistic consumer values advertising embodies are widely diffused through the society, thus suggesting the expected classical liberal interpretation of institutions being shaped by the individuals—i.e., the "individual in the society" rather than the "society in the individual." Yet, he was also troubled that "alternative articulations of values are relatively hard to locate,"[62] implying that other sets of values do not receive comparable institutional representation—a clear contradiction to atomism.

Now, it can be argued that at the base of the argument is a vision of the individual that suggests a passiveness in responding to values other than those articulated so relentlessly through advertising's ubiquity. Thus, from this perspective, advertising re-presents "some of the things that people hold dear as *all* of what they value."[63] And if individuals are willing to accept the reinforcement of some values to the diminishment of alternatives that they also "have or aspire to," then advertising is powerful indeed, as it relentlessly reinforces *some* values at the expense of others.

Schudson's rich perspective, then, suggests several analytical modes. Among the more interesting:

1. Advertising's economic impact is not nearly as important as its potential interaction with the societal value structure.
2. Although it could be considered relatively benign in the sense that its values are generally our values, advertising's long-run effect is troublesome due to its pervasiveness and the singularity of its value themes.

3. Its influence is particularly magnified in certain population segments—e.g., children, immigrants—and becomes even more powerful because of its assimilation as part of popular culture through comedy routines, movies, books, commonplace daily exchanges, etc.
4. Advertising's effect may be all the more influential because it is so easily accepted as part of our institutional environment and *not* taken seriously, largely because its forms are often subject to derision, and, perhaps of greatest importance, *because we are so comfortable with its values.*

So we are offered the perspective of advertising as capitalist realism. The individual messages are clearly the stuff of the self-interests of individual advertisers. Yet the advertising aggregate makes an important—and certainly controversial—contribution to our symbolic marketplace.

Pollay and Holbrook—The "Mirror" Controversy

Students of advertising in contemporary society are well served by two substantial and insightful articles appearing in the *Journal of Marketing* in 1986 and 1987. In "The Distorted Mirror: Reflections on the Unintended Consequences of Advertising," Richard W. Pollay offered a sweeping review of scholarly thought from "all North American authors known to have written on the cultural character of advertising."[64] Their ideas, he contended, "constitute a major indictment of advertising."[65] Somewhat over a year later, Morris B. Holbrook responded with "Mirror, Mirror, on the Wall, What's Unfair in the Reflections on Advertising?"[66] As with our other works in this chapter, the serious student is encouraged to read the originals. Herewith, however, are summaries and commentary.

Pollay

By the "unintended consequences of advertising," Pollay meant those effects of advertising that transcend "the pedestrian one of affecting sales, and despite the fact that many of the forms of advertising are transparent in intent to even quite unsophisticated subjects."[67] The array of scholars whose assessments he reviewed included psychologists, sociologists, anthropologists, educators, communication specialists, linguists, semanticists, philosophers, theologians, political scientists, economists, and historians. A summary statement of the general range of criticisms was afforded by this segment from the 1980 MacBride UNESCO report:

> Regarded as a form of communication, it [advertising] has been criti-
> cized for playing on emotions, simplifying real human situations into
> stereotypes, exploiting anxieties, and employing techniques of intensive
> persuasion that amount to manipulation. Many social critics have stat-
> ed that advertising is essentially concerned with exalting the materialis-
> tic virtues of consumption by exploiting achievement drives and emula-
> tive anxieties, employing tactics of hidden manipulation, playing on
> emotions, maximizing appeal and minimizing information, trivializing,
> eliminating objective considerations, contriving illogical situations, and
> generally reducing men, women, and children to the role of irrational
> consumer. Criticism expressed in such a way may be overstated but it
> cannot be entirely brushed aside.[68]

Certainly an entire course could be devoted to the dissection of this
litany, but it does provide an inventory of some of the concerns these
scholars had expressed. Clearly, of course, some of these matters are not
"unintentional" at all—e.g., playing on emotions, maximizing appeal,
minimizing information, and so forth are conscious sales tactics—but
certainly many others would seem to be beyond the usual narrow intent
of most sales-seeking advertising messages—i.e., they're not part of the
goals meant to be achieved by the advertiser.

Why the concern? In part, Pollay contended, because advertising is (1)
pervasive, appearing in many modes and media; (2) *repetitive*, reinforcing the same or similar ideas relentlessly; (3) *professionally developed*, with
all the attendant research sophistications to improve the probabilities of
attention, comprehension, retention, and/or behavioral impact; and (4)
delivered to an audience that is increasingly detached from traditional
sources of cultural influence like families, churches, or schools.[69]

Focusing on the common defense of advertising that it must, of necessity, "be in harmony with its culture"—hence acting as a cultural mirror—
Pollay contended that (1) any culture is a mosaic of multiple values; (2)
a culture is characterized in substantial measure by the relative importance of these values; and (3) not all cultural values are employed and
echoed in advertising.

"To most observers," he asserted, "the image presented in the cultural
mirror of advertising is not unambiguously worth imitating." Among
other concerns, it's heavy on the seven deadly sins and light on the seven
cardinal virtues.[70] Recognition that there are historical forces other than
advertising (e.g., urbanization, industrial expansion) that can lead to the
same outcome (e.g., the ascendancy of materialistic values), he contend-

ed, "does not alleviate our concern about advertising's continuing cultural role."[71]

Not surprisingly, then, Pollay called for research to complement the deductive conclusions of the surveyed scholars, which "constitute the conventional wisdom of nonbusiness academics and are better thought of as hypotheses than conclusions."[72] If advertising, he argued, "reflects" some values at the expense of others, "it becomes a serious research question which values are subjected to this selective reinforcement and which suffer from neglect, however benign."[73]

Holbrook

Calling Pollay's lengthy exploration "a unique and valuable contribution to the marketing literature," Holbrook countered that "if we search through Pollay's discussion to find the slender logical threads that underlie the attack on advertising, we might discover that they fail to support its heavy weight."[74] Figure 3-1 depicts the conceptualization Holbrook used to address the issues.

Monolithic versus Pluralistic

Holbrook contended that an "emergent assumption" from Pollay's analysis is that advertising works like a collective, univocal, and global force in which media, ad agencies, and marketing strategists somehow man-

Figure 3-1. Holbrook's Perspective on Pollay's "The Distorted Mirror"

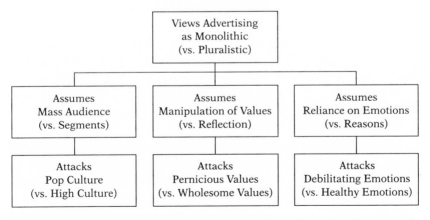

Source: Morris B. Holbrook, "Mirror, Mirror, on the Wall, What's Unfair in the Reflections on Advertising?" *Journal of Marketing* 51 (July 1987): 97.

age (whether intentionally or unintentionally) to create television commercials, print ads, and other promotional communications that join in concert to foster certain communication ends and objectives.[75]

Yet, Holbrook contended, the organizations involved in advertising are "bastions of pluralism" with explicit agendas to "(1) be different; (2) seek a unique niche; (3) avoid head-to-head competition; and (4) protect proprietary secrets." He added, "A communication system based on self-interest rather than central planning could not be otherwise."[76] Thus, he contended, the thrust of Pollay's argument was perhaps fatally weakened with such a challenge to what he saw as its central underlying assumption.

Mass Audience versus Segments

Pollay, Holbrook asserted, assumed advertisers attempt to influence mass markets, yet modern advertising practice emphasizes a "general repudiation of mass marketing."[77] As audiences are considered as segments rather than a homogeneous mass, differences, rather than similarities, are emphasized, and the prospects for monolithic control are weakened.

Pop Culture versus High Culture

"We cannot safely conclude," Holbrook asserted, "that advertising appeals only to the lowest common denominator of pop culture by dealing excessively in social stereotypes."[78] Thus, the "pluralism" argument reasserts itself when, depending on the segment addressed, it is in the advertiser's best interest to shatter rather than support stereotypes by emphasizing the individuality of lifestyles, particularly when it is harmonious with the advertiser's projected "image"—e.g., the quirkiness of Saturn owners and the determined individuality of Nike cross-trainers. Also, he observed, "some advertising escapes the pop-culture level of entertainment to approach the high-culture status of Art." This should not, he added, be surprising, "in light of the tremendous creative talent and energy" involved.[79]

Manipulation versus Reflection of Values

Citing the work of Boyd, Ray, and Strong,[80] Holbrook contended that generally advertisers find it an easier communication task to "augment or reposition" existing beliefs than to substitute one belief for another. (For example, these days it's easier to convince individuals that "healthier" food choices are a good idea rather than promoting the "If it tastes good, eat it" philosophy.) Thus, he contends, "most advertising appears

to mirror or reflect rather than to mold or shape the values of its target
audience."[81]

Pernicious Values versus Wholesome Values

"For Pollay's version," Holbrook observed, "reading print ads or watching
TV commercials is the moral equivalent of sticking one's head in a toilet."[82]
In sharp contrast, Holbrook responded that most ads seem to reflect "fairly
wholesome values," including sociability, affection, generosity, health,
patriotism, ecumenism, personal enrichment, security, and temper-
ance"[83]—again, because it's in the self-interests of the advertisers to do so.

Reliance on Emotions versus Reason

Holbrook challenged Pollay's contention that advertising relies on emotional appeals by citing research and the viewpoints of practitioners that
"emotional appeals work best for some situations, products, or people,
whereas rational appeals work best for others."[84] Certainly, he argued,
there is ample evidence that "reason why" approaches are still common
in American advertising practice.

Debilitating versus Healthy Emotions

Even if emotional appeals are not the sole staple of advertising appeals,
Holbrook agreed with Pollay that the *consequences* of those emotional
appeals that are utilized should be of concern. Although he concurred
that some emotional responses to television commercials do encourage
sentiments of sadness, fear, and disgust, he also found commercials elic-
iting feelings of anticipation, acceptance, joyfulness, happiness, gratifi-
cation, pride, love, and appreciation. "Ask yourself," he concluded, "which
would leave you feeling more cheerful, watching two hours of randomly
selected television commercials or viewing 10 minutes of the evening
news?"[85]

Thus, Holbrook contended, the views represented in Pollay's article
"form a weak logical thread that snaps in several places from the burden
of trying to tie together its multifarious attacks on advertising."[86]

•   •   •

Pollay and Holbrook share ground with several of our other theorists.
Like Potter, they concentrate not on advertising's narrow economic effects but rather on advertising's values. Like Potter, the scholars Pollay

assessed apparently share the view that advertising *shapes* values (advertising "trains us to act as consumers," as Potter put it) as well as sharing the concern of Schudson that advertising *reinforces* some values to the exclusion of others.

By contrast, Holbrook could seem to be aligned to some extent with Sandage, who contended that advertising's institutional function is to "inform and persuade." And in the process of implementing this highly self-interested function, Holbrook could contend that advertisers emphasize differences rather than similarities, reasons as well as emotions, uplifting as well as worrisome appeals, etc., therefore undermining the presumed "monolithic" assumption central to Pollay's position.

Both also share a fundamental interest with Leiss and colleagues in advertising's "nonintended" consequences, such as advertising's implicit communications concerning interpersonal and family relations, the sense of happiness and contentment, sex roles and stereotyping, the uses of affluence, the fading away of older cultural traditions, influences of younger generations, the role of business in society, persuasion and personal autonomy, and many others.[87]

Again, Pollay would contend that advertising works to *shape* these dimensions as well as to *reinforce* those aspects of these facets of everyday life that are in concert with the overarching agenda of business—i.e., establishing and reinforcing materialistic values (or, as Schudson might put it, "capitalist realism"). Holbrook, by contrast, could contend the advertisers' agendas are varied, with techniques ranging along a continuum of emotional and rational appeals, many quite laudatory.

Holbrook stated that Pollay, "rather than revealing his own views," simply portrayed the "conventional wisdom" of those he analyzed.[88] Yet Pollay's own ideological assumptions seem reasonably apparent, as in his statement "Polemic stands on all sides of this issue are potentially tempered by research findings, which should illuminate our understanding of both the institution of advertising and the character of its target, the consumer."[89] And in calling for future research, Pollay stated: "Critical inquiry does not require researchers to believe that advertising will be absolved of all charges as much as it requires having faith that all institutions of advertising have some potential for self-correction and a capacity for moral action in the light of new knowledge."[90] Thus, in one case, the consumer is considered advertising's "target," with all the one-sided force that suggests; and in another, advertising is clearly positioned as guilty-until-proven-innocent, with the only possibility for redemption through self-corrective "moral action."

Holbrook's continuing theme of the diverse intents of advertisers undermining the "monolithic" assumption of Pollay's position can, on the other hand, be seen to raise as many questions as it addresses. For example, if marketing directives do suggest "difference" as a desirable strategy and the transmission of "fairly wholesome values" to aid the process, could these not also be considered merely the *means to the end of selling the product*, therefore reinforcing the agenda of goods = happiness implicit in so many of the objections of the scholars? And when Holbrook writes of advertising's intent to "augment or reposition people's beliefs" while concluding that "most advertising attempts to mirror or reflect rather than to mold," the questions can be raised of *what* is to be repositioned and *what* reinforced—e.g., a broad representation of the American value system or, as Pollay (and Schudson) contended, *some* commercially compatible values to the exclusion of many others?

Both researchers concluded with a call for value-free research in which, as Pollay put it, "we should study the consumer in the marketing environment as the biologist studies the fish."[91] Neither, however, seemed particularly optimistic, with Pollay expressing repeated concern that academics are "servants to marketing practice," and Holbrook noting the "contrasting ideological origins"[92] that lead these two researchers to their jousting.

The "mirror" issue is, as we have seen, in many ways an ideological litmus test, with those toward the *animal rationale* end of the neo-liberal continuum seeing advertising as a reflection of the will of the sovereign consumer and those toward the *animal symbolicum* end seeing advertising as shaper/selective reinforcer, envisioning a vulnerable populace.

Pollay seems to contend that because advertising is value laden in what is an undesirable dimension, individuals are influenced accordingly; on the other hand, Holbrook seems to be assuming that self-interested business practice, presumably directed by correctly reading potentially powerful "markets," will result in a reasonably representative value mix by the "natural" adjustment processes of the market. Thus, Pollay's focus was, to a great extent, on the product of the process (the *ads*), and Holbrook's focus was on the business *motives* behind them.

Given the ideologically sensitive nature of advertising thought, and the arabesques of its practice that we have encountered in preceding pages, there seems little doubt that there is unlikely to be any emergence of "pure" truth, as the phoenix from the flames, in the near future.

In the meantime, we are, we believe, well served by the paths to understanding illuminated by the theorists of this chapter.

_____ Summary

In an attempt to deepen our understanding of the nature of institutional analysis in relation to advertising, we've examined the views of a number of insightful theorists.

James Carey saw advertising performing the historically necessary function of providing market information, with the nature of that information, and its potential effects, clearly affected by its source and attendant assumptions about human nature.

Vincent Norris saw advertising emerging as an institution in the late nineteenth century with the rise of national (producer) advertising in an attempt to avoid price competition and seize market power from the dominant wholesalers.

David Potter found advertising the distinctive institution of abundance, training people to act as consumers in an abundant economy, but without social responsibility to counter social control.

Charles Sandage envisioned advertising informing and persuading individuals so they might make satisfying decisions in a largely responsive market.

Michael Schudson saw advertising as an expression of capitalist ideals—capitalist realism as compared to socialist realism—with significant influence due to its possibility of overwhelming other competing values with its sheer ubiquity and the comfort of its themes.

Finally, Richard Pollay and Morris Holbrook addressed the vexing question as to what extent advertising mirrors or shapes our society. Pollay enlisted the "conventional wisdom" of major scholars to characterize advertising as a "distorted mirror" with troubling images. Holbrook found advertising practice leading to diversity, with relatively benign consequences and an image of reasonable fidelity.

Each perspective, along with the visions offered in the preceding three chapters, provides us with analytic tools for arriving at greater understanding of the various dimensions of advertising in contemporary society. And it is to a tighter focus on several of these dimensions that we now turn.

Notes

1. Walton Hamilton, "Institution," *The Encyclopedia of the Social Sciences* (New York: Macmillan, 1932), 8:89.

2. Charles H. Sandage, "Some Institutional Aspects of Advertising," *Journal of Advertising* 1, no. 1 (1973): 9. Reprinted with permission by Board of Directors, *Journal of Advertising*.

3. Hamilton, "Institution," 8:87.

4. James W. Carey, "Advertising: An Institutional Approach," in *The Role of Advertising*, ed. C. H. Sandage and V. Fryburger (Homewood, Ill.: Richard D. Irwin, 1960), 14, emphasis in original.

5. Ibid., 3.

6. Ibid., 10.

7. Ibid., 13.

8. Ibid., 15.

9. Ibid.

10. Ibid., 11.

11. Ibid., 16.

12. Ibid.

13. Ibid., 17.

14. Vincent P. Norris, "Toward the Institutional Study of Advertising," *Occasional Papers in Advertising* (University of Illinois Department of Advertising) 1, no. 1 (Jan. 1966): 60.

15. Ibid., 63.

16. Ibid., 65.

17. Ibid., 66, emphasis in original.

18. Ibid.

19. Ibid., 67.

20. Norris, "Institutional Study," 68.

21. Ibid.

22. Ibid.

23. David M. Potter quoted in Sandage and Fryburger, *The Role of Advertising*, 18.

24. Ibid., 19.

25. Ibid., 21.

26. Ibid., 22.

27. Ibid.

28. Ibid.

29. Ibid., 24–25.

30. Ibid., 25; interpretation based on his statements.

31. Ibid., 26.

32. Ibid.

33. Ibid.

34. Ibid., 27–32.

35. Ibid., 34.

36. Ibid.

37. Ibid.

38. Sandage, "Some Institutional Aspects," 6–9.

39. Ibid., 6.

40. Ibid.

41. Ibid., 6–7.

42. Ibid., 7.

43. Ibid.

44. Ibid.

45. Ibid., 8.

46. Ibid.

47. Ibid.

48. Ibid., 7.

49. Michael Schudson, *Advertising: The Uneasy Persuasion* (New York: Basic Books, 1984).

50. Ibid., 210.

51. Ibid., 214.

52. Ibid., 215.

53. Ibid.

54. Ibid., 218.

55. Ibid., 221.

56. Ibid., 210.

57. Ibid., 227.

58. Ibid., 231–32.

59. Ibid., 232.

60. Ibid., 233.

61. Ibid.

62. Ibid., 232.

63. Ibid., 233.

64. Richard W. Pollay, "The Distorted Mirror: Reflections on the Unintended Consequences of Advertising," *Journal of Marketing* 50 (Apr. 1986): 18–36.

65. Ibid., 31.

66. Morris B. Holbrook, "Mirror, Mirror, on the Wall, What's Unfair in the Reflections on Advertising?" *Journal of Marketing* 51 (July 1987): 95–103.

67. Pollay, "Distorted Mirror," 21.

68. Ibid.

69. Ibid.

70. Ibid., 26.

71. Ibid., 31.

72. Ibid.

73. Ibid., 33.

74. Holbrook, "Mirror, Mirror," 96.

75. Ibid., 98.

76. Ibid.

77. Ibid.

78. Ibid., 99.

79. Ibid.

80. Harper W. Boyd Jr., Michael L. Ray, and Edward C. Strong, "An Attitudinal Framework for Advertising Strategy," *Journal of Marketing* 36 (Apr. 1972): 27–33.

81. Holbrook, "Mirror, Mirror," 100.

82. Ibid.

83. Ibid., 101.

84. Ibid.

85. Ibid.

86. Ibid., 102.

87. William Leiss, Stephen Kline, and Sut Ghally, *Social Communication in Advertising: Persons, Products, and Images of Well-Being* (New York: Methuen, 1986), 3.

88. Holbrook, "Mirror, Mirror," 95.

89. Pollay, "Distorted Mirror," 31.

90. Ibid., 33–34.

91. Ibid., 34.

92. Holbrook, "Mirror, Mirror," 102.

2

Issues of Consequence

4

Advertising and the Economy

Why have so many studied the economic effects of advertising for such a long period of time? The reasons are probably quite simple:

1. Advertising is a major business in the United States, with over $140 billion spent annually.
2. Advertising is a highly visible institution, its messages touching most businesses and consumers every day.
3. There is a common belief among many business people that advertising "sells" the product or service. If sales are down, advertising gets the blame; if sales are up, advertising gets the credit.

Basic Limitations of Many Economic Studies

Before beginning a discussion of some of the issues concerning the economic effects of advertising, it is necessary to look at some basic underpinnings of many economic studies related to advertising. In many of the studies, there is an implicit assumption that advertising works in isolation rather than in concert with other elements of the marketing mix (product, place, price, and promotion) and the promotion mix (advertising, personal selling, sales promotion, and public relations). By examining overall expenditure patterns of promotional mixes within the package goods industry, it becomes clear that advertising is not the predominant marketing variable economists frequently assume it to be. Analyzing it by itself can therefore lead to erroneous results. For example, even though the package goods industry spends large amounts of money on advertising, the data in table 4–1 reveals that substantial amounts of marketing re-

Table 4-1. Allocations to Trade Promotion, Advertising, and Consumer
Promotion (1981–91)

	Percentage Allocated to Promotional Category											
Promotional Category	1981	1982	1983	1984	1985	1986	1987	1988	1989	1990	1991	1992
Trade promotion	34	36	37	37	38	40	41	43	46	47	50	45
Advertising	43	39	37	36	35	34	34	33	29	28	25	27
Consumer promotion	23	25	26	27	27	26	25	24	25	25	25	28

Sources: Adweek's Marketing Week, Apr. 13, 1992, 26; *Advertising Age,* Apr. 5, 1993, 3, 43. See also Joe Mandese and Scott Donaton, "Media, Promotion Gap to Narrow," *Ad Age,* June 29, 1992, 16.

sources are being allocated to alternative promotional activities such as trade promotion and consumer promotion. Compared to the $140 billion spent on advertising per year, for example, $140 billion is also spent on sales promotion efforts.[1] It is difficult to imagine that anything but a synergistic effect on sales could be expected from the combination of marketing and promotion mixes.

Other studies fail to take into account the many external environmental factors that influence the effectiveness of a firm's marketing and advertising efforts. Consider the following environmental factors and a few respective examples of each:

DEMOGRAPHIC: Population characteristics such as age, ethnic and racial composition, family structure, and educational levels

ECONOMIC: Macro influences such as Gross Domestic Product, inflation, interest rates, and unemployment; micro influences such as personal disposable/discretionary income, propensities to consume/save, and attitudes regarding credit/debt

POLITICAL/LEGAL/
REGULATORY: Federal, state, and local governmental policies concerning issues such as unfair trade practic-

es and product safety; self-regulatory initiatives developed and implemented by such mechanisms as the NAD/NARB, BBB, CARU, and the media

TECHNOLOGICAL: Development of new products such as virtual reality software and High Definition Television (HDTV) as well as improvements that facilitate the marketing process, like graphics technology, scanner-generated databases and fiber-optic information/communication systems

SOCIOCULTURAL: Rate of diffusion for innovations, consumer socialization processes, lifestyle patterns, value orientations, and belief systems

When other external factors such as competition are considered, it is obvious advertising is susceptible to myriad societal forces that shape the contextual parameters of any market system on a local, national, or global level.

Another critical factor often ignored in studies attempting to determine the economic effects of advertising is the cooperative advertising allowance made to retailers. It has been estimated that in 1992 over $15 billion was available for use in various media, although only about 50 percent of that total was actually utilized by retailers.[2]

An additional handicap to research into the economic effects of advertising was pointed out by Oskar Morgenstern, who found that necessary data are often unavailable and, when available, are often inaccurate or untrustworthy.[3] For example, the industry classifications used in government data may group together firms producing unrelated products or firms may switch classifications without any change in the kinds of goods they produce.[4]

It is also unlikely that individual firms over time or firms within a particular industry are equally effective in the development and transmission of their advertising.[5] Not all copy platforms, basic research programs, or media strategies are equally productive.

Lastly, few economic scholars are conversant with basic material on consumer behavior such as that we will present in chapter 5. Definitions of what is information or how it is processed by the consumer are often ignored. In other instances, consumer behavior concepts are defined in a manner to suit a more "economic" view of the research process.

——— Two Schools of Thought about the Economic Effects of Advertising

Mark S. Albion indicates that economists use two principal models to describe the effects of advertising: the Advertising = Market Power school and the Advertising = Market Competition school. The first model views advertising as a persuasive communications tool that marketers use to make consumers less sensitive to price. This decreased price sensitivity will subsequently increase the firm's market power. The second model regards advertising as informative in nature and contends that it increases consumers' price sensitivity and stimulates competition among firms.[6]

The market power school believes advertising is capable of changing consumer tastes and building brand loyalty. Brand-loyal customers are not very price sensitive, as they do not perceive acceptable alternatives in the marketplace. Once the firm has been able to differentiate its product/service through advertising expenditures, the firm should be able to increase its prices to consumers, subsequently increasing its profits and reducing competition in the marketplace.

The market competition model holds that advertising provides basic information to the marketplace, information that will increase price sensitivity, lower prices, and reduce any potential monopoly power. S. I. Ornstein described the market competition model as follows:

> The essence of this new view is that advertising provides information on brands, prices, and quality, thus increasing buyer knowledge, reducing consumers' search costs, and reducing the total costs to society of transacting business. By increasing information, advertising increases the number of substitutes known to buyers, thereby increasing price elasticity of demand and reducing price-cost margins. Far from being a barrier to entry, advertising facilitates entry by allowing previously unknown products to gain rapid market acceptance. . . . Advertising serves consumers by increasing product variety and by permitting firms to exploit economies of scale in production and distribution—which in turn yield lower consumer prices.[7]

The two approaches are summarized in table 4–2.

These two approaches have some major flaws. As discussed by Albion,[8] the market power model assumes that advertising is probably the sole cause of brand loyalty and price insensitivity. But there are other elements in the marketing mix or promotion mix, such as packaging, better product quality, personal selling, and sales promotion, that could

Table 4-2. Two Schools of Thought on the Role of Advertising in the
          Economy

Advertising = Market Power		Advertising = Market Competition
Advertising affects consumer preferences and tastes, changes product attributes, and differentiates the product from competitive offerings.	Advertising	Advertising informs consumers about product attributes and does not change the way they value these attributes.
Consumers become brand loyal and less price sensitive and perceive fewer substitutes for advertised brands.	Consumer Buying Behavior	Consumers become more price sensitive and buy best "value." Only the relationship between price and quality affects elasticity for a given product.
Potential entrants must overcome established brand loyalty and spend relatively more on advertising.	Barriers to Entry	Advertising makes entry possible for new brands because it can communicate product attributes to consumers.
Firms are insulated from market competition and potential rivals; concentration increases, leaving firms with more discretionary power.	Industry Structure and Market Power	Consumers can compare competitive offerings easily and competitive rivalry is increased. Efficient firms remain, and as the inefficient leave, new entrants appear; the effect on concentration is ambiguous.
Firms can charge higher prices and are not as likely to compete on quality or price dimension. Innovation may be reduced.	Market Conduct	More informed consumers put pressure on firms to lower prices and improve quality. Innovation is facilitated via new entrants.
High prices and excessive profits accrue to advertisers and give them even more incentive to advertise their products. Output is restricted compared to conditions of perfect competition.	Market Performance	Industry prices are decreased. The effect on profits due to increased competition and an increase in efficiency is ambiguous.

Source: Reprinted with permission of the publisher from Mark S. Albion, *Advertising's Hidden Effects:
Manufacturers' Advertising and Retail Pricing* (Westport, Conn.: Auburn House, an imprint of Greenwood
Publishing Group, Inc., 1983), 18.

contribute to the development of brand loyalty. Even if brand preference is established through integrated marketing communication efforts, there is no assurance it will be maintained. As the data indicate in table 4–3, brand loyalty for certain products often falls below 50 percent, even for industries in which brand leaders traditionally spend large amounts on advertising, such as the soft drink, automobile, and athletic shoe industries. For comparative purposes, a description of the top thirty leading national advertisers and their total ad expenditures for 1991 and 1992 are included in table 4–4. It is interesting to note brand loyalty is often strongest in the cigarette industry, which is legally prohibited from advertising on broadcast media and therefore utilizes sales promotion as a dominant factor in its marketing mix. According to an article in *Brandweek*, firms are indeed initiating marketing programs that emphasize an integrated approach to creating and sustaining brand loyalty—indicating a reliance on marketing components other than advertising. As stated: "Cut the price. Make the product better. Get out the word with advertising. And grab attention with promotions. Combined with the commitment to wring out every excess dollar of cost in the system . . . may be the formula for brandbuilding in the 90's."[9]

The market competition school assumes that consumers engage in a thorough and extensive search of product/service alternatives that is facilitated by advertising. The school also assumes that consumers are excellent judges of the merits of competing brands. Given our discussion to come in chapter 5, this assumption does not necessarily hold true.

——— Some Newer Approaches

Michael E. Porter and Robert Steiner have each developed new approaches to studying the economic effects of advertising. The main contribution of these two models has been the recognition of the retailer's role in both the sale of and the dissemination of information about the manufacturer's product to the ultimate consumer.

Porter divides retail goods into two sectors, convenience and nonconvenience. Convenience goods retailers (gasoline stations, convenience food stores, traditional supermarkets) provide display space for the manufacturer's product, but that is about the only service they offer. The manufacturer has already differentiated the product with the advertising to create demand and eventually develop brand loyalty among consumers. The manufacturer subsequently increases prices to the retailer,

Table 4-3. Loyalty to One Brand by Users of a Product
Category (percentages)

Product Category	Users Loyal to One Brand
Cigarettes	71
Mayonnaise	65
Toothpaste	61
Coffee	58
Headache remedy	56
Film	56
Bath soap	53
Ketchup	51
Laundry detergent	48
Beer	48
Auto	47
Perfume/after shave	46
Pet food	45
Shampoo	44
Soft drink	44
Tuna fish	44
Gasoline	39
Underwear	36
T.V.	35
Tires	33
Blue jeans	33
Batteries	29
Athletic shoes	27
Canned vegetables	25
Garbage bags	23

thereby reducing trade margins. Retailers will be willing to accept price increases because of higher product turnover. Consumers engage in a limited information search because of the lower cost of these items.[10]

Nonconvenience goods retailers (auto dealers, appliance stores, furniture stores) play a more significant marketing role. The retailer is often asked to provide information about the product, to demonstrate it, and to relate it to the store's image. More manufacturer advertising dollars are spent promoting the product to the trade (push strategy) in order to gain additional outlets. Consumers spend more time looking for the "best

Table 4-4. Top Thirty National Advertisers

Rank			Total U.S. Ad Spending		
1992	1991	Advertiser, Headquarters	1992	1991	% Change
1	1	Procter & Gamble Co., Cincinnati	$2,165.6	$2,150.0	+0.7
2	2	Philip Morris Cos., New York	2,024.1	2,071.3	−2.3
3	3	General Motors Corp., Detroit	1,333.6	1,476.8	−9.7
4	4	Sears, Roebuck & Co., Chicago	1,204.6	1,195.6	+0.8
5	5	PepsiCo, Purchase, N.Y.	928.6	903.9	+2.7
6	9	Ford Motor Co., Dearborn, Mich.	794.5	689.7	+15.2
7	11	Warner-Lambert Co., Morris Plains, N.J.	757.5	657.0	+5.3
8	21	Chrysler Corp., Highland Park, Mich.	756.6	547.1	+38.3
9	8	McDonald's Corp., Oak Brook, Ill.	743.6	695.7	+6.9
10	14	Nestlé SA, Vevey, Switzerland	733.4	643.4	+14.0
11	10	Eastman Kodak Co., Rochester, N.Y.	686.0	666.0	+3.0
12	6	Grand Metropolitan, London	680.2	746.5	−8.9
13	16	Unilever NV, London/Rotterdam	672.8	593.7	+13.3
14	7	Johnson & Johnson, New Brunswick, N.J.	659.6	733.2	+10.0
15	13	Toyota Motor Corp., Toyota City, Japan	648.9	649.0	−0.1
16	15	Time Warner, New York	637.9	617.1	+3.4
17	17	Kellogg Co., Battle Creek, Mich.	630.3	578.0	+9.1
18	12	AT&T Co., New York	623.7	649.3	−4.0
19	20	General Mills, Minneapolis	571.2	555.7	+2.8
20	22	Anheuser-Busch Cos., St. Louis	555.8	510.8	+8.8
21	18	Kmart Corp., Troy, Mich.	551.1	561.9	−1.9
22	30	J. C. Penney Co., Dallas	537.4	364.0	+47.6
23	24	American Home Products Corp., New York	531.6	449.2	+18.3
24	23	Walt Disney Co., Burbank, Calif.	524.6	495.0	+6.0
25	25	Sony Corp., Tokyo	507.9	445.8	+13.9
26	19	RJR Nabisco, Winston-Salem, N.C.	422.2	560.8	−24.7
27	27	Ralston Purina Co., St. Louis	411.5	393.7	+4.5
28	29	Coca-Cola Co., Atlanta	392.0	365.8	+7.2
29	28	May Department Stores Co., St. Louis	390.9	377.1	+3.7
30	33	Hershey Foods Corp., Hershey, Pa.	383.0	298.9	+28.1

Source: "Advertising Fact Book," *Advertising Age*, Jan. 3, 1994, 14.

buy." The brand name, developed through manufacturer advertising, may not be all important; store advertising and cooperative advertising may be just as important. As a result, manufacturer prices may be lower to maintain distribution in critical stores.[11]

The contributions of this model are clear. It stipulates that studying the economic effects of advertising is at best situational (convenience versus nonconvenience goods) and that advertising as economists generally study it may be more important for the convenience goods sector. It also involves the retailer as an important element in the system.

Steiner's dual-stage model also indicates that the retailer must be viewed as an integral part of the economics of advertising.[12] A scenario for Steiner's model would be as follows:

In the early stages of a product, it is generally unadvertised, and consumers exhibit no particular preference among a wide variety of close substitutes. Then, as Steiner describes the process:

> If a dealer in an unadvertised product category carries, say, 5 to 6 items, he is likely to be offered 100 by the manufacturers and finds he can select and substitute between them quite freely without a noticeable impact on his sales volume. As the retailer puts it, he can live without virtually any manufacturer product. Consequently, he plays one maker off against the next and ends up carrying the factory brands that afford him the greatest margin between retail list and factory invoice price. This causes factory demand curves to be extremely elastic and price to be depressed close to average unit cost.[13]

Consumer prices may well remain high because of the lack of competition at the retail level.

> If Manufacturer X now begins successfully to advertise his brand, the terms of trade shift decisively in his favor. Dealers find that the public expects them to handle the item. Hence, the trade's ability to stock a competing article in place of Brand X or to beat down the latter's price as a condition for carrying it is substantially diminished. As advertising expands the popularity of Brand X, its maker therefore finds he can increase its retail distribution with progressively fewer price concessions.[14]

Consumer prices may fall because of the increased competition at the retail level. Intense price competition could follow, driving retail margins to the new zero level, as retailers begin offering heavy discounts on the items or offer them as loss leaders to generate store traffic. Retailers will use these heavily advertised products in this way because consumers tend to use them as benchmarks in price comparisons. Factory prices at this stage might remain relatively constant or even increase.

Steiner indicates that at this point, one of three situations will probably occur:[15]

1. Manufacturer's brand domination
2. Mixed regimen
3. Private label domination

In the case of manufacturer's brand domination, it is possible that, from the point of view of the market power school, the heavily advertised brands will dominate the market and thus create major barriers to entry by new firms. Those controlling the market may see opportunities to offer a variety of new brands and advertise them heavily. Product differences would be relatively minor. Consumer prices would rise given the successful new differentiation effort. The aspirin and detergent markets might be good examples of this situation.

In a mixed regimen situation, retailers will market their own private labels in addition to manufacturer brands. Retailers can often negotiate low manufacturer prices for private labels because manufacturers want to maximize their productive resources and put excess plant capacity to use. Retailers subsequently receive higher gross profit margins on private label products even though consumer prices for private labels are substantially lower in most cases. Private labels are certainly making an impact as consumption of these products continues to increase, especially in the package goods business sector. A 1993 article in *Brandweek* notes: "Ten years ago, private label package goods started making in roads in the supermarket. But it wasn't until 1988 that store brands began to scare major marketers who always believed national brands would prevail."[16] In fact, it has been estimated that private label products are expected to increase their share of the consumer-goods market from 17 percent in 1993 to 20 percent in 1997.[17]

It is apparent that retailers are attempting to regain some control in their marketing environments by challenging manufacturer brands. It will be interesting to see how far private label penetration in the retail sector will advance.

Private label domination does occur in certain business segments. For example, supermarkets often sell produce and meat without a manufacturer label, likewise building material retailers often don't label their lumber.

It is imperative to remember, though, that private labels do cannibalize manufacturer brands. On one hand, manufacturers are gaining distribution overall by selling their excess capacity to retailers at discounted rates. On the other hand, they are doing so at the expense of their own manufacturer brands, which command higher wholesale prices from retailers. As levels of private label consumption continue to rise, profit margins for manufacturers may decline even if aggregate demand for specific product categories is increasing. In Steiner's model, advertising can be seen as increasing distribution and thus potential users while diminishing the gross margins earned by retailers. At the same time it allows factory prices to increase more than consumer prices.[18] The ability of marketing components such as advertising to maintain or stimulate demand for either private labels or manufacturer brands within product categories will be a key determinant in shaping future market dynamics regarding the relative power manufacturers, retailers, and consumers hold.

The Basic Economic Issues

As the basic economic issues are reviewed, it will become evident that the phrase "it depends" will play an important role. Often, only mixed conclusions will be reached for many of the issue areas. These mixed conclusions probably arise from the limitations discussed earlier in this chapter—viewing advertising as an isolated function, using inaccurate data, etc.—or from failing to recognize the thrust of the Porter and Steiner models.

Advertising and Price

Does advertising lead to lower prices or does it make items the consumer purchases more expensive? Before the price question can be answered, as Norris indicates, one must inquire about what kind of advertising is being discussed, retail or national.[19] His distinction between national and retail advertising is the same one that Porter and Steiner have made.

A number of studies have indicated that high levels of retail advertising increase price competition and may subsequently lower relative consumer brand prices.[20] Product groups including gasoline, drugs, and eyeglasses are often cited as examples. The proliferation of lower priced, yet heavily advertised food items included in value menus and special value combinations by many national fast food retailers also represent a price competitive situation accompanied by large promotional expenditures. As for national advertising, Norris concluded in his review of economic literature that national advertising raises the prices of goods and services.[21] Studies by William S. Comanor and Thomas A. Wilson[22] and J. J. Lambin[23] concluded that advertising decreases factory price sensitivity. The factory price versus consumer price (retail price) conclusions of these studies seem to be in agreement with the assumptions of both the Porter and the Steiner models.

Returns to Advertising

A mixed set of results is revealed when looking at the issue of efficiency in returns to advertising. Many economists and marketers have assumed there are increasing returns to advertising expenditures. For example, a campaign must reach a certain level of expenditure to generate the most efficient level of response.[24] Response in some form or another is a typical measure of advertising's "effectiveness" or efficient return to expenditures as a persuasive communication tool. It is assumed that large firms can more easily reach this level of response than can firms with more limited resources. But it does not necessarily mean that large firms can support their market share with relatively lower advertising costs than can smaller firms.[25]

Efficiencies in returns to advertising can occur because there is a threshold of awareness that advertising must cross. Though it is assumed a certain amount of message repetition is necessary before consumers become aware of a product or service, unfortunately no one knows exactly what that threshold is. The exact amount of message repetition needed to communicate effectively to consumers is often a function of such factors as risk, novelty, perceived differences in product alternatives, degree of confidence about a purchase, and the type of decision-making rules consumers employ (see chapter 5). If a high rate of repetition is required, many smaller firms could be excluded because they lack a substantial promotion budget.

Can larger firms produce "better" advertising? Through the use of marketing research and copy-testing procedures combined with the excellent creative departments at major advertising agencies, it may be possible for the large advertiser to produce more "effective" advertisements.

Evidence that larger advertisers receive dramatically different media discounts than smaller advertisers is also lacking.[26] Although such differentials did apparently occur as late as the seventies, the differentials now seem rather small.

Advertising's Effects on Profits

Leo W. Jeffres correctly pointed out: "Many economists believe that the true measure of market power is the price elasticity of demand. However, since it is so difficult to measure this factor, economists concentrate on the profit rates of manufacturers."[27]

Unfortunately, conclusions regarding the effect of advertising on profits are also clouded by measurement problems, cause-and-effect issues, and definitions of basic terms. Some authors have concluded that advertising has little effect on profit rates,[28] while others have found that advertising leads to higher profit rates.[29] Albion and Farris conclude that there is no overwhelming evidence to substantiate either the market power or market competition model, though a majority of the empirical studies find a positive relationship between advertising and profitability.[30] Because of these confusing results, researchers have often turned to another measure of the market power of advertising: concentration.

Advertising and Concentration

The concentration ratio that has been used in most of the studies in this area of research is based upon a ranking of the firms in an industry by order of size (usually sales or employees), beginning with the largest. The percentage of each firm's sales out of the total industry sales is first derived. Then the top X firms' percentages are added to obtain a concentration ratio. Published statistics usually give concentration ratios for the largest four, largest eight, and largest twenty firms in the industry.[31]

It is assumed, especially by the market power school, that advertising expenditures are related to these measures of market concentration. Advertising would cause these high concentration levels because:

1. Efficiencies in returns to advertising would enable large-scale advertisers to push smaller advertisers out of the market.
2. Increased capital requirements and brand loyalty would discourage potential entrants.[32]

F. Scherer,[33] H. Mann,[34] John Blair,[35] K. Lancaster, R. Batra, and G. Miracle,[36] and W. Mueller[37] found that advertising inequalities explain the largest share of the variance in market concentration. Many of these studies found the electronic media, especially television, to be a prime factor in increased levels of concentration. However, William S. Comanor and Thomas A. Wilson,[38] Mark S. Albion,[39] Stanley I. Ornstein and Steven Lustgarten,[40] and John M. Vernon[41] found no significant relationships between advertising and concentration. An interesting finding by Richard E. Caves, Michael E. Porter, and A. Michael Spence, with John T. Scott, was that advertising was highest in medium concentrated industries and lower in high and low concentrated industries.[42]

Norris would conclude that advertising does lead to higher levels of concentration in consumer goods industries.[43] There is, however, enough mixed evidence to indicate that the relationship may not be so simple.[44]

Again, there are probably specific industries and situations in which advertising can lead to higher levels of concentration, but a sweeping statement that advertising always develops concentration may not be possible.

Advertising and Aggregate Consumption

Several studies have investigated the effect of advertising on aggregate consumption. Richard Schmalensee found high correlations between advertising and aggregate consumption, correlations that were improved when advertising was moved from cause (preceding consumption) to effect (lagging behind consumption).[45] He points out, however, that in spite of an increase in the ratio of advertising to Gross Domestic Product, the ratio of household spending to household disposable income has remained stable over the long term.[46] He concludes that national advertising does not affect total spending for goods and services.[47]

For illustrative purposes, in 1993 personal consumption expenditures from the household sector ($4,237.2 billion) accounted for roughly 68.8 percent of the Gross Domestic Product ($6,158.8 billion). Table 4–5 provides GDP expenditures by sector. During 1993, personal disposable income equaled $4,580.3 billion. As a result, personal consumption ac-

Table 4-5. Gross Domestic Product Expenditures by Sector, 1993 (billions of 1993 dollars per year)

Sector	Expenditures	
Household sector (personal consumption expenses)	4,237.2	(+68.8%)
Government sector (purchases of goods and services)	836.4	(+13.6%)
Business sector (gross private domestic investment including depreciation)	1,118.2	(+18.2%)
Foreign sector (net exports)	–33.1	(–.5%)
TOTAL (GDP)	6,158.8	

Source: Roger LeRoy Miller, Economics Today (New York: HarperCollins, 1994), 179.

counted for approximately 92.5 percent of personal disposable income. If advertising expenditures are estimated at $140 billion, the advertising/ GDP ratio will equal about 2.3 percent.[48]

Other researchers, however, might cautiously disagree with Schmalensee. Indications that advertising does affect aggregate consumption have been reported by L. Taylor and D. Weiserbs[49] and Cowling and colleagues.[50] Rebecca C. Quarles and Leo W. Jeffres examined data for more than fifty nations to test the Galbraithian notion that advertising raises consumption to fit the needs for the industrial system against the competing argument that advertising is caused by consumption (see figure 4–1). Income and industrial development were seen as factors affecting advertising and consumption. They conclude: "We find little evidence for Galbraith's view of advertising as a high priest of materialism with the persuasive force to alter the spending and savings habits of people and nations. Instead, our analysis yields a picture of spending severely constrained by disposable income—a world where advertising has little room to maneuver in any efforts to draw spending from savings."[51]

Most of the evidence would seem to indicate that advertising is the result rather than the cause of consumption. The conclusion that advertising does not increase aggregate consumption may be based on the way that advertising budgets are traditionally established at the manufacturers' level. Many firms continue to use a percentage-of-sales method, which

Figure 4-1. Competing Views on the Relationship between Advertising and Consumption

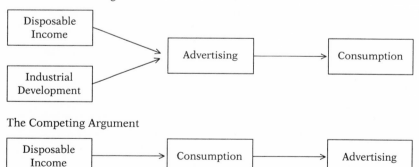

The Galbraithian Argument

The Competing Argument

will always view sales as the cause of advertising rather than as the result. Also, the studies on aggregate consumption have made an implicit assumption that advertising affects consumer attitudes and values concerning their saving and spending patterns. The two confounding factors introduced above can only lead to the conclusion that it simply is not clear whether advertising affects aggregate consumption patterns.

Advertising's Effect on Primary Demand

Primary demand is the demand for all the brands, advertised or unadvertised, within a given product category. Neil H. Borden's 1942 study concluded: "[So far as primary demand is concerned] from the many cases analyzed and from the industry studies, one clear and important generalization can be made, namely, that basic trends of demand for products, which are determined by underlying social and environmental conditions, are more significant in determining the expansion or contraction of primary demand than is the use or lack of use of advertising."[52]

H. Grabowski concluded that "the main impact of advertising is on a consumer's choice of brands or products within a particular class rather than across product classes."[53] Lambin probably best critiqued knowledge in this area: "In only four product markets out of ten have statistically significant (barely, at low levels) industry advertising effects been observed on primary demand. . . . Those four product classes are all in the early stages of the life cycle, where product-related social, economic, and technological forces are favorable to the spontaneous expansion of demand."[54]

The finding that advertising can speed growth rates (not cause dramatic shifting between product categories) under favorable conditions within a given product category gives the critics of advertising another reason to condemn the institution. In fact, either a positive or negative finding in this area would lead advertising to be damned. If advertising simply leads consumers to change from one brand of aspirin to another or from one brand of dishwashing detergent to another, it is a social waste. If advertising does increase primary demand, then advertising "can quite easily be accused of being nothing more than an antisocial tool, the properties of which range from those of a propaganda device of Orwellian proportions, an uncontrolled, insidious, pervasive activity capable of changing consumers' 'desires' to the more academic ideas of Chamberlain and Galbraith that it is a means by which capitalist corporations control demand."[55] Some Marxists and radical scholars argue that advertising has played a historical materialist role in making monopoly capitalism function through demand management[56]—e.g., advertising helps to create homogeneous markets on a global scale for transnational corporations.[57] The implicit assumption in their arguments is that "advertising is effective in reorganizing consumer demand and in creating artificial wants."[58]

Summary

Is advertising a social waste or does it benefit society and the individual consumers who comprise that society? There is no firm answer to the question. As Norris states, "The most obvious and perhaps the only certain conclusion to be drawn from this plethora of studies is that there is manifold disagreement among the students of the economic effects of advertising."[59]

B. Chiplin and B. Sturgess underscore the point at the end of *Economics of Advertising:* "Our discussions have indicated that there is no consensus in economics concerning the net benefit or cost of advertising to society. Much here depends on the value judgments of the particular individual. There are, therefore, no clear-cut policy recommendations."[60]

There is hope of finding more definitive results through the recent contributions made by Porter, Steiner, and Albion and Farris. They have broadened the economic horizon by adding the retailer component, recognizing that there are different types of consumer goods, and explicitly recognizing the difference between demand at the retail and factory levels with regard to price. If one thing is certain, it is that the market economy is dynamic, constantly evolving, and full of uncertainty. It is important in this regard to continually analyze the economic effects of major market components such as advertising.

Notes

1. Joe Mandese and Scott Donaton, "Media, Promotion Gap to Narrow," *Ad Age,* June 29, 1992, 16.

2. J. Thomas Russell and W. Ronald Lane, *Kleppner's Advertising Procedure* (Englewood Cliffs, N.J.: Prentice-Hall, 1993), 421.

3. Oskar Morgenstern, *On the Accuracy of Economic Observations* (Princeton: Princeton University Press, 1963).

4. Richard Schmalensee, *The Economics of Advertising* (Amsterdam: North

Holland, 1972), 146.

5. David Ogilvy and J. Raphaelson, "Research on Advertising Techniques That Work and Don't Work," *Harvard Business Review* 60 (July–Aug. 1982): 14–18.

6. Mark S. Albion, *Advertising's Hidden Effects: Manufacturers' Advertising and Retail Pricing* (Boston: Auburn House, 1983), 16–17.

7. S. I. Ornstein, *Industrial Concentration and Advertising Intensity* (Washington, D.C.: American Enterprise Institute, 1977), 2–3.

8. Albion, *Advertising's Hidden Effects*, 17–21.

9. Fara Warner, "The New Formula: Brandbuilding for the 90's," *Brandweek*, Oct. 18, 1993, 16–22.

10. Mark S. Albion and Paul W. Farris, *The Advertising Controversy: Evidence on the Economic Effects of Advertising* (Boston: Auburn House, 1981), 139.

11. Ibid.

12. Ibid., 144–45.

13. Robert Steiner, "A Dual Stage Approach to the Effects of Brand Advertising on Competition and Price," in *Marketing and the Public Interest*, ed. John Cady (Cambridge, Mass.: Marketing Science Institute, 1978), 131.

14. Ibid., 134.

15. Ibid., 131–35.

16. Warner, "New Formula," 20

17. Ibid., 18.

18. Albion and Farris, *Advertising Controversy*, 149.

19. Vincent P. Norris, "The Economic Effects of Advertising: A Review of the Literature," in *Current Issues of Research in Advertising*, ed. James H. Leigh and Claude Martin Jr. (Ann Arbor: Division of Research, Graduate School of Business Administration, University of Michigan, 1984), 93.

20. See ibid., 93–94; and Albion and Farris, *Advertising Controversy*, 153–70.

21. Norris, "Economic Effects," 105.

22. William S. Comanor and Thomas A. Wilson, *Advertising and Market Power* (Cambridge, Mass.: Harvard University Press, 1974).

23. J. J. Lambin, *Competition and Market Conduct in Oligopoly over Time* (Amsterdam: North Holland, 1976).

24. Albion and Farris, *Advertising Controversy*, 103.

25. Kenneth D. Boyer and Kent M. Lancaster, "Are There Scale Economies in Advertising?" *Journal of Business* 59 (July 1986): 509–26.

26. John L. Peterman, "Differences between the Levels of Spot and Network Advertising Rates," *Journal of Business* 52 (Oct. 1979): 549–62.

27. Leo W. Jeffres, *Mass Media: Processes and Effects* (Prospect Heights, Ill.: Waveland Press, 1986), 319.

28. See R. Ayanian, "Advertising and Rate of Return," *Journal of Law and Economics* 18 (Oct. 1975): 479–501; and H. Block, "Advertising and Profitability: A Reappraisal," *Journal of Political Economy* 82 (Mar.–Apr. 1974): 267–86.

29. See Comanor and Wilson, *Advertising and Market Power;* and John M. Vernon and Robert E. M. Nourse, "Profit Rates and Market Structure of Advertising Intensive Firms," *Journal of Industrial Economics* 22 (Sept. 1973): 1–20.

30. Albion and Farris, *Advertising Controversy*, 127–33.

31. Richard Caves, *American Industry: Structure, Conduct, Performance* (Englewood Cliffs, N.J.: Prentice-Hall, 1964), 8.

32. Albion and Farris, *Advertising Controversy*, 60.

33. F. Scherer, *Industrial Market Structure and Economic Performance* (Chicago: Rand McNally, 1980), chap. 14.

34. H. Mann, "Advertising, Concentration, and Profitability: The State of Knowledge and Directions for Public Policy," in *Economic Concentration: The New Learning*, ed. Harvey Goldschmid, H. Mann, and J. Weston (Boston: Little, Brown, 1974).

35. John Blair, *Economic Concentration: Structure, Behavior, and Public Policy* (New York: Harcourt Brace Jovanovich, 1972), 311, 321–31.

36. K. Lancaster, R. Batra, and G. Miracle, "How the Level, Intensity, and Distribution of Advertising Affect Market Concentration," in *Proceedings of the 1982 Conference of the American Academy of Advertising*, ed. Alan Fletcher (Lincoln, Nebr.: American Academy of Advertising, 1982).

37. W. Mueller, "Changes in Market Concentration of Manufacturing Industries, 1946–1977," *Review of Industrial Concentration* 1 (Spring 1984): 1–14.

38. See Comanor and Wilson, *Advertising and Market Power.*

39. Mark S. Albion, "The Determinants of the Level of Advertising and Media Mix Expenditures in Consumer Goods Industries," ms., Harvard University, Jan. 1976.

40. Stanley I. Ornstein and Steven Lustgarten, "Advertising Intensity and Industrial Concentration—An Empirical Inquiry, 1947–1967," in *Issues in Advertising: The Economics of Persuasion*, ed. David G. Tuerck (Washington, D.C.: American Enterprise Institute for Public Policy Research, 1978), 217–53.

41. John M. Vernon, "Concentration, Promoting, and Market Share Stability in the Pharmaceutical Industry," *Journal of Industrial Economics* 19 (July 1971): 146–266.

42. Richard E. Caves, Michael E. Porter, and A. Michael Spence, with John T. Scott, *Competition in the Open Economy* (Cambridge, Mass.: Harvard University Press, 1980).

43. Norris, "Economic Effects," 88–92.

44. E. Woodrow Eckard Jr., "Advertising, Competition, and Market Share Instability," *Journal of Business* 60 (Oct. 1987): 539–52.

45. Richard Schmalensee, "Advertising and Economic Welfare," in *Advertising and the Public Interest*, ed. S. F. Divita (Chicago: American Marketing Association, 1974), 266.

46. Ibid., 264.

47. Ibid., 285–86.

48. Roger LeRoy Miller, *Economics Today* (New York: HarperCollins, 1994), 179.

49. L. Taylor and D. Weiserbs, "Advertising and the Aggregate Consumption Function," *American Economic Review* 62 (Sept.–Dec. 1971): 642–55.

50. Keith Cowling, *Advertising and Economic Behaviour* (London: Macmillan, 1975).

51. Rebecca C. Quarles and Leo W. Jeffres, "Advertising and National Consump-

tion: A Path Analytic Re-examination of the Galbraithian Argument," *Journal of Advertising* 12, no. 2 (1983): 13; Jeffres, *Mass Media*, 316. For a discussion of Galbraith's view on advertising, see Michael Schudson, "Criticizing the Critics of Advertising: Towards a Sociological View of Marketing," *Media, Culture, and Society* 3 (Jan. 1981): 3–12.

52. Neil H. Borden, *The Economic Effects of Advertising* (Chicago: Irwin, 1942), 433.

53. H. Grabowski, "The Effects of Advertising on Intraindustry Shifts in Demand," *Explorations in Economic Research: Occasional Papers of the National Bureau for Economic Research* 4 (Winter–Spring 1977–78): 675–701.

54. Lambin, *Competition*, 136.

55. P. Kyle, "The Impact of Advertising on Markets," *International Journal of Advertising* 1 (Oct.–Dec. 1982): 345–59, quotation from 345.

56. Dallas W. Smythe, "Communications: Blindspot of Western Marxism," *Canadian Journal of Political and Social Theory* 1 (Fall 1977): 1–27.

57. Noreene Z. Janus, "Advertising and the Mass Media: Transnational Link between Production and Consumption," *Media, Culture, and Society* 3 (Jan. 1981): 13–23.

58. See Editorial, *Media, Culture, and Society* 3 (Jan. 1981): 1–2.

59. Norris, "Economic Effects," 116.

60. B. Chiplin and B. Sturgess, *Economics of Advertising* (London: Holt, Rinehart, and Winston with the Advertising Association, 1981), 134.

5

Advertising and Its Audience

This chapter will depart from many others written on the same topic. We will not discuss demographic characteristics of audiences, identify the types of consumers who tend to watch more television, or include any of the wealth of information that syndicated services provide on media and product usage patterns.

Instead of describing the advertising audience in general, we will center our discussion on the concept of *information*. The views of Carey and Sandage, reviewed in chapter 3, suggest that advertising is an institution that attempts to transmit different types of market information, information that presumably matches buyers and sellers in the marketplace. This reflects a lengthy Western philosophical tradition of broadly defining "information." Thus, consumer information can be functional in nature, such as the amount of hot water that various kinds of dishwashers use, or it can be aesthetic or symbolic, such as whether a cologne or aftershave lotion suits one's self-image.

We will focus on the impact of advertising information on the individual consumer. By individual consumer, we mean the average consumer who must enter the marketplace to buy anything from salt to a new automobile. This definition excludes those who buy professionally for others—e.g., purchasing agents. These institutional buyers have been excluded because we wish to focus our discussion on typical consumer advertising, for it is here that advertising's role is most praised and damned.

Since this chapter will view advertising as an informational medium, we will see how individual consumers acquire information and subsequently use it in order to make final purchase decisions. It is felt that this perspective offers the potential for considerable understanding of the interaction between advertising and the individual.

_____ The Basic Informational Functions of Advertising

Twenty years ago, Jagdish N. Sheth outlined four basic functions of advertising—precipitation, persuasion, reinforcement, and reminder.[1] It remains a valid list today.

Precipitation induces consumers to move from a state of indecision to one in which purchase of a particular brand is a definite possibility. Advertising's main function is to create general awareness and brand knowledge among large groups of potential customers. It attempts to intensify existing needs and wants.

When new products are introduced into the marketplace, there is usually an initial burst of advertising. The advertising usually indicates that a new product is available, tells something about its unique features, and indicates where it may be purchased. This is typical of the precipitation function.

Persuasion is seen as the mechanism by which advertising actually induces purchase. By using appeals to basic human emotions such as love, hate, fear, and self-esteem, or by using appeals to reason by discussing product attributes as benefits, the advertisement attempts to induce purchase.

For example, advertisers of home-security systems hope their messages reach those who have recently been victimized by crime or know of someone who has. By utilizing a strong appeal to fear combined with product attributes and benefits, there is an attempt to get these potential consumers to move to an immediate purchase of the security system, based on their past disturbing experience with crime. The consumer has a need for information, the advertiser has a need to inform the consumer of how his or her product will satisfy the consumer's needs.

The *reinforcement* mechanism provides information that legitimizes previous choices. Information is given that indicates the wisdom of the existing choice or validates a previous decision to reject a particular product.

Automobile companies often do an excellent job of reinforcement advertising. Usually, after a new car has been purchased, the buyer is made a member of a special club formed by the company. Each month the buyer receives a magazine that offers glowing information about the car just purchased. This information reinforces the idea that this was the right purchase decision.

Finally, the *reminder* mechanism is said to act as a triggering cue for habitual brand behavior (brand loyalty, brand equity) learned from prior experiences and exposure to information. With products that are purchased frequently, customers need to be reminded about a particular brand because of the many conflicting messages they will hear about competing brands. The large volume of advertising done for the popular soft drinks and fast-food establishments is an example of reminder advertising.

Figure 5–1 demonstrates the sequential nature of the four advertising mechanisms. It is hypothesized that consumers typically move through these four mechanisms in making initial purchases. Not all consumers, however, will cycle completely through to the reminder stage. Some will remain at reinforcement. This usually occurs for infrequently purchased products such as autos and color television sets. Some consumers will become satiated or bored with an existing product. When satiation or boredom occurs, it is believed that they will enter the first stage of the cycle again and begin to search for new product alternatives. For example, a person may become "tired" of a sofa and seek to buy a new one, feeling it will "liven up" the living room. Others will perceive there to be a "better offer" in the marketplace and thus will also recycle through the full process.

The key concept in the Sheth model is information, and it seems apparent that these four informational functions are performed in part through advertising. The consumer can be seen as constantly in the marketplace for products and services. Thus, there is a constant need for information. Likewise, marketers are constantly trying to supply that information, so as to gain sales and profits. This, in turn, provides a market system characterized by the active exchange of information, goods, and services.

_____ The "Imperfect" Information System of the Marketplace

The marketplace information system can be viewed in a simplified perspective as having two major components—advertisers and consumers. Theoretically, information brings advertisers and consumers together, thereby "matching" those with information (marketers) and those who

Figure 5-1. Basic Advertising Mechanisms

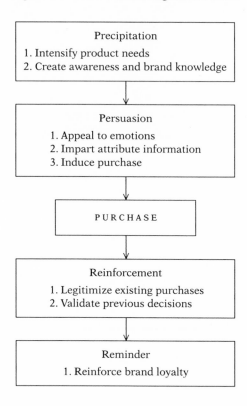

desire it (consumers). Yet, the market does not exhibit a "perfect" matching of buyers and sellers by objective standards. Hundreds of new products fail each year, retail outlets constantly end up carrying too much of the wrong product (or too little of the right one), and consumers often complain that they are unable to find what they want at the price they wish to pay. Although the market clearly "works" in a satisfactory manner much of the time, some understanding can be gained by suggesting it still performs at less than an optimal level considering the quality and quantity of messages available. Why?

Several possibilities exist: (1) advertisers are not transmitting *enough* information; (2) advertisers are transmitting the *wrong* information to the wrong audiences at the wrong times; (3) advertisers transmit too much information; (4) consumers do not *seek* out sufficient information;

and (5) consumers make "poor" decisions even when *given* adequate information.

On the basis of this perspective, let us now examine the two major components of the marketplace information system.

Advertisers

The information transmitted by advertisers is always of a persuasive nature. Since all advertisers attempt to present their products or services in the most favorable light, the information transmitted will not be perfectly objective. But then, no information is perfectly objective. All communication has a motive; all humans interpret communication. Consumers are selectively perceptive, active interpreters and equipped with diverse processing motives that completely invalidate the notion of "the communication of objective facts." No such communication exists, in advertising or anywhere else.

For example, auto manufacturers do not emphasize in their advertising that driving can be dangerous. Nor do food product advertisers discuss the presence of certain additives in their products or brag about their high fat content or their loads of refined sugar. But who would expect them to, when such a discussion would likely make the product less appealing.

Critics have often taken issue with the persuasive nature of advertising, claiming that it subverts the consumer's "rational" decision-making processes. But, as Borden has argued, "whether one likes persuasion or not, it appears inevitable in a free society."[2] As Carey suggested, the persuasive nature of advertising communications is an institutionally understandable part of our market economy. The market economy basically presumes that firms will operate in their own self-interest to produce sales and profits; persuasive advertisements are a vehicle to achieve that end. Consumers explicitly know that an ad is an ad and implicitly understand its basic rhetorical intent, as well as most of the "rules" of this persuasive "game."

Closely related to the persuasion issue is the issue of frequency. Frequency—the repetition of many commercial messages—is something that all consumers are aware of and many are annoyed by. Recognizing that their messages are among hundreds attempting to attract the attention of consumers, advertisers use the technique of repetition to attract their share of attention. They are trying to be "heard above the crowd," to "break through the clutter."

Although advertisers view repetition as an important technique in selling products, they are often unsure about how much repetition to use. Sometimes an ad is repeated too many times, sometimes not often enough. It is usually quite difficult to determine the optimal expenditure of media dollars. In fact, there is no reason to think that any advertiser really knows just how much to repeat any message. Advertisers usually err on the side of more, rather than less.

Related to repetition is the issue of occasion—the time of day that an advertisement is presented. Advertisers are naturally in constant search of their most cost-effective audience. However, many consumers complain about the promotion of certain kinds of products at the dinner hour—laxatives or hemorrhoid preparations, for example. Again, the advertiser is presumably acting in self-interest. Large numbers of people are viewing television during the dinner hour, and many of these people are users or potential users of these products. Since advertisers want to reach as many potential customers as possible, they see the dinner hour as an ideal time for them to transmit their messages. Still, there is always a significant amount of "wasted" placement in any media schedule.

In addition to "puffing" their products, repeating their ads too often, or placing them at "inappropriate" or less than optimal times, advertisers may direct their messages to the wrong audience. The advertiser may have perceived the market to be the twenty-to-thirty-year-old group when, in fact, the major market for the product is consumers forty to fifty years of age. This misdirected information may not effectively reach the "prime market" and consequently will be of little value to either advertiser or consumer.

At other times advertisers send messages that consumers do not understand or interpret incorrectly. For example, consumers may have seen an ad for a paint sale at a local hardware store. The ad may have failed to state clearly enough that only certain colors were on sale, leaving some consumers with the impression that the sale prices applied to all colors of paint. The subsequent visit to the hardware store will prove unsatisfactory for both the advertiser and the consumer.

In sum, advertisers do not always transmit "perfect" information for either their own or consumers' interests. Because of practices such as attempting to induce purchase through partial information, making mistakes in frequency rates and timing, developing poor messages, and transmitting information to the wrong audience, less than optimal information may be offered by advertisers to consumers.

Consumers

Consumers, as well, are "imperfect" in the way they go about gathering and processing information. They are not the rational beings that classical economists had thought they were. Although there is evidence that consumers approach some buying decisions in a deliberate manner, there is also reason to believe that a good deal of purchasing behavior involves little conscious decision making.

Much decision making does not follow the systematic approaches presented in formal consumer behavior models. Rarely does a consumer proceed smoothly from need recognition to information acquisition to purchase. The decision process may take place over a long period of time with incomplete and often ambiguous data, and the final decision may be made with something less than total confidence.[3]

A consumer's ability to process bits of information is also imperfect. At any given time, individuals can probably actively process only a limited amount of information.[4] When the buying environment is very complex, it is easy to become confused. Take, for example, the process of deciding which house to buy. After looking at many different houses and collecting a myriad of data, how many consumers base their final decision on an essentially minor feature, such as whether a fence is part of the property? For some home buyers, the mass of information about unique support features, insulation, wiring, landscaping, fireplaces, size of lot, and heating and cooling systems can be too much to deal with. So, they buy a house because "it feels right." They have somehow reduced an overwhelming amount of data into a more manageable set of feelings, or summary judgments. They have made a decision. Whether this was sufficiently "rational" to please economists is beyond determination, but it is certainly characteristic of a good many consumer decisions.

Consumer behavior is aptly described by James A. March and Herbert A. Simon's concept of "bounded rationality": Faced with a very complex environment and limited resources (time, money, cognitive capabilities), consumers attempt to resolve buying problems in ways that are satisfactory rather than optimal.[5] In Raymond A. Bauer's view of consumer behavior, "consumers characteristically develop decision strategies and ways of reducing risk that enable them to act with relative confidence and ease in situations where their information is inadequate and the consequences of their actions are in some meaningful sense incalculable."[6]

Thus, it appears that neither consumers nor advertisers always operate in an optimal manner in the marketplace. Yet, given this less than ideal performance on the part of both major components of the market information system, it is interesting to note that the system continues to function and has given apparently adequate service to many consumers and advertisers. The *perfect* marketplace has never existed—and never will. That does not mean, of course, that it is fruitless to search for ways to improve the existing mechanism.

One approach may be to look more closely at exactly *how* consumers use the information available to make buying decisions. Given some kind of descriptive model, it may be possible to better understand the "human" workings of the market, and thus be more adequately equipped to offer suggestions for improvement.

_____ How Consumers Gather and Use Information

Of course consumers do not rely solely upon advertising to gather product brand information. There are five primary sources of information, both internal and external, available to consumers:[7]

1. *Memory* of past searches, personal experiences, and low-involvement learning (internal information)
2. *Marketer-dominated sources,* such as advertising, personal selling, etc.
3. *Consumer-dominated sources,* such as family and friends
4. *Neutral sources,* such as *Consumer Reports* and various state and local government publications
5. *Experiential sources,* such as inspections or product trials

The acquisition of information from these types of sources is illustrated in figure 5–2.

When Are These Information Sources Used?

The internal information sources are the primary ones used by consumers, especially in cases where the consumer is involved in a very limited problem-solving situation or is brand loyal.[8] In fact, when we talk about consumer "information processing" and "decision making," we sometimes forget that the consumer does not "reinvent the wheel" each time she or he makes a decision. A distinction has emerged in the consumer behavior literature between decisions made "on-line" versus those that are "memory based." For a very long time, researchers and regulators assumed that all of the original information from ads was recalled and systematically

Figure 5-2. Information Sources for a Purchase Decision

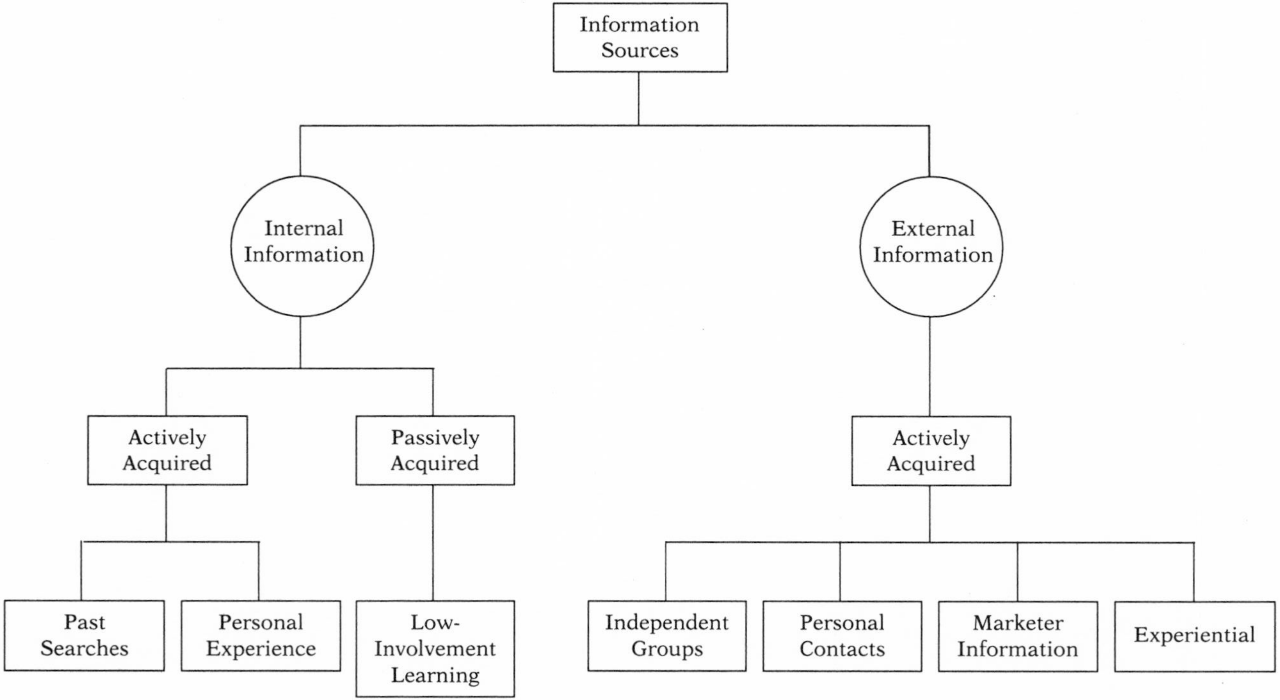

Source: Adapted from H. Beales, M. B. Mazis, S. C. Salop, and R. Staelin, "Consumer Search and Public Policy," *Journal of Consumer Research* 8 (June 1981): 12.

evaluated every time a consumer made a decision. More recent work in social cognition indicates that consumers often rely on previously made judgments, rather than on attitudinal attribute weightings and evaluations.[9] Finally consumer researcher knowledge caught up with what most anyone on the street knew: sometimes we make decisions and then rely on them, while completely forgetting why we decided the way we did. This means that the original information supplied by the marketer becomes far less important, from an informational-decision-making standpoint, after the first decision is made. With subsequent decisions, the probability of merely retrieving the judgment increases significantly.

In memory-based decision making, a decision is retrieved. Consumers remember that they buy Brand X Beer, but can't remember why. The fact that they can't remember doesn't mean that they are simply dupes of the advertising machine, but it does mean that they don't have to make that decision again. If such a mental method did not exist, an average trip to the grocery store would take about a year. It may not be a thorough method, but it is efficient, and very human.

Mass media or market-dominated sources have been found to be important in the early stages of the decision process, when buyers are informing themselves about possible alternatives (Sheth's precipitation function);[10] but these sources are frequently found to be of limited direct value in consumers' decisions (Sheth's persuasion function).[11]

There has been some research on the effect of product characteristics on information sources used. Research on the diffusion of information indicates that there is a tendency for buyers of new and high-involvement products to prefer consumer-dominated sources.[12] Robert B. Settle found that for complex and socially visible products the preferred sources of information were conversations with experts and close friends. For durable and multipurpose products, the preferred information source was personal experience.[13]

The neutral channels are vastly underutilized. One study found 6 percent or less of female consumers utilize neutral sources in the purchase of small appliances, clothing, and food items;[14] while other researchers found that neutral sources were valued sixth (out of six choices) in importance in the purchase of men's shirts and television sets.[15] Sharon E. Beatty and Scott M. Smith found that a search of neutral sources was influenced by time, availability, and ego involvement. They concluded that people perceive neutral sources as time consuming, and that under time pressure, people may avoid this type of search. Examining ego involvement, they found that if a product is really important to a person's ego, a neutral source may be sought out.[16]

It is clear that consumers rarely rely on a single source of information. Instead they use multiple information sources that are complementary rather than competitive, and their use depends upon the situation in which consumers find themselves.

However, no matter which channel(s) consumers use, there still is often some motivation to gather information. The next section will deal with these motivating forces.

Determinants of the External Search Effort by Consumers

Let us first turn to some of the basic reasons why consumers seek information before making a purchase. The area of external search activity has a long history of study. Beatty and Smith have developed a rather complete analysis of many of these works. Their conclusions for over seventy reviewed articles were:

1. Consumers tend to engage in more searches when purchasing higher priced, more visible, and more complex products—i.e., products that intrinsically create greater perceived risk.
2. Searches are also influenced by individual factors, such as the perceived benefits of the search (e.g., enjoyment, self-confidence, role), demographic aspects, and product knowledge possessed.
3. Searching efforts tend to be further influenced by factors in the marketplace, such as time pressure impinging on the shopper.[17]

Although it would not be appropriate for this text to review all the possible determinants of external search activity in depth, some of the more interesting findings that supplement and extend Beatty and Smith's work will now be reviewed.

Risk

In every buying decision, consumers have identified (however vaguely) a need and a product or service that will satisfy that need. Many buying decisions involve some perceived risk: as Bauer puts it, "Consumer behavior involves risk in the sense that any action of a consumer will produce consequences which he cannot anticipate with any approximate certainty."[18] How many times have we thought about buying something and yet been very unsure which purchase would be most satisfactory for the money involved?

Perceived risk is apparently a function of at least two factors—uncertainty and consequences.[19] Consumers may be uncertain about their goals. For example, a consumer who has identified the need for a new car might be unsure whether economy or comfort is a more important goal. Even if the consumer has established economy as the basic goal, there is still uncertainty about exactly what type of car will be best. A Ford Escort? A Honda Accord? Thus, uncertainty deals with basic buying goals (economy versus comfort) as well as with final specification of an exact product (Escort versus Accord) that will satisfy the overall goal.

The consequences of a purchase is the second factor that can generate perceived risk. Consequences can be defined as "the amount that would be lost if the consequences of the act were not favorable."[20] If you buy the Escort, will it impress your friends as you hoped? You may also have had certain expectations of how well the Escort would perform. For example, you may be fearful that the car might require more maintenance than you anticipated.

The major types of risk that consumers may perceive in making product/service decisions have been categorized as follows:[21]

1. FUNCTIONAL RISK. The product/service will not perform as expected. "Will the Accord get excellent highway gas mileage?"
2. PHYSICAL RISK. Using the product will involve risk to oneself or others. "Will the lawn mower be safe for my teenage son to operate?"
3. FINANCIAL RISK. The product/service will not be worth its cost in terms of money to acquire it. "Will buying a new home cause financial hardship?"
4. SOCIAL RISK. The product/service will be an embarrassment to oneself. "Will others like my new entertainment center?"
5. PSYCHOLOGICAL RISK. The consumer's final choice will bruise the ego. "Will I really be happy in this apartment?"
6. TIME RISK. The time spent in searching may be wasted if performance is not expected. "Will I have to return this and go shopping again?"
7. OPPORTUNITY LOSS. Risk that by taking one action the consumer will miss out on doing something else he or she would prefer doing. "Instead of purchasing a BMW I could have taken a trip to Europe."[22]

In general, consumers can reduce perceived risk by (1) reducing the amount at stake or (2) decreasing uncertainty through information acquisition. Reducing the consequences (the amount at stake) of a decision is a somewhat more difficult strategy to follow for most consumers than reducing uncertainty. To use our earlier example, it may be very difficult for a person to say that she does not care what her friends think of her new Escort if social esteem is important to her. It would also be difficult for her to minimize a poor maintenance record when it has cost her dearly to make repairs. Therefore, it appears more likely that consumers will tend to seek to reduce uncertainty through information acquisition or to avoid the uncertainty altogether.

Some more specific risk-avoidance strategies include the following:[23]

1. Information seeking from memory, market, consumer, or neutral dominated sources of information
2. Development of brand loyalty toward a product/service instead of purchasing new or untried products/services
3. Trusting of well-known brand names when experience has been minor in a product category (brand image)
4. Trusting of stores to provide only good-quality products/services (store image)
5. Choosing of the most expensive item or model
6. Reliance upon private laboratory tests, money-back guarantees, warranties, and pre-purchase trial (reassurance)

One study, however, found that risk-reduction strategies employed by consumers vary by product class. Brand loyalty was the best strategy for shampoos, detergents, and canned mushrooms, while money-back guarantees and store images were the best risk-reduction strategies for electrical appliances. Comparison shopping was the reduction strategy for dresses and dishes.[24]

The impression should not be left that all consumers act to reduce or avoid risk. Different individuals have different levels of tolerance for risk, each acting to reduce risk to a personally acceptable level. Certain consumers, in fact, have been found to act in a way that increases risk.[25] The Sheth model, discussed earlier, indicated that consumers who become satiated or bored by a product will accept the risk involved in seeking new product alternatives. Thus, consumers can have two entirely different strategies concerning risk: acting to decrease it or acting to increase it. The novelty factor below will expand the discussion on increasing risk.

Novelty, Variety Seeking

Novelty is another factor that motivates consumers to seek information.[26] All dimensions of newness in the market, such as new products or new advertising (appeals, media) can be viewed as stimuli that will motivate consumers to seek information. For many consumers, novelty is a change of pace from the usual way of doing things and thus holds intrinsic appeal. The new safer tire, the newly designed auto, or the unusual advertisement may all attract the initial attention of the consumer. Quite often, the consumer will attempt to find out more with the possibility of eventually buying.

Number of Alternatives

The greater the number of alternatives (products, stores, brands) available to the consumer to resolve a particular problem, the more external searching there is likely to be.[27]

Store Distribution

The number, location, and distances between retail outlets can affect the number of store visits a consumer will make to gather information.[28] When stores are clustered together, as often happens with auto dealers or appliance stores or in shopping malls, the consumer will generally visit more of them, since there will be a reduction in the time and energy to make such visits.

Greater Differences in Product Alternatives

When the consumer perceives important differences between brands based on differences in features, style, or appearance, more external searching for information will occur.[29] Dissimilarities in products/services may lead the consumer to perceive substantial benefits from searching for information. Such benefits may not be as evident when products/services are perceived as having parity. Highly differentiated products for which many consumers engage in extensive information searching include clothing,[30] new furniture,[31] and autos.[32]

Education, Occupation, and Income of Consumers

The external search for information has been found to be related to education, occupation, and income.[33] A positive relationship has been found between the level of education and the amount of information searching for such items as major appliances[34] and homes,[35] while a negative relationship was found for sporting equipment and shirts.[36] The more elevated the occupation, the more external searching was found for the purchase of durable goods;[37] but the lower the income, the less searching there was for small appliances.[38]

Age of the Consumer

External searching tends to decrease as the age of the consumer increases.[39] This may in part be that the older consumer has become more familiar with a host of products/services that the younger consumer is just encountering.

Attitudes toward Shopping

"Attitudes toward shopping reflect the individual's beliefs about the value and benefit achieved through shopping activities for the product category being purchased. This variable is not equivalent to simple shopping enjoyment, but it is a strong motivating predisposition to shopping and could be viewed as indicating 'shopping involvement.'"[40] The literature shows a strong positive relationship between attitudes toward shopping and actual search behavior.[41]

Degree of Confidence

If consumers are confident about a purchase, they are not likely to seek much information. An example would be a consumer who is loyal to a particular brand of coffee. When coffee is on the grocery list, a favorite brand is automatically chosen from the supermarket shelf. Because of previous satisfactory experience with the brand, there is no motivation to seek information about the purchase. Many new car buyers, based on a satisfying experience with a brand of auto, repurchased that brand with very little information.[42] Conversely, a consumer who is not confident about a purchase (e.g., buying a home computer for the first time) will probably seek information about both the product class and the brands available.

William L. Moore and Donald R. Lehmann found that the greater the number of previous purchases, the less information was required.[43] However, Peter D. Bennett and Robert M. Mandell found that past experience with a product reduces the need for information only as long as the consumer is satisfied with the product.[44] It may be that confidence and risk are closely related. If the consumer is very confident about an upcoming purchase, it may also be that little or no risk is perceived. Thus, in either instance, little information seeking will occur.

Involuntary Situation

A final factor that motivates information seeking is the involuntary situation. When the refrigerator or dryer breaks for the last time, consumers are forced into the marketplace to gather information. Generally, consumers perceive more risk than is actually present in the involuntary situation.[45]

Given these ten motivations for information seeking, we shall attempt to review some of the factors that affect how much information consumers will gather.

How Much Information Do Consumers Gather?

We do know consumers actively gather information in the marketplace. Often, however, the amount of information that *could* be gathered and processed is overwhelming. For example, on any drugstore shelf, there are a dozen or more brands of shampoo. Each has a different price, different ingredients, different functions (for dry, normal, or oily hair; for dandruff; for body), and different quality-price associations. Information is readily available on the shampoo package and from prior learning about the products through advertisements and personal experience. Friends may have offered advice on which products are good. Hence, with little effort, the consumer can be exposed to a plethora of valuable product information.

Although the amount of external searching that consumers undertake before making a purchase has been measured in a number of ways in the literature (number of stores visited, number of information sources consulted, number of alternatives considered, number of different types of information used, and time duration of the purchase decision), it is clear that for most consumers the amount of external research conducted is very limited. We shall review the first two of these measurement types.

J. W. Newman found that one-stop shoppers accounted for approximately 60 percent of the purchases of new autos; 60–80 percent of the purchases of various items of apparel and small appliances; and 85 to 90 percent of the purchases of cookware, towels, sheets, and toys.[46]

R. A. Westbrook and C. Farnell reported on retail store shopping patterns used by purchasers of major appliances and found that 31 percent of all buyers visited only one outlet, while 15 percent visited two stores and 19 percent visited three retail outlets. Thirty-five percent visited four or more stores.[47]

Concerning number of information sources utilized for the purchase of autos, J. Newman and R. Staelin[48] reported the following:

1. Fifteen percent of the buyers consulted no external information source.
2. Thirty percent of the buyers consulted only one external information source.

3. Twenty-six percent consulted two information sources.
4. Eighteen percent used three information sources.
5. Twelve percent utilized four or more information sources before purchase.

Del I. Hawkins, Roger J. Best, and Kenneth A. Coney[49] classify durable-goods purchasers into three groups of information search types:

1. NONSEARCHERS. Fifty percent of the consumers conduct little or no search prior to purchase.
2. LIMITED INFORMATION SEARCHERS. Thirty-eight percent of the consumers conduct limited information searches.
3. EXTENDED INFORMATION SEARCHES. Only about 12 percent are involved in extensive information searching prior to purchase. These individuals tend to have higher incomes, are heavy users of a variety of media vehicles, are opinion leaders, and have favorable overall attitudes toward business.

Other equally important factors are the time and money it takes to gather information. How many times have we bought the first item we saw because we simply did not have the time or inclination to "look around"? We may have known about a store that offered the same product at a better price, but it was "just too far away." Thus, in many instances, information is not sought by consumers because the added costs of search (time and money) are too high in light of the expected benefits this information will provide for making a final decision.[50]

One note of caution is appropriate. It would appear from the previous studies that many consumers, because they conduct little or no external searching, are not searching at all. What many of these studies fail to note is the amount of internal searching (memory) each consumer engages in prior to making a purchase.[51] Visiting few stores and reviewing only a few brands may also indicate that consumers have various decision-making rules that immediately limit their set of store and brand alternatives. We will now discuss these decision-making rules.

Decision-Making Rules That Consumers Use

Consumers use decision-making rules when they attempt to evaluate and select alternatives they have discovered in the search process. Some consumers average out some of the very good features with some of the less attractive features of a product in determining overall brand preference. The brand that rates highest on the sum of the consumer's judgment of the relevant evaluative criteria will be chosen. This is known as the *linear compensatory* rule.[52] This form of decision making appears to be used in more complex high-involvement situations.

The following rules are called *noncompensatory*, since very good performance on one evaluative criterion cannot compensate for poor performance on another evaluative criterion:

1. THE DISJUNCTIVE RULE. This rule establishes a minimum level of desired performance for each relevant attribute. The number of attributes will be small, and the level of desired performance will generally be high. All brands that surpass the performance for any attribute are considered acceptable. The consumer would say, "I'll consider all (or buy the first) brands that perform really well on any attribute I consider to be important."[53]
2. THE CONJUNCTIVE RULE. A consumer will consider a brand only if it meets acceptable standards on all key attributes. If the washing machine meets the consumer's requirements for amount of water utilized and permanent-press features but is above a set limit on cost, it will be eliminated from the alternatives.[54]
3. THE LEXICOGRAPHIC RULE. The consumer rank-orders all the key brand attributes by perceived importance. After comparing the brands on the most important attributes, the one that is highest is selected. If there is a tie, brands are then evaluated on the second most important attribute.[55]

Certainly, these are not the only decision-making rules that consumers employ. For many purchase situations, prior learning as a result of product trial may be utilized. Assessment of attributes may not be important, and the consumer may choose the brand with the best overall impression. Leon G. Schiffman and Leslie Lazar Kanuk call this the *affect referred rule*.[56]

Consumers may use only one rule or combine them in myriad ways to reach final purchase decisions. Low-involvement purchases probably involve simple decision-making rules, such as the conjunctive, the disjunctive, or the lexicographic, since consumers may attempt to minimize the mental cost of such decisions.[57] High-involvement decisions may utilize complex rules such as the linear compensatory and may involve different rules at different stages of the decision-making process.[58] Table 5–1 may help to clarify the above discussion.

Table 5-1. Use of Decision-Making Rules in Choosing a Brand of Automobile

Rule	Verbal Description	Percentage Using Rule
Disjunctive	I chose the car that had a really good rating on at least one characteristic.	0
Conjunctive	I chose the car that didn't have any bad ratings.	0.6
Lexicographic	I looked at the characteristic that was most important to me and chose the car that was best in that characteristic. If two or more of the cars were equal on that characteristic, I then looked at my second most important characteristic to break the tie.	60.7
Compensatory	I chose the car that had a really good rating when you balanced the good ratings with the bad ratings.	32.1
Disjunctive-conjunctive	I first eliminated any car that didn't have at least one really good score and then chose from the rest the product that didn't have a really bad score on any characteristic.	0
Conjunctive-disjunctive	I first eliminated the cars with a bad rating on any characteristic and then chose from the rest the one with a high score on any characteristic.	0
Disjunctive-compensatory	I first eliminated any car that didn't have at least one really good rating and then chose from the rest of the cars that seemed the best when you balanced the good ratings.	1.1
Conjunctive-compensatory	I first eliminated the cars with a really bad rating on any characteristic and then chose from the rest the one that seemed the best overall when you balanced the good ratings with the bad ratings.	5.4

Source: Derived from M. Reily and R. Holman, "Does Task Complexity or Cue Intercorrelation Affect Choice of an Information Processing Strategy: An Empirical Investigation," in *Advances in Consumer Research Four,* ed. W. D. Perrault Jr. (Chicago: Association for Consumer Research, 1977), 189.

How Does Information Influence Purchase?

There are many conflicting views of how information can influence a purchase decision. We shall review five theories that have received some support from a host of studies conducted in the area. The approaches to be discussed view the influence process as occurring through the interaction of cognitive, affective, and conative elements. The cognitive component includes attention, awareness, comprehension, learning, interest, and beliefs; the affective component is concerned with interest, attitude, feeling, and evaluation; the conative factor deals with behavior—trial, action, and adoption.

The Learning Hierarchy

One view of the process, the learning hierarchy, states that information transmitted and subsequently gathered by consumers must first create changes in the cognitive component (awareness, attention, comprehension). In other words, the consumer must first attend to and understand the information. If this is successfully accomplished, then changes in the affective component (attitude) may occur (reorganization of belief structure). Once a favorable attitude toward purchase of the brand occurs, changes in the conative component (intentions to behave, trial, etc.) will occur (see figure 5–3). Michael L. Ray refers to this sequence as the "learn-feel-do" hierarchy.[59]

As Ray indicates, the learning hierarchy exists only in special circumstances. It is most likely to occur in situations in which there are audi-

Figure 5-3. The Learning Hierarchy

Cognitive Changes

1. Attention
2. Awareness
3. Comprehension
4. Beliefs

Affective Changes

1. Attitude
2. Evaluation
3. Feelings

Conative Changes

1. Intentions
2. Actual behavior

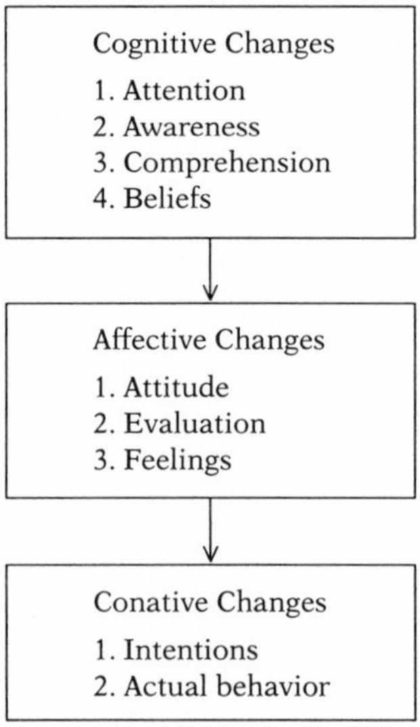

ence involvement, product differentiation, and emphasis on the mass media in communication, and in which the product is in the early stages of the product life cycle.[60] Product examples include portable television sets, autos, washing machines, and pocket calculators.[61]

The Dissonance-Attribution Hierarchy

Another view of the organization of the cognitive, affective, conative structure is called the dissonance-attribution hierarchy. This is the exact reverse of the learning hierarchy—"do-feel-learn" instead of "learn-feel-do"; in the dissonance-attribution hierarchy, behavior occurs first, then attitude change, and finally learning[62] (see figure 5–4).

Although studies in dissonance theory have been applied to this model, Ray indicates that attribution theory may be a more adequate explanation of this hierarchy. The reasoning for this approach would be as follows: People determine that they have attitudes by perceiving their own behavior. If someone has made a brand choice, this person will say, "I must have a positive attitude toward that brand because I have chosen it." If, after choice and attitude change, individuals are exposed to marketing messages, they will tend to choose the information that will support their attitude. Product examples might be autos and home-entertainment equipment.[63]

Figure 5-4. The Dissonance Attribution Hierarchy

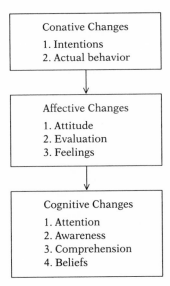

Conative Changes
1. Intentions
2. Actual behavior

Affective Changes
1. Attitude
2. Evaluation
3. Feelings

Cognitive Changes
1. Attention
2. Awareness
3. Comprehension
4. Beliefs

The dissonance-attribution hierarchy has been found to occur when the following conditions exist:

1. Low differentiation for complex alternatives
2. Non-mass media, personal sources important
3. Mature stage in the product life cycle
4. Situation crucial[64]

The Low-Involvement Hierarchy

A third approach is called the low-involvement hierarchy, or "learn-do-feel"[65] (see figure 5–5). The low-involvement hierarchy views information as first changing the cognitive component, then bringing about actual behavior changes, and then finally affecting attitude. The view holds that television viewers, for example, are not involved with the advertising. Thus, there is little perceptual defense against the commercial messages. Although television commercials will probably not change attitudes, they may, after a great deal of repetition, make possible a shift in cognitive structure. Consumers will thus be better able to recall the name of a product or service that has been advertised. The next time they are in a store, that name could come to mind and result

Figure 5-5. The Low-Involvement Hierarchy

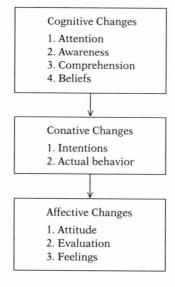

in a purchase. After consumers have used the product, it is contended, an attitude shift will occur. If product usage is satisfactory, a more favorable attitude toward the product will develop; if product usage is unsatisfactory, an unfavorable attitude will develop. Examples of products that often fit this profile are soaps, mouthwashes, and gum—often heavily advertised products.

Low involvement is likely to occur under the following conditions:[66]

1. Low differentiation
2. Mass media important
3. Mature stage in the product life cycle

The Batra-Ray model[67] (shown in figure 5–6) is another more recent view of how information can influence a purchase decision. The first stage in the model, affective response, indicates that determinants of attitude toward the ad, A_{ad}, are not all cognitively based reactions to the advertising stimulus.[68] Advertisements, in addition to providing product, benefit, or attribute information, can also provide "music, humor, affectionate vignettes, story elements, role portrayals, and the like."[69] These later elements can evoke moods within the consumer that are simply the consumer's affective state at the time of exposure.[70]

Figure 5-6. The Batra-Ray Model

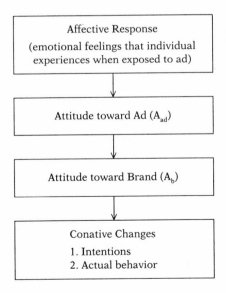

Given that advertisements can "set the right mood, through some emotional appeal," these affective responses will influence A_{ad}. A_{ad} can best be defined as liking the advertising execution or production. The model then indicates that A_{ad} could influence attitude toward the brand, A_b, which in turn could lead to some conative changes, such as more positive behavioral intentions or actual behavior.

More recent research indicates that the model may work best in situations in which the consumer is unfamiliar with the brand.[71] For familiar brands, it may be that the emotional execution acts by changing the level of confidence or degree of accessibility that the consumer has in the A_b.[72]

In sum, this model implies that it is not always what you say but how you say it that is important. This emotional strategy utilized by many advertisers is often viewed as a "say nothing" message by critics of advertising, but the Batra-Ray model indicates that these messages can indeed communicate with the audience.

The Experiential-Based Model

Our last model of how information can influence decision is shown in figure 5–7. This model is based upon an alternative view of the buying process, one that emphasizes the experiential side of consumption rather than the view that consumers actively process information in a rational, thoughtful manner. The experiential model views consumers as feelers, in addition to thinkers, who consume many types of products for the sensations, feelings, images, and emotions they generate.[73]

Olli T. Shtola believes that products/services/events should be classified into utilitarian and esthetic groups.[74] Utilitarian products/services/events might include many traditional food products, soaps, garbage bags, and motor oil; while esthetic products/services/events might include movies, art, novels, operas, and casinos.[75] The experiential view, then, focuses on the symbolic, hedonic, and aesthetic nature of consumption and regards the consumption experience as a phenomenon directed toward the pursuit of fantasies, feelings, and fun.[76]

Some additional examples might help to clarify the model. When women look to purchase nail polish or eye makeup or men look to purchase cologne, a host of options are presented at the cosmetic counter of a department store. Observing consumers reviewing the hundreds of shades of nail polish and eye makeup or "consuming" the many scents of cologne, one wonders how a decision is made concerning a particu-

Figure 5-7. The Experiential-Based Model

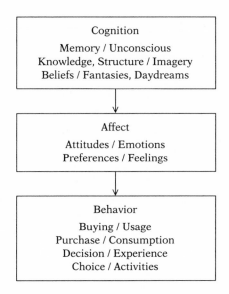

Note: Terms on the left-hand side indicate traditional terms used in information processing, while those on the right-hand side indicate experiential concepts.

Source: Morris B. Holbrook and Elizabeth C. Hirschman, "The Experiential Aspects of Consumption: Consumer Fantasies, Feelings, and Fun," *Journal of Consumer Research* 9 (Sept. 1982): 133.

lar shade of blue or scent of cologne. When asked how the decision was made, comments often arise such as: "It's me!" or "It is just right!" Is it a decision based entirely upon bits of information or one that is influenced by the fantasies and feelings generated by the individual? Women's lingerie, for example, is often purchased for the fantasies, feelings, and emotions that it generates rather than for functional purposes.

This experiential model is still in its evolutionary stages and thus is open to many interpretations. Grant McCracken provides another view.[77] He would describe the experiential-based model as being meaning based rather than information based. The meaning-based model assumes a purchase is made in the broader cultural context. Consumer goods, in their anticipation, choice, purchase, and possession, are important sources of meaning with which consumers construct their lives. They are looking for things that help shape the meaning of themselves, their family, and their communities. McCracken's view is compatible with the cultural view of advertising expressed by Carey.

It is also compatible with that of Linda Scott,[78] who views advertising as a socially embedded text, which does carry meaning the way a glass carries wine. According to Scott, an ad has no set meaning, and thus no predefined bundle of "information." There is no "the meaning" of an ad. Its meaning depends on who is reading it. This is not to say something as banal as "everyone has a different reading," but more that different audiences will have different readings. For example, men probably don't get the same meaning from a tampon ad as do women. Why? Because the experience of being a woman privileges the reading of the ad. Men just can't understand it in the same way. The same could be said of ads read by communities of readers defined by ethnicity, age, etc. The point is that much of the meaning of an ad is in the reading, as well as in the writing.

——— Summary

We have attempted to look at the information system in the marketplace via advertisers and consumers. Advertisers send messages to consumers with varying degrees of efficiency and professionalism. Consumers in turn receive some of the messages from advertisers, but they also look to their own memories, the advice and opinions of friends, and neutral sources of information.

If we take an "objective" stance, such as that of classical economists, we would have to say that the system of information flow in the marketplace leaves much to be desired. Advertisers, predictably, operate in their own self-interest by sending only the information they wish to send, when they wish to send it, and often with uncertain guidance as to the proper "mix" of message content and frequency.

Consumers, for their part, frequently fail to meet the standards of the "economic person." They do not always collect all the information they could when deciding which product to buy. Often they rely on shortcuts; they may look to price as an indicator of quality or they may become brand or store loyal. They not infrequently stop processing information when they become confused and may make "snap" decisions just to "get it over with." They may buy in pursuit of fantasies, feelings, and fun.

But from another vantage point, the market of information flow tends to operate in a generally acceptable manner. If we accept our existing economic system, it is perfectly logical for advertisers to operate in their own self-interest by transmitting persuasive communications that are repeated often. They are attempting to induce sales to ensure the continued existence of the firm.

Although consumers do not always try to find perfect solutions to their purchase decisions, they operate in ways that often lead to subjective satisfaction on their part. Consumers will often informally balance the cost of seeking additional information with the benefits they hope it will bring to the final purchase decision. If it appears that additional information is not needed, they will not collect it. This does not necessarily mean that they are not "rational," but only that they are operating from a set of decision-making rules that they have found acceptable in making purchases. If consumers attempted to behave in the rational manner that classical economists have posited, they probably would spend a great deal of their time gathering information. Consumers are constantly seeking products and services that will allow them more leisure time. It is not different with information seeking. Consumers are always seeking ways to reduce search time, yet still reach acceptable decisions.

This is not to say that consumers do not buy products that are unacceptable for their existing needs. When this happens, it is very difficult to determine whether it is the fault of the "imperfect" market sources or the fault of the "imperfect" consumer. For example, if you make a mistake in a purchase decision, it may be easier to blame the advertisements than to accept the blame yourself.

Advertising can be viewed as being involved in a market service. It provides a type of information that helps match buyers and sellers in a general system emphasizing the self-interest of the participants. It is clearly not "perfect" and could certainly be improved. But any steps toward improvement must rest on an understanding of the ways consumers actually utilize information.

More and more information is apparently not the answer. Consumers will continue to use shortcuts in their purchasing behavior. What is apparently needed is not more, but better information. Unfortunately, neither critics nor supporters of advertising are exactly sure what "better" information is. There is little prospect that we can make the consumer the perfect information procuring and processing system. All we can hope for is to make the consumer a better information system, given the "recalcitrance and perversity" of human nature.

Advertising can be made more informative, but that is only one side of the issue. The consumer must also be improved through better education, learning not only how to obtain information but also how to use it. Most of all, the consumer must *want* to use the information.

Notes

1. Jagdish N. Sheth, "Measurement of Advertising Effectiveness: Some Theoretical Considerations," *Journal of Advertising* 3, no. 1 (1974): 8–11.

2. Neil H. Borden, *The Economic Effects of Advertising* (Chicago: Irwin, 1942).

3. Raymond L. Horton, *Buyer Behavior: A Decision-Making Approach* (Columbus: Charles E. Merrill, 1984), 12.

4. See Jacob Jacoby, Donald E. Speller, and Carol A. Kohn, "Brand Choice Behavior as a Function of Information Load," *Journal of Marketing Research* 11 (Feb. 1984): 63–69; William L. Wilkie, "Analysis of Effects of Information Load," *Journal of Marketing Research* 11 (Nov. 1974): 467–68; and Gerald Zaltman and Melanie Wallendorf, *Consumer Behavior: Basic Findings and Management Implications,* 2d ed. (New York: John Wiley and Sons, 1983), 351–53; Thomas E. Muller, "Buyer Response to Variations in Product Information Load," *Journal of Applied Psychology* 69 (1984): 300–306.

5. James A. March and Herbert A. Simon, *Organizations* (New York: John Wiley and Sons, 1958), 203–4.

6. Raymond A. Bauer, "Consumer Behavior as Risk Taking," in *Dynamic Marketing for a Changing World,* ed. Robert S. Hancock (Chicago: American Marketing Association, 1960), 389, 398.

7. Del I. Hawkins, Roger J. Best, and Kenneth A. Coney, *Consumer Behavior: Implications for Marketing Strategy* (Plano, Tex.: Business Publications, 1986), 574.

8. E. C. Hirschman and M. K. Mills, "Sources Shoppers Use to Pick Stores," *Journal of Advertising Research* 20 (Feb. 1980): 47–51.

9. See Robert Wyer Jr. and Thomas K. Srull, *Social Cognition: Memory in Its Social Context* (Hillsdale, N.J.: Erlbaum, 1991).

10. Carol A. Kohn Berning and Jacob Jacoby, "Patterns of Information Acquisition in New Product Purchases," *Journal of Consumer Research* 1 (Sept. 1974): 8–12; George Kotona and Eva Mueller, "A Study of Purchase Decisions," in *Consumer Behavior: The Dynamics of Consumer Reactions,* ed. L. H. Clark (New York: New York University Press, 1955), 35–87.

11. D. F. Midgley, "Patterns of Interpersonal Information Seeking for the Purchase of a Symbolic Product," *Journal of Marketing Research* 20 (Feb. 1983): 74–83; T. A. Swartz and N. Stephens, "Information Search for Services," in *Advances in Consumer Research Eleven,* ed. T. C. Kinnear (Chicago: Association for Consumer Research, 1984), 31.

12. Horton, *Buyer Behavior,* 271.

13. Robert B. Settle, "Attribution Theory and Acceptance of Information," *Journal of Marketing Research* 9 (Feb. 1972): 85–88.

14. Thomas S. Robertson, "The Effect of the Informal Group upon Member Innovative Behavior," in *Marketing and the New Science of Planning*, ed. Robert L. King (Chicago: American Marketing Association, 1968), 334–40.

15. Ben M. Enis and Gordon W. Paul, "Store Loyalty as a Basis for Market Segmentation," *Journal of Retailing* 46 (Fall 1970): 46.

16. Sharon E. Beatty and Scott M. Smith, "External Search Effort: An Investigation across Several Product Categories," *Journal of Consumer Research* 14 (June 1987): 83–95.

17. Ibid., 84.

18. Bauer, "Consumer Behavior," 87.

19. Leon G. Schiffman and Leslie Lazar Kanuk, *Consumer Behavior* (Englewood Cliffs, N.J.: Prentice-Hall, 1987), 214.

20. Donald F. Cox, ed., *Risk Taking and Information Handling in Consumer Behavior* (Boston: Division of Research, Graduate School of Business Administration, Harvard University, 1967).

21. List of risks taken from Schiffman and Kanuk, *Consumer Behavior*, 214–15, unless otherwise noted.

22. John C. Mowen, *Consumer Behavior* (New York: Macmillan, 1987), 75.

23. Schiffman and Kanuk, *Consumer Behavior*, 217–18.

24. C. Derbaix, "Perceived Risk and Risk Relievers: An Empirical Investigation," *Journal of Economic Psychology*, no. 3 (1983): 19–38.

25. Cox, *Risk Taking*, 9.

26. M. Venkatesan, "Cognitive Consistency and Novelty Seeking," in *Consumer Behavior: Theoretical Sources*, ed. Scott Ward and Thomas S. Robertson (Englewood Cliffs, N.J.: Prentice-Hall, 1973), 355–84; L. McAlister and E. Pessemier, "Variety Seeking Behavior: An Interdisciplinary Review," *Journal of Consumer Research* 9 (Dec. 1982): 311–22.

27. D. R. Lehmann and W. L. Moore, "Validity of Information Display Bounds: An Assessment Using Longitudinal Data," *Journal of Marketing* 44 (Nov. 1980): 450–59.

28. P. Nelson, "Advertising Is Information," *Journal of Political Economy* (July–Aug. 1974): 729–54; G. S. Cost and L. V. Domingurz, "Cross-Shopping and Retail Growth," *Journal of Marketing Research* 14 (May 1977): 187–92.

29. D. Cox and S. Rich, "Perceived Risk and Consumer Decision Making—A Case of Telephone Shopping," *Journal of Marketing Research* 1 (Nov. 1964): 32–39.

30. W. Dommermuth and E. Cundiff, "Shopping Goods, Shopping Centers, and Selling Strategies," *Journal of Marketing* 31 (Oct. 1967): 32–36.

31. B. Le Grand and J. Udell, "Consumer Behavior in the Marketplace—An Empirical Study in the Television and Furniture Fields," *Journal of Retailing* 39–40 (Fall 1964): 32.

32. J. Newman and R. Staelin, "Prepurchase Information Seeking for New Cars and Major Household Appliances, *Journal of Marketing Research* 9 (Aug. 1972): 249–57.

33. N. Capon and M. Burke, "Individual, Product Class, and Task-Related Factors in Consumer Information Processing," *Journal of Consumer Research* 7 (Dec. 1980): 314–26.

34. George Katona and E. Mueller, "Study of Purchase," *Cooking Appliance Purchase and Usage Patterns* (New York: Newsweek, 1978), 27.

35. D. Hempel, "Search Behavior and Information Utilization in the Home Buying Process," in *Marketing Involvement in Society and the Economy*, ed. P. McDonald (Chicago: American Marketing Association, 1969), 241–49.

36. George Katona and E. Mueller, "A Study of Purchasing Decisions," in *Consumer Behavior: The Dynamics of Consumer Reaction*, ed. Lincoln H. Clark (New York: New York University Press), 30–87.

37. Katona and Mueller, "Study of Purchase."

38. Jon C. Udell, "Prepurchase Behavior of Buyers of Small Electric Appliances," *Journal of Marketing* 30 (Oct. 1966): 50–52.

39. Hempel, "Search Behavior," 241–49; Katona and Mueller, "Study of Purchase"; Newman and Staelin, "Prepurchase Information Seeking," 249–57.

40. Howard Schuman and Michael P. Johnson, "Attitudes and Behavior," *Annual Review of Sociology* 2 (1976): 161–207.

41. Beatty and Smith, "External Search Effort," 83–95; Calvin P. Duncan and Richard W. Olshausky, "External Search: The Role of Consumer Beliefs," *Journal of Marketing Research* 19 (Feb. 1982): 32–43; Girish N. Punj and Richard Staelin, "A Model of Consumer Information Search Behavior for New Automobiles," *Journal of Consumer Research* 9 (Mar. 1983): 366–80.

42. Peter D. Bennett and Robert M. Mandell, "Prepurchase Information-Seeking Behavior of New Car Purchases: The Learning Hypothesis," *Journal of Marketing Research* 6 (Nov. 1969): 430–33.

43. William L. Moore and Donald R. Lehmann, "Individual Differences in Search Behavior for a Nondurable Product," *Journal of Consumer Research* 7 (Dec. 1980): 296–307.

44. Bennett and Mandell, "Prepurchase Information-Seeking Behavior," 430–33.

45. B. Fishhoff, P. Slovic, and S. Lichtenstein, "Which Risks Are Acceptable?" *Environment* 21 (Jan. 1971): 17–38.

46. J. W. Newman, "Consumer External Search: Amount and Determinants," in *Consumer and Industrial Buying Behavior*, ed. A. Woodside, J. Sheth, and P. Bennett (New York: Elsevier North Holland, 1977), 79–94.

47. R. A. Westbrook and C. Farnell, "Patterns of Information Source Usage among Durable Goods Buyers," *Journal of Marketing Research* 16 (Aug. 1979): 303–12.

48. Newman and Staelin, "Prepurchase Information Seeking," 249–57.

49. Hawkins, Best, and Coney, *Consumer Behavior*, 577–79.

50. Newman, "Consumer External Search," 79–94; B. Marby, "An Analysis of Work and Other Constraints on Choice Activities," *Western Economic Journal* 8 (Sept. 1970): 213–25; T. Lanzetta and U. Kanareff, "Information Cost, Amount of Payoff, and Level of Aspiration as Determinants of Information Seeking in Decision Making," *Behavioral Science* 7 (1962): 459–73.

51. James R. Bettman, *An Information Processing Theory of Consumer Behavior* (Reading, Mass.: Addison-Wesley, 1979), chap. 5.

52. Hawkins, Best, and Coney, *Consumer Behavior*, 625–26.

53. Ibid., 622–23.

54. Ibid., 620–21.

55. Ibid., 624–25.

56. Schiffman and Kanuk, *Consumer Behavior*, 644–45.

57. S. M. Shugan, "The Cost of Thinking," *Journal of Consumer Research* 7 (Sept. 1980): 99–111.

58. N. K. Malhotra, "Multi-Stage Information Processing Behavior," *Journal of the Academy of Marketing Science* 10 (Winter 1982): 54–71.

59. Michael L. Ray, *Advertising and Communication Management* (Englewood Cliffs, N.J.: Prentice-Hall, 1982), 184–85.

60. Ibid.

61. Michael L. Ray, "Marketing Communications and the Hierarchy-of-Effects," in *New Models for Mass Communications,* ed. Peter Clarke (Beverly Hills, Calif.: Sage, 1973), 152.

62. Ray, *Advertising and Communication Management*, 185–86.

63. Ibid., 186.

64. Ibid., 187.

65. Ibid.

66. Ibid.

67. Rajeev Batra and Michael Ray, "Affective Responses Mediating Acceptance of Advertising," *Journal of Consumer Research* 13, no. 2 (Sept. 1986): 234–49.

68. Richard J. Lutz, "Affective and Cognitive Antecedents of Attitudes toward the Ad: A Conceptual Framework," in *Psychological Processes and Advertising Effects*, ed. Linda Alwitt and Andrew Mitchell (Hillsdale, N.J.: Lawrence J. Erlbaum, 1985), 47.

69. Batra and Ray, "Affective Responses," 234–35.

70. Lutz, "Affective and Cognitive Antecedents," 54.

71. Karen A. Machleit and R. Dale Wilson, "Emotional Feelings and Attitudes toward the Advertisement: The Roles of Brand Familiarity and Repetition," *Journal of Advertising* 17, no. 3 (1988): 32–33.

72. Russell H. Fazio and Mark P. Zanna, "Direct Experience and Attitude-Behavior Consistency," *Advances in Experimental Social Psychology* 14 (1981): 161–202.

73. M. P. Venkatraman and D. J. MacInnis, "The Epistemic and Senovy Exploratory Behaviors of Hedonic and Cognitive Consumers," in *Advances in Consumer Research Twelve*, ed. Elizabeth Hirschman and Morris Holbrook (Ann Arbor: Association for Consumer Research, 1985), 102–7.

74. Olli T. Shtola, "Hedonic and Utilitarian Aspects of Consumer Behavior: An Attitudinal Perspective," in *Advances in Consumer Research Twelve*, ed. Hirschman and Holbrook, 7–10.

75. Morris B. Holbrook and Elizabeth C. Hirschman, "The Experiential Aspects of Consumption: Consumer Fantasies, Feelings, and Fun," *Journal of Consumer Research* 9 (Sept. 1972): 132–40.

76. Ibid., 132.

77. Grant McCracken, "Advertising: Meaning or Information?" in *Advances in Consumer Research Fourteen,* ed. Melanie Wallendorf and Paul Anderson (Provo, Utah: Association for Consumer Research, 1987), 121–24.

78. See Linda Scott, "Reader-Response Theory: From Text to Mind," *Journal of Consumer Research* 21 (Dec. 1994): 461–80.

6

Advertising and the Media

By exposing advertisements to the largest possible group of people, national advertisers attempt to persuade *enough* people to buy a product. If the advertising effort increases sales of a product sufficiently, the promotional expense is recaptured and a profit is made. The mass media—newspapers, magazines, television, and radio—have traditionally been enlisted toward this end.

In this chapter we will explore social aspects of the mass media as defined here, the trend toward micromedia, and the resulting implications for advertisers.

Given this perspective, the reader should not expect this chapter to deal with the more functional material, such as factors in media selection: reach, frequency, media exposure models, and the differences between the various media vehicles.

We will not touch on issues such as the alleged bias toward the interest of advertisers in editorial content and the economic implications of the advertising "subsidy," for instance. These are covered elsewhere, and the curious reader is encouraged to pursue more specialized sources.[1]

Instead, we will focus on advertising as *commercial* speech, the mass media as distributors of speech, the problems that ensue, and the future of advertising and the media.

As we move through the chapter, consider two important questions: (1) How does advertising, as a source of revenue, affect the availability (existence and price) of the media and (2) How does advertising affect the quality (content, for example) of the media?

———— Commercial Speech

The First Amendment specifically states, "Congress shall make no law . . . abridging the freedom of speech, or of the press." However, the definition of "speech" is open to interpretation.

The Supreme Court defines commercial speech as "expression related solely to the economic interest of the speaker and its audience."[2] The court deems commercial speech to be substantially more subject to government regulation than noncommercial speech.

Noncommercial forms of speech include, but are not limited to, news, opinion, and political speech in the form of advertisements for specific candidates.

It is the consideration of this dichotomy that has been the subject of debate in a number of court decisions. The "good" of the people, it is argued, must be considered when establishing the rights of the advertiser to interact with the public through the various media.

———— Media Theory

As Americans we assume, to an extent, a libertarian view of the manner in which the mass media function in our society. We expect the media, which are such an integral part of our society, to promote unfettered communication among themselves. In another respect, most Americans also expect the media to be "responsible" when communicating, which is a more neo-liberal than libertarian assumption. There is subsequently a dichotomy between the inalienable "rights" associated with libertarianism and the "responsibilities" that can arise from a neo-liberal perspective.

Libertarian theory (i.e., based on classical liberalism) characterizes the manner in which the media are presumably expected to function in a democratic society. Although libertarian writings refer mainly to "the press," Fred S. Siebert's summary of the theory correctly extends the definition of "press" to include *all* media.

> The press is not an instrument of government, but rather a device for presenting evidence and arguments on the basis of which the people can check on government and make up their minds as to policy. Therefore, it is imperative that the press be free from government control and influence. In order for truth to emerge, all ideas must get a fair hearing; there must be a "free market place" of ideas and information. Minorities as well as the strong must have access to the press. This is the theory of the press that was written into our Bill of Rights.[3]

Under the libertarian theory, the free press (mass media) is expected to perform certain functions for the benefit of society. Theodore Peterson has detailed these functions as follows:

> (1) servicing the political system by providing information, discussion, and debate on public affairs; (2) enlightening the public so as to make it capable of self-government; (3) safeguarding the rights of the individual by serving as a watchdog against government; (4) servicing the economic system, primarily by bringing together the buyers and sellers of goods and services through the medium of advertising; (5) providing entertainment; (6) maintaining its own financial self-sufficiency so as to be free from the pressures of special interests.[4]

According to this theory people have the inalienable right to be free to express themselves without the fear of reprisal from government. Emphasis is therefore placed on the freedom to speak.

No specific mention of freedom of speech is included in the functions listed above. This may at first seem strange in light of the fact that freedom of speech and freedom of the press have been, almost universally, linked together. However, the freedom to speak is necessary to the function of a free press and vice versa. Freedom, in itself, is more a state of affairs than a function.

There would be little value in upholding the freedom to speak if the instruments for distributing speech were controlled.

The Mass Media as Distributors of "Speech"

Members of the media have generally conceived freedom of speech to be freedom for the media to speak as they wish without fear of government restraints or penalty. Such freedom would then prohibit the government from acting as a gatekeeper to open or close the gate at its will with respect to what news, ideas, and concepts should be passed on to the people.

Even then, it is idealistic to expect the media to speak for (or to) all citizens, including the corporate ones. The media do, however, attract a variety of audiences who utilize specific vehicles for a multitude of reasons at any given time. In other words, the dissemination of information is difficult to control by a single medium because people acquire information from various media. Table 6–1 illustrates media usage patterns for 1992 based on hours per year individuals spent with each media on average.[5]

Table 6-1. Media Usage

Medium	Hours per Person per Year
Television	1,555
Radio	1,150
Recorded music	233
Newspapers	172
Consumer magazines	85
Home video	46
Movies	9

Source: U.S. Bureau of the Census, *Statistical Abstract of the United States: 1994* (Washington, D.C.: GPO, 1994).

The pervasiveness of media within households is illustrated in table 6–2.[6]

There is no guarantee a balance of power either among the various media or between media and their audiences will automatically occur as a result of audience exposure to and utilization of diverse media sources.

Sandage asserts that the freedom of each individual to speak to large numbers of the population is essential to freedom of speech. If the media can control what an individual or group wishes to say, then freedom effectively does not exist. Perhaps society should expect the media, particularly the media with the largest audiences, not only to be free to speak as they wish but also to serve as distributors of speech by lay citizens who wish to reach large numbers of people.

Table 6-2. Pervasiveness of Media

Households with television sets	98.3%
Average number of sets per home	2.1
Households with cable television	60.2%
Households with VCRs	75.0%
Households with radios	99.0%
Average number of radios per home	5.6

Source: U.S. Bureau of the Census, *Statistical Abstract of the United States: 1994* (Washington, D.C.: GPO, 1994).

The issue of a presumed balance of power generates a variety of criticisms. One such criticism revolves around the ability of an advertiser to influence the content published or produced in the different media. If an advertiser can affect what gets published, it is argued that freedom of speech does not exist.[7]

It is an accepted fact that commonly used media rely on advertising a great deal to underwrite their operations. As segmentation techniques become more sophisticated, the media will continue to deliver even more defined audience segments based on their programming or content. To what extent, then, is content produced to attract certain types of advertisers? Alternatively, to what degree is control exerted by advertisers regarding radio and television programming, editorial content of magazines or newspapers, etc.

The *Daily Spectrum* in St. George, Utah, once apologized in print for a story it ran on how to bargain when buying a car after local car dealers launched an ad boycott of the paper.[8] Similar documented incidents involve other newspapers, TV stations, radio stations, and magazines.[9] The question remains whether advertisers can influence the content of different media vehicles. If they can, and presumably they do, freedom of the press and freedom of speech would exist only to the extent permitted by an influential advertiser. Peterson's sixth function would be unfulfilled because special interests, in the form of big business (instead of government), would control the information flow to the public.

The dissemination of information to the public sphere through the mass media seems particularly susceptible to environmental influence. To better ascertain the nature of this influential ability, let us consider the following issues and how they relate to newspapers, magazines, television, and radio:

1. Media concentration
2. Media as gatekeepers
3. Diversity
4. Agenda setting
5. Spiral of silence
6. Cultivation theory

Media Concentration

Overall, American media ownership has been contracting. The emergence of some new media, such as cable, is inviting more people into the media arena by creating opportunities for new firms; the general trend, however, is for fewer companies to own more media enterprises and for fewer companies to own more than one medium.[10]

For example:

1. There were 1,586 daily newspapers in the United States in 1992. Of this amount, 1,205, or 76 percent, were chain owned, while only 381, or 24 percent, were individually owned. The average or mean number of dailies per chain was 9.1 in 1992.[11]

2. Although cable systems continue to penetrate the television market, network affiliates accounted for 53 percent of the nation's TV stations:[12]

ABC affiliates	15.2 percent
CBS affiliates	14.6 percent
NBC affiliates	14.0 percent
FOX affiliates	9.4 percent

3. Time Warner has extensive ownership in all the major media except newspapers.

Here is a partial list of its holdings:[13]

Magazines: *Time, Life, People, Fortune, Sports Illustrated, Money*
Books: Book of the Month Club, Warner Books, Oxmoor House, TimeLife
Music: Warner Bros. Records, Atlantic Records, Electra Entertainment, Columbia House
Cable Television: Time Warner Cable, Paragou Communications
Television: Lorimar Television, Warner Bros. Television, 42 percent interest in BHC Inc., operator of seven TV stations
Cable TV Programming: HBO, Cinemax
Motion Pictures: Warner Bros.
Video: Warner Home Video

These examples provide evidence that concentration of media ownership is definitely occurring in the mass media. So how does this affect the quality of the media?

Pam Eversole found that newspapers that were once competitive but were made monopolies by chains had "higher prices and lower quality."[14] The Brookings Institution showed that though chain-owned papers charge 7 percent more for ads than independent papers, chains operating in areas where there are competitive papers have advertising rates

15 percent lower than those for their other chain-owned papers.[15] Kristine Keller found that there was 23 percent less news content in chain-owned than in independent papers,[16] while Daniel Wackman and colleagues found that 85 percent of chain papers publish uniform political endorsements.[17] Stephen Hess found that chains have about one-third the number of correspondents that individual papers have and that chain correspondents have significantly less education than those working for independent newspapers.[18]

Are the media being adversely affected by the increase in media concentration? There would appear to be cause for concern.

The Media as Gatekeepers

It is in their nature for the media to function as gatekeepers. Recent court decisions have interpreted freedom of the press to mean freedom to publish or broadcast, therefore solidifying the idea that publishers and broadcasters make the ultimate decisions concerning what should and should not go into or on their newspapers, magazines, or radio or television stations. This certainly includes advertising space and air time. The basic premise that the media use in rejecting news or advertising materials is the "best interest" principle. Presumably, materials that are not in the best interest of the particular media vehicle or the public it serves should not be used. The problem is whether media management is in a position to (or should) judge what is in the best interest of the public. Again libertarian theory states that publishers are free to publish or not, according to their own best interest because the invisible hand will take care of the public's best interest. The social responsibility theory says publishers have an obligation or duty to consciously serve the public interest because the invisible hand doesn't always work.

What is interesting, however, is that the courts have generally restricted government actions to influence news or editorial content and advertising placed in the media. These areas have been granted some First Amendment protection. In its purest form, these rulings can be expressed in the statement "above all else, the First Amendment means that the government has no power to restrict expression because of its message, its ideas, its subject matter, or its content."[19]

Although commercial speech has more limited First Amendment protection than news or editorial material,[20] it seems ironic that advertising messages protected from government interference may subsequently not appear because media decide they should not.

Have the media made use of their gatekeeping function? That is, have they interjected their subjective (personal or arbitrary) judgments in the news-gathering function, as well as in the selection of which advertisements to run? D. M. White,[21] W. Gieber,[22] and A. Hetherington[23] seem to believe they have.

The *Baltimore Sun* killed a story describing imminent labor negotiations between hospital workers and the management of Johns Hopkins Hospital in Baltimore. Apparently, a director of the *Sun* was a director of Johns Hopkins Hospital and a director of the Mercantile Safe Deposit and Trust Company, which held 61.3 percent of the shares of the newspaper company.[24]

The media can also exercise their gatekeeping function when it comes to traditional advertisements. In the classic case *Shuck v. The Carroll Daily Herald*, the court held:

> The newspaper business is an ordinary business. It is a business essentially private in its nature—as private as that of the baker, grocer, or milkman, all of whom perform a service on which, to a greater or lesser extent, the communities depend, but which bears no such relation to the public as to warrant its inclusion in the category of business charged with a public use. If a newspaper were required to accept an advertisement, it could be compelled to publish a news item. If some good lady gave a tea, and submitted to the newspaper the proper account of the tea, and the editor of the newspaper, believing that it had no news value, refused to publish it, she, it seems to us would be a person engaged in business to compel a newspaper to publish an advertisement.

Thus, a newspaper is strictly private enterprise, the publishers thereof have a right to publish whatever advertisements they desire and refuse to publish whatever advertisements they do not desire to publish.[25]

The many decisions since have added nothing to this ruling. Other cases have established that publishers can classify advertisements as they see fit[26] and change ads to meet their standards of acceptability.[27] Therefore, barring a pattern of refusal that points to an intent to harm a competitor, any news medium may refuse commercial advertising for any reason or for no reason.[28]

There are occasions when individuals or groups in our society perceive that they have a serious grievance and wish to make those grievances known to the larger population. Besides seeking more traditional press coverage of their concerns, they may also wish to buy space or time in the media for an advertisement to explain their cause. Just as traditional ads may be rejected by privately owned media, so may "cause" oriented advertisements. Any attempt by the government to tell an owner of a privately held media vehicle that an ad must be accepted could be construed as taking of property without due process of law, thereby violating the Fifth Amendment. Further, an attempt by the state to tell media owners that they must accept an advertisement violates the freedom of the press guaranteed by the First Amendment.[29] Thus, anti–Vietnam war messages, ads by gay rights activists, and information about family planning have regularly been rejected by many media owners over the past decades.

The issue in these cases resides in determining the extent to which the media exercise their gatekeeping function and how this editorial prerogative affects the public at large.

The Question of Diversity

It may be contended that the central issue in the dissemination of ideas and information in the libertarian or neo-liberal media environment is that of diversity. The essence of diversity is best stated by Jeffres:

> Diversity as a goal is not merely a matter of philosophical or legal niceties. It is grounded in the lessons of experience. First, a free flow of ideas is essential to the political liberty and is essential in developing ideas of potential value to society. The notion of diversity in communication is not new; the challenge is in implementing diversity. Viewed as communication systems rather than industries, the major function of the mass media is to circulate ideas which have consequences for every aspect of society. The circulation of ideas is an evolutionary process. From an enormous variety of possibilities, some ideas are introduced into the system, some are developed or modified as they circulate and some are deleted. Writers introduce ideas but so do producers and directors, networks and advertisers, and local outlets. Public officials may introduce ideas when they give speeches, hold press conferences, or generate interest to attract coverage. Members of the public who normally serve as audiences may also introduce ideas when placed before the microphones and cameras in the studio or on the street.[30]

Of all the ways ideas enter the social discussion, the mass media may be the most important.

Two schools of thought address how to achieve Jeffres's description of diversity. The first school is skeptical of any regulation, and it assumes that the free and open marketplace is the best possible environment in which diversity can flourish. The premise of this position is that a fluid, competitive marketplace will permit all sectors of the population to enter the system and provide needed information-communication services. One consideration is how to provide profit incentives to attract the risk capital that will be needed to accomplish the goal of additional information-communication services. The key measurement criterion to judge success would be the quantity of channels. This school believes that if there is a sufficient quantity of channels, and the freedom to open new ones, an acceptable level of diversity can be achieved.[31]

The second school argues

> that in this era of giant national and transnational corporate dominance, it is absurd to presuppose that there is sufficient equitable distribution of economic power to allow market forces alone to assume equitable distribution of services. The political decision-making process is so manipulated by powerful corporations that it is virtually impossible for citizens' groups, consumers, minorities and the poverty sector of society to participate significantly in the policy-making process. Access to information is such a basic human right and communication so central in the development of national cultures that these should be considered a common good and a public trust. Information should not be considered simply a marketplace commodity distributed only to those with capacity to pay.[32]

The question here, then, is how the economically and socially less powerful can gain access to information carriers (media). For this school of thought, what is important is not the *quantity* of channels but their *quality*.

Thus, a case may be made that in order to achieve true diversity in the sense of individuals being confronted with challenging (new, provocative, unfamiliar) points of view, access needs to be gained in a qualitative sense. In short, rather than striving for more media vehicles, we might best reach diversity by attempting to enrich the "marketplace of ideas" within the existing media structure. And that, of course, requires a fresh look at the media as gatekeepers.

Agenda Setting

As the issue of diversity was concerned with the free flow of ideas or the knowledge base of the audiences, the issue of agenda setting deals with the distribution of knowledge. The simplest definition of agenda setting might be this: The media don't tell you what to think, but they do tell you what and whom to think about. The evidence for this statement consists of data showing a correlation between the order of importance given in the media to issues and the order of significance attached to the same issues by the public.[33] Such a phenomenon has been found for both the press and advertising.[34] Caution should be exercised, however, in assuming cause and effect.

The relevance of agenda setting for advertising is that a major goal of many advertisers is to focus consumers' attention on which values, products, brands, or attributes to think about rather than to try to persuade consumers what to think about these.[35] Max Sutherland and John Galloway proposed a two-step model: Prominence of products or ideas in the media, accomplished through heavy advertising, should increase the salience of the brand; and second, this salience should influence such behavioral outcomes as purchasing. Products that are prominent (heavily advertised) in the media would have a status conferred upon them and would be seen as the more popular products. Just as the ordinary person does not appear on television, neither does the ordinary product.[36]

To test their theory that media advertising can engage in such agenda setting and produce images that advertised products are superior, the authors surveyed homemakers about a variety of products. No less than 25 percent of the respondents indicated that what they thought was a popular brand was related to advertising frequency. The brand thought to be the most popular was also shown to bear a strong relationship with top-of-mind awareness.[37]

Shailendra Ghorpade, in his study of the 1984 Helms-Hunt senatorial campaign in North Carolina, found that the advertising campaigns of the two candidates did affect behavior. Advertising salience translated into salience in the public mind and salience in the public mind affected the behavioral outcome (voting).[38]

Could it be that large advertisers, such as Procter and Gamble, Ford Motor Company, RJR/Nabisco, McDonald's Corporation, and Anheuser-Busch, have achieved such predominant market share in some product categories because they have "set the agenda" for the consumer? When it comes to hamburgers, cigarettes, and beer, we know what to think about.

Spiral of Silence

Elizabeth Noelle-Neumann stated that because journalists in the media tend to concentrate on the same major news stories, the audience receives similar information from many fronts. The media, as a result, tend to present a consensus to the public. As this opinion gains ascendancy, others will be perceived as losing ground. If members of the audience believe that their opinions are in accordance with the dominant trend, perhaps they will feel their opinion can be expressed openly and publicly outside of their family and immediate friends. If these same individuals feel that their opinions have become in the minority, they may well be less confident of their positions and therefore will be less likely to express their opinions openly. The more frequently the topic arises, the weaker their positions appear, and in a spiral-like process, opinions become increasingly suppressed as people fear that expressing their opinions could result in negative judgments from others.[39] Carrol J. Glynn and Jack M. McLeod lend additional support for this theory.[40]

Although no research has been conducted to determine the relationship between the spiral of silence and advertising, speculation on the relationship is possible. As the press, over the past several years, has come to a consensus concerning the clear superiority of Japanese products (such as autos and electronic equipment) over American-built products, it has become less and less popular to voice an opinion among consumers concerning the quality of American products. Has this suppression of opinion led to less purchase of American products because they are really inferior or because it is not the popular thing to do?

Relationship between Agenda-Setting and Spiral of Silence

There may be a relationship between agenda setting and the spiral of silence. A paradigm adopted from Sutherland and Galloway is shown in figure 6–1.

Figure 6-1. Relationship between Agenda-Setting and Spiral of Silence

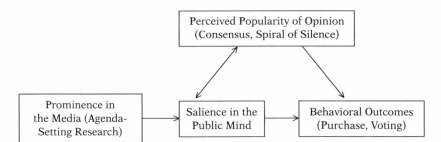

Source: Adapted from Max Sutherland and John Galloway, "Role of Advertising: Persuasion or Agenda-Setting?" *Journal of Advertising Research* 25, no. 5 (Oct. 1981): 29.

This model indicates that the producer could follow a twofold strategy to bring about purchase: (1) develop sufficient advertising frequency to help set the agenda for the consumer and (2) cultivate a strong relationship with the business and popular press to develop a perceived consensus of the superiority of the product. Thus, advertising and public relations are necessary complements of the communication process.

Sufficient advertising frequency would be dependent upon the financial resources of the producer, although the development of highly creative, memorable advertisements could offset limited resources. Cultivation of the press to develop consensus would be more difficult for the popular press than the business press due to the sheer diversity of the popular press. For the business press, however, there are often only a few key publications. Getting positive recommendations in these publications could well trigger the spiral of silence. One example might be computer software; a few critical recommendations from lay editors or feature writers might well develop a consensus feeling among potential buyers, particularly those buyers who rely on the "experts" for their decisions instead of on their own technical knowledge.

The Cultivation Process

George Gerbner, Larry Gross, Michael Morgan, and Nancy Signorielli posit that television is a centralized system of storytelling. It is part of our daily lives; its drama, advertisements, news, and other programs bring a relatively coherent world of common images and messages into every American home. "Television cultivates from infancy the very predispositions and preferences that used to be acquired from other primary sources. Transcending historic barriers of literacy and mobility, television has become the primary common source in socialization and everyday information (mostly in the form of entertainment) of an otherwise heterogeneous population. The repetitive pattern of television's mass-produced messages and images form the mainstream of a common symbolic environment."[41] What television does, then, is to present the audience with the myths, ideologies, "facts," and relationships that serve to define and legitimize the social order.[42]

This cultivation process takes place in two ways: mainstreaming and resonance.[43] Mainstreaming is the process by which television brings diverse groups into the mainstream of American values. These groups tend to be heavy viewers of television and by this heavy viewing tend to develop common outlooks or viewpoints. For example, viewing heavy doses of violent crime on television might affect those who have had little experience with it to become more fearful of crime and thus develop similar views to those who already live in high-crime neighborhoods. Resonance occurs when the experiential environment of an individual closely resembles the reality presented by television. Social perceptions that previously existed are consequently reinforced or intensified by television. For instance, resonance could increase fear of crime for those heavy viewers who are already afraid. "When one's everyday environment is congruent with and reinforces television's messages,"[44] the result, according to Gerbner and colleagues, would be a "double dose" of the reality of crime.

Although Gerbner and other researchers have mainly focused on television programming, there is no reason to believe that advertising messages do not play the same role. Advertisers are storytellers who convey common messages and images. Although the advertisements may appear diverse, the common messages "Buy! Buy! Buy!" "Thin Is Beautiful!" "Things Can Make You Happy!" "You Deserve the Best," "You Deserve a Break," and "You Are What You Consume" have cultivated the images of what Americans should be like. The American consumer has, to some extent, been as mainstreamed by American advertisements as it has been by television programming.

The Future of Media

Newspaper readership has been declining steadily over the past thirty years. The newspaper business sector has, for the most part, reacted by offering more color and more sensational stories. Magazines have lost circulation but their future is more promising because they can deliver specialized audiences to advertisers.

The use of television, including cable, has gained ground along with radio and direct mail. It would seem that audiences are seeking out more entertaining means of information retrieval about the world.

Such things as interactive media, personal computers (with modems), picture phones, and various new means of broadcast distribution are now being developed. They will undoubtedly have an effect on how we receive information. Keeping up with these developments poses a challenge for future advertisers.

While newspaper and magazine circulations are decreasing, the number of magazines is increasing. The viewership of television is rising while the number of stations (channels) is increasing. The use and effectiveness of direct mail is progressing as well, as evidenced by the boom in catalog sales.

The result of these trends is for individual media to have smaller, more specific audiences. The cross section of the population is smaller but made up of more "dedicated" people. *Time* magazine may attract a larger number of readers but *Snow Country* magazine caters to a more defined group with a specific reason for reading.

By taking all of these variables into consideration an argument can be made for the emerging dominance of micromedia.

Some advertising agents find this trend disturbing. How will messages be communicated to large numbers of people at relatively low prices? Advertisers will presumably continue to develop more precise segmentation procedures due to ongoing advances in information systems, etc. This will in turn generate incredible specificity in audience characterization. The old principle of persuading *enough* people of a large heterogeneous group may have to give way to the opportunities presented by even more narrowly defined markets. Micromedia would best serve a method of persuading enough people of small homogenous groups. It would require more planning but would likely be more effective, producing a higher effort-response ratio.

_____ Summary

The debate over the protection of commercial speech and noncommercial speech may never be resolved. The courts support the press's freedom to act on its own prerogative concerning content. The issues of concentration and media diversity were discussed in this chapter as possible impediments to the freedom of speech—both commercial and noncommercial. It was also made clear that the media act as gatekeepers for issues concerned citizens would like to transmit. Advertisers, agencies, and the media can set the agenda for consumers about what and who to think about, bring them to a consensus on many matters, and help to establish a common set of cultural images and values.

It should be noted that these influences are just that—influences. Many other factors continue to influence the consumer when in the marketplace, such as family, friends, peers, reference groups, and one's own individuality. The media and advertising is only one aspect of each person's environment.

Notes

1. For further information see Vincent P. Norris, "Consumer Magazine Prices and the Mythical Advertising Subsidy," *Journalism Quarterly* 59, no. 2 (Summer 1982): 205–11; and R. C. Smith, "The Magazine's Smoking Habit," *Columbia Journalism Review* 16 (Jan.–Feb. 1978): 29–31.

2. *Central Hudson Gas and Electric Corp. v. Public Service Commission. supra* n. 1, at 561.

3. Fred S. Siebert, Theodore Peterson, and Wilbur Schramm, *Four Theories of the Press: The Authoritarian, Libertarian, Social Responsibility, and Soviet Communist Concepts of What the Press Should Be and Do* (Urbana: University of Illinois Press, 1956), 34.

4. Ibid., 74.

5. Shirley Biagi, *Media Impact: An Introduction to the Mass Media* (Belmont, Calif.: Wadsworth, 1994), 276; *The Veronis* (Suhler and Associates Communication's Industry Forecast), June 1992, 12.

6. U.S. Bureau of the Census, *Statistical Abstract of the United States,* 113th ed. (Washington, D.C.: GPO, 1993), 561.

7. Biagi, *Media Impact,* 17; *The Veronis,* June 1992, 56.

8. *Consumer Reports,* Apr. 1992, 208.

9. A related article: Ronald K. L. Collins, "Advertiser 'Censorship' Must Be Outlawed," *Advertising Age,* Apr. 13, 1992, 22.

10. Warren K. Agee, Phillip H. Ault, and Edwin Emery, *Introduction to Mass Communications* (New York: HarperCollins, 1994), 64–65, 71–72.

11. Biagi, *Media Impact,* 511.

12. Ibid., 515.

13. Agee, Ault, and Emery, *Introduction,* 79.

14. Pam Eversole, "Consolidation of Newspapers: What Happens to the Consumer?" *Journalism Quarterly* 48 (Summer 1971): 245.

15. *Strass Editor's Report,* Dec. 13, 1968, 1.

16. Kristine Keller, "Quantity of News in Group Owned and Independent Papers: Independent Papers Have More" (Master's thesis, Graduate School of Journalism, University of California, Berkeley, 1978).

17. Daniel B. Wackman, Donald M. Gilmore, Cecile Graziano, and Everett E. Dennis, "Chain Newspaper Autonomy as Reflected in Presidential Campaign Endorsement," *Journalism Quarterly* 52 (Autumn 1975): 411–20.

18. Stephen Hess, "Chains Tend to Hire," *The Washington Reporters* (Washington, D.C.: Brookings Institution, 1981), 136–66. See also D. Weaver and C. G. Wiholt, *The American Journalist* (Bloomington: University of Indiana Press, 1986).

19. *Police Dept. of Chicago v. Mosely,* 408 U.S. 92, 96 (1971).

20. *Virginia State Board of Pharmacy v. Virginia Citizens Consumer Council,* 425 U.S. 748 (1976); *Central Hudson Gas & Electric Corp. v. Public Service Comm'n,* 433 U.S. 350 (1977).

21. D. M. White, "The Gatekeeper: A Case Study in the Selection of News," *Journalism Quarterly* 27 (Fall 1950): 383–90.

22. W. Gieber, "Across the Desk: A Study of Sixteen Telegraph Editors," *Journalism Quarterly* 33 (Fall 1956): 423–33.

23. A. Hetherington, *News, Newspapers, and Television* (London: Macmillan, 1985).

24. Ben H. Bagdidian, *The Media Monopoly* (Boston: Beacon Press, 1983), 3–4.

25. *Shuck v. The Carroll Daily Herald*, 247 N.W. 813 (1933).

26. *Staff Research Associates v. Tribune Co.*, 346 F. ad 372 (7th Cir. 1965).

27. *Camp-of-the-Pines v. New York Times*, 53 N.Y.S. ad 475 (S. Ct., Albany Co., 1945).

28. Ralph L. Holsiger, *Media Law* (New York: Random House, 1987), 428.

29. Ibid., 428–29. See also *Chicago Joint Board, Amalgamated Clothing Workers of America, AFL-CIO v. Chicago Tribune Co.*, 307 F. Supp. 422 (N.D. Ill. 1969).

30. Leo W. Jeffres, *Mass Media: Processes and Effects* (Prospect Heights, Ill.: Waveland Press, 1986), 76.

31. Robert A. White, "What Kind of Media Diversity?" *Communication Research Trends* 4, no. 1 (1983): 7.

32. Ibid.

33. Dennis McQuail, *Mass Communication Theory: An Introduction* (Beverly Hills, Calif.: Sage, 1987), 275. See also G. E. Lang and K. Lang, *The Battle for Public Opinion: The President, the Press, and the Polls during Watergate* (New York: Columbia University Press, 1983) for an expanded version of this concept.

34. Jeffres, *Mass Media*, 296.

35. Max Sutherland and John Galloway, "Role of Advertising: Persuasion or Agenda Setting?" *Journal of Advertising Research* 25, no. 4 (1986): 26.

36. Ibid., 27; Jeffres, *Mass Media*, 296.

37. Sutherland and Galloway, "Role of Advertising," 28. See also P. M. Carrick, "Why Continued Advertising Is Necessary," *Journal of Marketing* 23 (1959): 386–98.

38. Shailendra Ghorpade, "Agenda Setting: A Test of Advertising's Neglected Function," *Journal of Advertising Research* 26, no. 4 (1986): 26.

39. Elizabeth Noelle-Neumann, "The Spiral of Silence: A Theory of Public Opinion," *Journal of Communication* 24 (Spring 1974): 43–51; Elizabeth Noelle-Neuman, "Turbulences in the Climate of Opinion: Methodological Applications of the Spiral of Silence Theory," *Public Opinion Quarterly* 41 (Summer 1977): 143–58; Jeffres, *Mass Media*, 281.

40. Carrol J. Glynn and Jack M. McLeod, "Public Opinion du Jour: An Examination of the Spiral of Silence," *Public Opinion Quarterly* 40 (1976): 731–40.

41. George Gerbner, Larry Gross, Michael Morgan, and Nancy Signorielli, "Living with Television: The Dynamics of the Cultivation Process," in *Perspectives on Media Effects*, ed. Jennings Bryant and Dolf Zillman (Hillsdale, N.J.: Lawrence Erlbaum Associates, 1986), 18.

42. Ibid.

43. Ibid., 30.

44. Ibid.

7

Advertising and Regulation

This chapter will deal with the question What forces should be allowed to regulate the institution of advertising? Should it be regulated by natural market forces, organized market forces (consumerism), self-regulatory forces, governmental forces, or media forces (see figure 7-1)? Are these mutually exclusive approaches or synergistic when operating simultaneously?

Figure 7-1. The Forces of Regulation

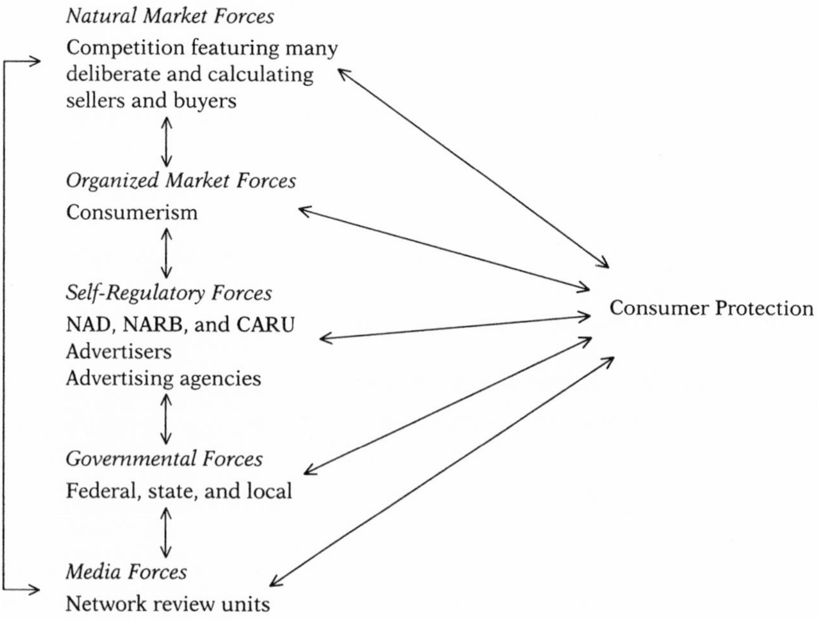

Natural Market Forces
Competition featuring many
deliberate and calculating
sellers and buyers

Organized Market Forces
Consumerism

Self-Regulatory Forces
NAD, NARB, and CARU
Advertisers
Advertising agencies

Governmental Forces
Federal, state, and local

Media Forces
Network review units

Consumer Protection

_____ Natural Market Forces

As discussed in chapter 1, the market is presumed, in the best of worlds, to be entirely self-regulating. Consumers will always seek out the lowest prices for products or services. If consumers find some advertising to be inadequate, they will turn away from it and seek other competitive advertising sources that will satisfy their information needs.

Advertisers will promote their products or services in their own self-interest, and this advertising will be successful only if it is in agreement with the self-interest of potential buyers. If advertisers find their messages are deficient in this regard, they will alter their practices or lose their competitive advantage.

It is the simple yet complex world of Adam Smith. There may be some short-term aberrations; but in the long run, the market will make appropriate adjustments if allowed to run its own course. Or could it be that the long run does not matter, as significant damage could be done in the short run?

_____ Organized Market Forces (Consumerism)

Consumerism can be defined in many different ways. Betty Furness has described it as follows: "Consumerism is an effort to put the buyer on an equal footing with the seller. Consumers want to know what they're buying. What they're eating. How long a product will last. What it will and will not do. Whether it will be safe for them and/or the environment."[1]

A somewhat broader view is offered by David Aaker: "Consumerism is an evolving set of activities of government, business, independent organizations, and concerned consumers that are designed to protect the rights of consumers. It is an evolving, dynamic movement with an enlarging scope and changing spokesmen and issues. It is action oriented and, therefore, more than an analysis of problems."[2]

History of the Consumer Movement

Is consumerism a new idea? Certainly not. Consumers were attempting to cooperate in a number of ways to improve their situation as early as 1844. For it was in this year that poor weavers in Rochdale, England, formed the first "co-op" of consumers.[3]

Although many groups and individuals were active in consumer issues during the late 1800s in this country, it was not until Upton Sinclair's *The*

Jungle[4] that consumerists were generally able to see tangible results of their efforts. This book, along with articles in the *Ladies Home Journal, Collier's Weekly,* and *Good Housekeeping* concerning patent-medicine abuses, ushered in the era of the "muckrakers," writers who investigated and publicized alleged corruption and improper practices in industry and government.[5]

Sinclair's book dealt with the unsanitary conditions and fraud that existed in the meat-packing industry. This powerful exposé, combined with the leadership of Dr. Harvey W. Wiley, chief of the Bureau of Chemistry in the Department of Agriculture, helped lead to the passage of the Pure Food and Drug Act of 1906, which made it unlawful to transmit between states adulterated or misbranded food or drugs. This law was a landmark in that it represented the first major shift in the attitude of the federal government from a philosophy of *caveat emptor* (Let the buyer beware) to one of *caveat venditor* (Let the seller beware).[6]

Advertising, of course, received its share of attention during the muckrakers' period. In the early 1900s, *Printer's Ink* magazine established a set of legal standards to help eliminate misleading and deceptive advertising. Many consumerists lobbied for this model statute, and it subsequently became law in many states. A far more important piece of legislation that dealt with advertising was passed by Congress in 1914. Titled the Federal Trade Commission Act, it was established primarily to deal with antitrust matters and unfair methods of competition. The newly formed commission quickly interpreted the act as a weapon against deceptive interstate advertising practices.[7]

Certainly, this is not a complete picture of what happened during this tumultuous era. It can be said, however, that for the first time large numbers of consumers were made aware of the potentially dangerous consequences of consumption. The edifice of the market had begun to show signs of strain.

The thrust of the consumer movement was reduced by the period of affluence that followed in the twenties. Many of the heated issues were set aside or forgotten, and many of the existing laws were not adequately enforced, owing in part to key court decisions. For example, in *FTC v. Raladam Co.,*[8] the court held that the Federal Trade Commission must find that not only consumers but also competitors were injured by the misrepresentation. This was a situation (the competitor's injury) that was extremely difficult to prove in court.

With the publication of *Your Money's Worth* by Stuart Chase and Frederick J. Schlink in 1927, the movement again came alive. The book became a best-seller because of such comments as bar soap for women is made with "a little creosol, a common and cheap disinfectant recommended by the government for disinfecting cars, barns, and chicken yards."[9] Over the next decade, this book seemed to spawn a series of others that criticized advertising and indicated that the consumer was being deceived. They included *Skin Deep*[10] and *Eat, Drink, and Be Wary.*[11]

Of the attacks made on advertising, many were bitter and far-reaching. These challenges were different from previous ones in that critics struck at the very existence of advertising rather than merely its excesses or the products that advertising promoted.

Thus, the spotlight turned once again to the imperfect marketplace. Spurred by the devastating effects of the Great Depression, consumers and governmental bodies were again ready to take action. More consumer-oriented legislation was passed than ever before, including the Securities Act of 1933 (which provided potential investors with protection against deceptions concerning new issues of corporate securities), the Federal Food, Drug, and Cosmetic Act of 1938 (which strengthened the Pure Food and Drug Act of 1906), and the Wheeler-Lea amendments to the Federal Trade Commission Act of 1914 (which extended "unfair methods of competition" to include deceptive acts or practices).[12] The Wheeler-Lea amendments eliminated the problems of the *Raladam* decision for the FTC.

Consumer Research and Consumers' Union were born; Sears, Roebuck and Macy's began testing products before selling them; *Good Housekeeping* checked products to ensure that advertising claims were accurate; the American Medical Association tested proprietary drugs; and the National Bureau of Standards tested products before government purchase.[13]

But the movement, which had lasted almost two decades, faltered again. The postwar recovery and the increasing affluence of the fifties moved consumers into a period of complacency.

The most recent consumer movement had its beginnings in the sixties. An influential book again served as a trigger mechanism; *Hidden Persuaders*[14] by Vance Packard argued that the consumer was being manipulated unconsciously by advertising. Other best-sellers during this time frame included John Kenneth Galbraith's *The Affluent Society*,[15] Rachel Carson's *Silent Spring*,[16] and Ralph Nader's *Unsafe at Any Speed.*[17]

For some, President John F. Kennedy's watershed message to Congress on March 15, 1962, began the "new consumerism cycle." In that speech, he enumerated four basic consumer rights:[18]

1. The right to safety
2. The right to be informed
3. The right to choose
4. The right to be heard (redress)

The above-mentioned books, Kennedy's address, and a number of other underlying currents, including (1) technology which produced products that were considerably less than 100 percent reliable; (2) a series of revelations about the ingredients used in frankfurters and hamburgers; (3) the condition of our fisheries and water supplies; (4) reports about corruption of public officials on an unprecedented scale; (5) soaring medical and dental costs; and (6) special tax privileges for the few, all combined to generate and nurture the new consumerism.[19]

New consumer laws included the Fair Packaging and Labeling Act of 1965 (to regulate the packaging and labeling of consumer goods), the Child Safety Act of 1966 (to strengthen the Hazardous Substance Labeling Act of 1960 by preventing the marketing of potentially harmful toys), the Consumer Credit Protection Act of 1968 (to require disclosure of annual interest rates and their finance charges on consumer loans and credit buying, including revolving charge accounts), the Federal Boat Safety Act of 1971 (to provide for a coordinated national boating safety program),[20] and the Magnuson-Moss Warranty-Federal Trade Commission Improvement Act of 1975 (to improve warranties and warranty information for consumers and allow the FTC to order restitution for consumers).[21]

The post of special assistant for consumer affairs was established under President Johnson, while new bureaucracies were created, including the Consumer Product Safety Commission, the Environmental Protection Agency, and the Occupational Safety and Health Administration. Ralph Nader became institutionalized by establishing far-flung organizations throughout the country to deal with consumer matters. Some women boycotted stores to protest high meat prices, while other people formed Action for Children's Advertising, a potent lobbying group that attempted to correct abuses in advertising directed at children.

Throughout the eighties, the American public became less approving of consumerist activities. Some negative views include a 1982 Harris Poll that found a greater mistrust of consumer activists than in the seventies. In 1977, 22 percent of the respondents had agreed with the statement that activists such as Ralph Nader were out of touch with consumer interests.[22] In the 1982 poll, the percentage in agreement had more than doubled, to 45 percent.

The Outlook for Consumerism

As we move through the nineties and into the twenty-first century, how will consumerism fare? The nineties have brought about a resurgence of consumer activism. The activist organizations are no longer intimidated by big business or big brands. Any type of product and company can be called into question about products and activities. This viewpoint is not necessarily new and is best explained by Jack Mongoven, issue strategist: "Ever since the civil movement, the Vietnam War and the ecological efforts of the 1960 and 1970s, activist organizations have become major participants in the public policy development process. They are the voices of change. They foreshadow the direction political movements will take. They are voices listened to in legislative bodies."[23] Consumer activists are increasing their numbers and attracting even more politicians to support various causes. However, the most effective tool of a nineties consumer group is the media.

"Publicity is key in the war on intimidation,"[24] and consumer groups increasingly are becoming experts in advertising, public relations, and event marketing. This integral approach gives activists' messages salience and allows the messages to reach thousands more consumers in half the time. David Phillips, executive of Earth Island, an organization that works to protect dolphins from tuna nets, created a video news release that aired on three television networks and CNN. This video gained "more public support overnight than in 17 years of campaigning."[25] The targeted tuna companies immediately responded by "not buying tuna caught using methods that kill dolphins."

Although big businesses still need to keep an eye on their brands, consumers are focusing more on health and environmental issues. "Health and environmental concerns have come into the mainstream agenda. Consumer activism once perched safely on the periphery shows signs of evolving into a more broad based active consumerism."[26] A January 1993 Gallup Poll found that in terms of noneconomic issues, health and health care issues are rapidly increasing in importance. The public is almost as concerned about health care as it is about unemployment.[27]

Activists have also put increasing pressure on companies to develop products and packaging that are environmentally friendly. Consumers in the United States are actively searching for goods that do nothing to harm the environment. Companies, in turn, can increase their credibility by supporting environmental issues in their day-to-day operations.

The relatively calm consumer movement of the eighties has definitely adopted a more aggressive stance to communicate its agenda in the nineties. The integrated media that activists have recently discovered allow them to saturate the public with their messages. To stay ahead now, not only do businesses need to monitor competitors' advertising practices but they must also stay abreast of campaigns designed to expose harmful activity.

Returning to our original question—How will consumerism fare?—the prognosis for the time is quite good. However, the consumer movement is a myriad of ideas and organizations. It ranges from national organizations to highly specialized, local groups. Some elements of the movement view the consumer as *animal rationale,* while others call for more "individual consumerism" through education. Some areas will prosper, while others will not, and the heyday of the movement is more "business beware" rather than "buyer beware."

—— Self-Regulatory Forces

Self-regulation is not new to the institution of advertising. During the last two decades of the 1800s, the *Ladies Home Journal* and *Good Housekeeping* developed advertising acceptance policies. In the early 1900s, the *Printers' Ink Model Statute* was developed and later became the model for many state advertising laws. During the 1920s, better business bureaus were established to help deal with such practices as false comparisons, misleading statements, false claims as to quality, and "bait and switch" advertising.

Is self-regulation an admission that natural market forces are insufficient to regulate the marketplace or is it simply a reaction to increased concern on the part of consumerists and governmental agencies? Eric J. Zanot provides a perspective:

> Apparently self-regulation has been a response and a reply to forces impinging upon the trade from the outside. Self-regulation can be considered a reaction by the trade to downturns in the economy, criticism from the public or, especially, the threat of legislation. Although the altruistic motive of protecting consumers undoubtedly enters to some degree, the primary motive behind self-regulation is thought to be enlightened self-interest. Although this analysis does not permit tight cause-

and-effect statements, it appears that the trade has used self-regulation to not only eradicate false and deceptive advertising but also to dampen public criticism and forestall government legislation.[28]

The National Advertising Division and the National Advertising Review Board

Whatever the reason for the establishment of self-regulatory mechanisms, it is still important to review the major ones and discuss their effectiveness. In 1971, the American Association of Advertising Agencies, the American Advertising Federation, the Association of National Advertisers, and the Council of Better Business Bureaus (CBBB) established the National Advertising Review Council (NARC), which in turn established two operating arms, the National Advertising Division (NAD) of the Council of Better Business Bureaus and the National Advertising Review Board (NARB).

"The NAD/NARB system focuses on truth and accuracy in advertising; it deals almost exclusively with cases of false and misleading advertisements (print) and commercials (broadcast). Complaints related to unfairness, social responsibility, taste and morality are not handled by the NAD, although the NARB has issued a few papers about such issues as safety and women in advertising."[29]

The NAD/NARB does not have codes or guidelines of its own but instead relies heavily upon those of the CBBB and the FTC. The exception is children's advertising.[30]

The NAD is the investigative arm of the NARC. It operates on a full-time basis and is staffed by people with backgrounds in advertising. It essentially receives complaints or questions about the truthfulness of national advertising from a variety of sources, including competitors, consumers, and local better business bureaus. The NAD also has its own monitoring system.

From 1991 to 1993, competitor challenges accounted for 65.4 percent of the cases investigated, while only 17.1 percent of contested advertising claims were initiated by the NAD monitoring system. The remaining sources of complaints were consumers (10 percent), local better business bureaus (2.9 percent), and other sources (4.6 percent).[31]

When a complaint is received, the NAD may contact the advertiser in question and request material to substantiate the claims made in the advertisement. If it finds the substantiation inadequate, it urges the advertiser to modify or withdraw the advertising. If a satisfactory resolution cannot be found by either the advertiser or the NAD, the case is referred to the NARB.

The NARB is composed of seventy members, including forty national advertisers, twenty advertising agencies, and ten representatives from the public sector.

When a case is referred to the NARB, five members are assigned (one public) to the case. If the final decision of these five members is not accepted by the advertiser (assuming it is a negative one from the advertiser's point of view) the NARB will refer the matter to the FTC. In addition to referring the case to more traditional legal channels, the board will make public the facts of the disputed case along with any statement the advertiser might wish to make. Tables 7–1 and 7–2 present data on the activity of the NAD since its establishment in 1971.

Between 1971 and 1990, the NAD investigated 2,519 cases. During this period, 1,041 (41.3 percent) of contested advertising claims were substantiated. In addition, the NAD negotiated a modification or discontinuance of an advertisement in 1,453 (57.7 percent) of the cases while referring a mere 24 (0.95 percent) of investigated cases to the NARB.[32]

In 1991 the NAD introduced the two new headings "Referred to Government Agency" and "No Substantiation Received" to their decision reporting format.[33] Table 7–3 provides data on case activity of the NAD since the change was implemented.

Of the 240 cases investigated by the NAD from 1991 to 1993, 61 (25.4 percent) of ad claims were substantiated, 153 (63.8 percent) were modified or discontinued, and 14 (5.8 percent) were referred to the NARB. The NAD also referred 8 (3.3 percent) of the cases to governmental agencies and received no substantiation in 4 (1.7 percent) cases.[34] To illustrate current case characteristics, a description of NAD activity during 1993 by product/service classification is depicted in table 7–4.

The Children's Advertising Review Unit

In 1974, the NAD created the Children's Advertising Review Unit (CARU), which is funded by major children's advertisers. The CARU attempts to review advertising through the eyes of children, taking into account that they may lack the sophistication and understanding of adult audiences. The CARU tries to ensure that children's advertising is fair, with the word *fair* encompassing such issues as social values, product presentation, pressure of purchase, endorsements, safety, and premiums.[35]

Table 7-1. Sources of Complaints Handled by the NAD, 1971–93
(percentages)

	NAD Monitoring[a]	Competitor Challenges	Local BBBs[b]	Consumer Complaints	Other[c]
1971	10	2	53	9	26
1972	10	6	20	25	39
1973	51	8	15	14	12
1974	40	11	22	13	14
1975	35	27	16	15	7
1976	52	25	10	10	3
1977	56	21	11	9	3
1978	48	36	12	2	2
1979	34	39	9	16	2
1980	45	37	12	6	0
1981	43	35	12	8	2
1982	39	39	10	9	3
1983	37	42	11	5	5
1984	31	45	10	9	5
1985	37	41	10	11	1
1986	27	43	15	12	3
1987	30	40	13	13	4
1988	36	40	9	9	6
1989	26	43	13	12	6
1990	18	54	10	8	10
1991	14	71	2	6	7
1992	12	72	3	11	2
1993	24	54	3	14	5

Source: National Advertising Division, *NAD Case Report* (New York: National Advertising Division, Council of Better Business Bureaus, 1985); ibid. (1986, 1987, 1988, 1989, 1990, 1991, 1992, 1993, 1994).

a. Based on incoming cases; year 1982 forward based on published reports.

b. Half of all BBB referrals are estimated to be consumer initiated.

c. Includes organized consumer groups, professional or trade associations, and federal and state regulatory agencies.

Ads are evaluated against the CARU guidelines, which were revised in 1983. The staff makes subjective judgments about ads, sometimes with the advice of the CBBB's legal staff. In addition, seven academic advisers are occasionally consulted on specific cases.

Table 7-2. Cases Closed by the NAD, 1971–90

	Substantiated	Modified/ Discontinued	Referred to NARB	Suspended Pending FTC Litigation	Total
Mid-1971 through 1973	191	126	9	0	326
1974	75	65	2	0	142
1975	72	101	0	0	173
1976	67	95	1	0	163
1977	94	60	1	0	155
1978	64	99	0	0	163
1979	63	99	1	0	163
1980	57	78	0	0	135
1981	68	80	1	1	150
1982	61	79	0	0	140
1983	46	64	0	0	110
1984	22	83	0	0	105
1985	31	70	2	0	103
1986	26	80	1	0	107
1987	32	65	1	0	98
1988	27	75	1	0	103
1989	26	76	2	0	104
1990	19	58	2	0	79

Source: National Advertising Division, *NAD Case Report* (New York: National Advertising Division, Council of Better Business Bureaus, 1985); ibid. (1986, 1987, 1988, 1989, 1990, 1991).

CARU's guidelines regarding children's advertising are based upon the following principles:

1. Advertisers should always take into account the level of knowledge, sophistication, and maturity of the audience to which their message is primarily directed. Younger children have a limited capability for evaluating the credibility of information they receive. Advertisers, therefore, have a special responsibility to protect children from their own susceptibilities.

2. Realizing that children are imaginative and that make-believe play constitutes an important part of the growing up process, advertisers should exercise care not to exploit that imaginative quality of chil-

Table 7-3. Cases Closed by the NAD, 1991–93

Decision	1991		1992		1993	
	Number	Percent	Number	Percent	Number	Percent
Substantiated	16	18	14	22	31	36
Modified/discontinued	66	75	37	57	50	57
Referred to NARB	4	5	10	15	0	0
Referred to government agency	2	2	4	6	2	2
No substantiation received	0	0	0	0	4	5
TOTAL	88	100	65	100	87	100

Source: National Advertising Division, *NAD Case Report* (New York: National Advertising Division, Council of Better Business Bureaus, 1992); ibid. (1993, 1994).

dren. Unreasonable expectations of product quality or performance should not be stimulated either directly or indirectly by advertising.

3. Recognizing that advertising may play an important part in educating the child, advertisers should communicate information in a truthful and accurate manner with full recognition that the child may learn practices from advertising that can affect his or her health and well-being.

4. Advertisers are urged to capitalize on the potential of advertising to influence behavior by developing advertising that, wherever possible, addresses itself to positive and beneficial social behavior, such as friendship, kindness, honesty, justice, generosity, and respect for others.

5. Care should be taken to incorporate minority and other groups in advertisements in order to present positive and pro-social roles and role models wherever possible. Social stereotyping and appeals to prejudice should be avoided.

6. Although many influences affect a child's personal and social development, it remains the prime responsibility of the parents to provide guidance for children. Advertisers should contribute to this parent-child relationship in a constructive manner.[36]

As agents of persuasive communication, the advertising industry's "special responsibility" to children is clearly acknowledged and accepted within

Table 7-4. 1993 NAD Cases

Product Service Category	Substantiated	Modified/ Discontinued	Referred to NARB	Referred to Government	No Substantiation Received	Total
Appliances/consumer electronics	0	2	1	0	0	3
Automobiles/accessories/ rentals	1	3	0	0	0	4
Commercial products/ services	0	1	1	0	1	3
Cosmetics/toiletries	8	7	2	0	0	17
Drugs/health/health aids	4	8	0	0	1	13
Finance	2	0	0	0	0	2
Foods/beverages	9	10	2	0	1	22
Home furnishings	0	2	0	0	0	2
Household products	3	3	0	0	0	6
Houseware/garden products	0	1	0	0	0	1
Jewelry	0	1	0	1	0	2
Miscellaneous	0	1	0	0	0	1
Pets/pet products	2	1	0	0	0	3
Retail chains	1	1	0	0	1	3
Sport/hobby equipment	1	3	0	0	0	4
Travel	0	0	0	1	1	2

Source: National Advertising Division, *NAD Case Report* (New York: National Advertising Division, Council of Better Business Bureaus, 1994).

the context of these self-regulatory principles. Yet this accountability appears to be somewhat diffused when it is stated, for example, that "prime responsibility" for children's guidance ultimately lies with their parents and "many influences affect a child's personal and social development." The principles do, however, point out the necessity of developing and maintaining a conjoint effort between parents and the ad industry to effectively address the special concerns of children's advertising. Sociocultural issues are also being addressed by incorporating initiatives that foster positive role portrayals and character representations.

To get a better idea of current CARU activity, the following information is offered as an illustrative example. Self-regulatory monitoring by CARU during 1993 produced a total of seventy-one informal inquiries. Of these, sixty-one involved commercials for the toy industry, six for the food industry, and four fell into the "other" category.[37] Table 7–5 provides data on case activity by CARU for 1993 regarding the nature of these inquiries and subsequent decision results. To give an example of the amount of advertisements that falls under CARU monitoring per month, roughly 1,350 TV advertisements were reviewed in November 1993 (of which 13 came to the attention of CARU) and 1,600 were reviewed in December 1993 (of which 6 came to the attention of CARU).[38] These data suggest that a very small percentage of ads are investigated, and when inquiries do occur, they are either substantiated or modified/discontinued. This suggests a high level of compliance by advertisers with the self-regulatory initiatives and mechanisms of CARU.

Table 7-5. CARU Activity in 1993

	Decision	
Nature of Inquiry	Substantiated	Modified/Discontinued
Product presentation	30	12
Disclosure	0	14
Most selling	0	3
Sales pressure	0	3
Safety	2	4
Premium offers	0	3
TOTAL	32	39

Source: National Advertising Division, *NAD Case Report* (New York: National Advertising Division, Council of Better Business Bureaus, 1994).

───── Governmental Forces

Our focus in this discussion of government forces will be the federal level. Although all states and some local jurisdictions attempt to deal with
advertising, their approaches are often so varied that it is impossible to
arrive at a common position regarding their efforts.

Before we begin a discussion of the formal regulatory process, it is
necessary to stress the importance of the mood of Washington in legislation and enforcement. The philosophy of the White House during any
given administration strongly influences what legislation will be passed
and what areas of enforcement the Justice Department and the Federal
Trade Commission will concentrate on.

The mood of Washington under the Clinton administration is one of
openness to ideas and the wishes of the American public. One primary
concern is the elimination of waste in the federal government. This problem was handled by a nationwide "brainstorming session—including
citizen participation."[39] In this situation, taxpayers were asked to "evaluate and improve the federal government."[40] Clinton wants to hear what
the people have to say and wishes to adapt new regulations to address
their concerns.

Despite the lack of attention to National Advertising Regulation during the eighties, when the value of the proposed regulation was submit-
ted to a cost-benefit analysis, the nineties began with highlights of specific
areas for future concern. Janet Steiger, the FTC chair, said the following
issues would be targeted:

1. Promotional practices of the tobacco and alcohol industries
2. Health claims in food advertising
3. Children's advertising (toy advertising and telephone services)
4. Advertising directed toward the elderly regarding health, safety, and
   financial security
5. Environmental "green claims"[41]

Thus far in the nineties the FTC has addressed these prominent issues:

- In the past, the tobacco industry faced a broadcast ban of advertisements and was restricted to advertising only in print and on billboards. This ban has been further defined to prohibit using a tobacco product's brand name, logo, selling message, color, or design
  feature in any area of a televised event. In other words, if an event is

sponsored by a tobacco company and it is televised, the participants, the equipment, and the arena may not depict any element of the company's image.[42]

- In order to eliminate false advertising claims, the FTC has decreed that thirty-minute television shows that appear to be independent news programs must disclose every fifteen minutes that the "infomercial" is a paid advertisement. The words "The program you are watching is a paid advertisement for [the product or service]," will occur within the first thirty seconds of the program, every fifteen minutes after that, and every time product ordering is presented.[43]
- Several cases of deceptive practices in the 900–number telephone services have been cited. The FTC is proposing legislation that would regulate the advertisement of goods and services sold through the telephone services. Common carriers would be required to submit information relating to the services provided.[44]
- Within the expanding interest in saving the environment, the FTC wants to ensure that environmental marketing claims are not deceptive to the consumer and that the claims are adequately substantiated. Several investigations have focused on ozone safety, degradibility, and pesticide-free claims. The companies must provide adequate support for the claims they make.[45]

Despite the emphasis in the eighties on government regulation that (1) produced benefits that outweighed costs and (2) provided the least expensive solution to the problem,[46] Congress passed the Federal Trade Improvement Act in 1980. This act revised the manner in which the FTC could improve trade rules and regulations, provided for congressional review of the commission's actions, and removed "unfairness" as the basis for trade rules dealing with advertising.[47] Deception had to be present to justify a new industrywide trade rule or court litigation.

During the eighties, the commission adopted new standards for defining deception in advertising. The FTC will find deception if there is a representation, omission, or practice that is likely to mislead the consumer acting reasonably in the circumstances and lead to the consumer's detriment.[48]

Finally, important tools adopted in the seventies remain "on the books" as regulatory options for the Federal Trade Commission. Some continue to be used, while others are in need of refinement. Some of the most important ones are:

1. ADVERTISING SUBSTANTIATION. This policy states that it is illegal to advertise an affirmative claim for a product without having a reasonable basis. Claims must be substantiated if they relate to a product's safety, performance, quality, or price.[49] The commission continues to actively enforce this policy.

2. CORRECTIVE ADVERTISING. This FTC strategy would require advertisers who have made deceptive or unfair claims to spend a certain amount of future advertising dollars to make statements to correct the deception. Listerine was required to spend $10 million to communicate the message "Listerine will not help prevent colds or sore throats or lessen their severity." The effectiveness of this remedy in the present form has been questioned by some researchers, although several excellent modifications for this remedy have been suggested.[50]

3. REDRESS OF CONSUMER INJURY. The Magnuson-Moss Act authorizes the FTC to bring civil actions to redress consumer injury. This could include rescission for contracts, refund of money, return of property, and payment of damages. The FTC can only bring such actions if there has been a violation of a trade regulation or if there is a violation of a cease-and-desist order.[51] The commission has also developed a policy to notify consumers of redress situations.

4. AFFIRMATIVE DISCLOSURE. This policy requires marketers and advertisers to inform potential customers of certain facts about the product or service offered. These disclosures would deal with the deficiencies or limitations of the product or service as well as any positive characteristics. The most widespread use of this policy is in cigarette advertising and labeling.

5. UNIQUENESS CLAIMS. Even substantiated claims may not be used if (unsupported) uniqueness is implied in an advertisement. Wonder Bread advertised that it "helps build strong bodies in twelve ways." While technically true, every bread appears to contribute to growth in much the same way.[52]

Although most current federal government policies continue to point toward a "tightening of the control mechanisms," it is likely that an administration change in the future will mean a switch to a "back to the basics" policy and a focus on deregulation. For the time being, regulations are generated with high consumer involvement. However, the pendulum will always continue to swing.

Current Complementary Natures of the FTC and the NAD/NARB

J. J. Boddewyn indicates several similarities between the forces of self-regulation and governmental forces:[53]

1. Limited outside participation
2. Emphasis on "hard issues and criteria"
3. Choice of cases to handle
4. Shared standards

Concerning limited outside participation, the FTC is primarily composed of civil servants, although the commission has occasionally utilized outside expert witnesses and advisers. The NAD does not use outsiders except as expert advisers and as one member of the five-member panels that review advertising complaints. Both of these organizational structures appear to allow little room for outside participation in the fundamental processes of either organization.

Both the FTC and the NAD/NARB tend to focus on "hard" cases and refuse to handle "soft" issues, such as taste, social responsibility, and morality. The NARB currently has a policy to consider the content of messages for reasons other than truth and accuracy. The NAD/NARB, however, has generally declined to handle such cases because "there is no government agency to which such cases could be referred."[54]

Both bodies also tend to select similar types of cases; each tries to choose cases that set precedents and send important signals to businesses. "Both emphasize cases of poorly substantiated and misleading advertisements, . . . and they both use a case-by-case approach now that the FTC has largely abandoned the pursuit of broad trade regulation rules and industry-wide rounds."[55]

Finally, concerning the issue of shared standards, the NAD/NARB has repeatedly acknowledged that FTC and FDA rules and rulings constitute many of its own main standards. FTC Commissioner Patricia Bailey referred to the NAD/NARB self-regulatory program as "now grounded in FTC precedent and policy."[56]

——— Media Forces

In 1979, a civil antitrust suit was brought against the National Association of Broadcasters (NAB) charging that its television-code rules that regulate television advertising were anticompetitive and in restraint of trade. In 1982, a consent decree was signed by all parties that basically eliminated the NAB code. There are now no formal standards concerning

1. The number of commercial minutes per hour
2. The number of commercials per hour
3. The number of consecutive commercials at each commercial interruption
4. The number of products that can be promoted in a commercial lasting less than sixty seconds
5. The purchase of network time for liquor ads
6. The actual consumption of beer or wine on television[57]

Although there are no longer any specific prohibitions in the areas maintained above, some are still being enforced by individual networks, such as time for liquor ads and consumption of beer or wine on television. All the networks have also maintained their guidelines for deceptive advertising. Advertisements will not be broadcast by networks unless they meet standards of truth, fairness, and adequate substantiation.[58]

However, guidelines concerning the number of commercials per hour, per minute, and the number of products that can be promoted in commercials lasting less than sixty seconds are not being upheld. There are now more advertising messages in a given hour, and the fifteen-second commercial spot is an acceptable industry practice.

Some critics also believe that many cable stations are adhering to even less rigid standards for what is considered deceptive advertising. For example, some toy manufacturers have complained that toy ads on independent cable networks often violate basic network standards.

It would appear that self-regulation on the media's part is in some disarray. The removal of the NAB code and the factionalization of media outlets present continuing problems.

Summary

Returning to the question at the beginning of the chapter—What forces should be allowed to regulate the institution of advertising?—it is clear that there will always be some combination of forces involved in regulation. The exact mix of these forces is dependent on the tenor of the times. Since shifts in sociopolitical attitudes change the mix from decade to decade, one probably should not expect to find a consistent stream and heritage of regulation. A certain amount of instability in the marketplace is inevitable for both advertisers and consumers.

The swing of the sociopolitical pendulum toward a tightening of regulation has allowed consumerism to play a greater role in regulation. Consumers are now asked for direction and suggestions regarding the regulation of the economic marketplace. In this scenario, government must intervene on behalf of the consumer to guide issues of the day.

Will this feeling about the marketplace spill over to the self-regulatory mechanisms currently in place? How will the consumer fare in an environment of the twenty-first century? As discussed in chapter 2, depending on the sets of assumptions the reader makes about such fundamental matters as human nature, the proper role of the market, and the presence of government, the resultant feeling may be one of optimism or pessimism.

Notes

1. Betty Furness quoted in William T. Kelley, ed., *New Consumerism: Selected Readings* (Columbus: Grid, 1973), vi.

2. David Aaker quoted in ibid., iv.

3. Eugene R. Beem, "The Beginnings of the Consumer Movement," in *New Consumerism*, ed. Kelley, 13.

4. Upton Sinclair, *The Jungle* (1906; New York: Viking Press, 1946).

5. Beem, "Beginnings," 17–18.

6. Ibid., 18–19.

7. Francis J. Charlton and William A. Fawcett, "The FTC and False Advertising," *Kansas Law Review* 17 (June 1969): 599–606.

8. *FTC v. Raladam Co.*, 283 U.S. 643.

9. Stuart Chase and Frederick J. Schlink, *Your Money's Worth* (New York: Macmillan, 1927), 254.

10. Mary C. Phillips, *Skin Deep* (New York: Vanguard Press, 1934).

11. Frederick J. Schlink, *Eat, Drink, and Be Wary* (New York: Covici-Friede, 1935).

12. Marshall C. Howard, *Legal Aspects of Marketing* (New York: McGraw-Hill, 1974), 10–11.

13. Beem, "Beginnings," 28.

14. Vance Packard, *Hidden Persuaders* (New York: McKay, 1957).

15. John Kenneth Galbraith, *The Affluent Society* (Boston: Houghton Mifflin, 1958).

16. Rachel Carson, *Silent Spring* (Boston: Houghton Mifflin, 1962).

17. Ralph Nader, *Unsafe at Any Speed* (New York: Grossman, 1965).

18. James F. Engel, Roger D. Blackwell, and Paul W. Minard, *Consumer Behavior* (New York: Dryden Press, 1986), 583.

19. "MIN's Historical Perspective on Consumerism," *Media Industry News Letter,* May 11, 1972, 7.

20. Ralph M. Gaedeke and Warren W. Etcheson, *Consumerism Viewpoints from Business, Government, and the Public Interest* (San Francisco: Canfield Press, 1972), 374–75.

21. Dorothy Cohen, *Advertising* (Glenview, Ill.: Scott Foresman, 1988), 600.

22. "New Harris Consumer Study Causes Few Shocks in Adland," *Advertising Age,* May 30, 1977, 2.

23. Jack Mongoven quoted in Arion N. Pattakos, "Growth in Activist Groups: How Can Business Cope?" *Long Range Planning,* June 1989, 98.

24. David Kiley, "The Whole World Is Watching," *Adweek's Marketing Week,* July 23, 1990, 18.

25. Ibid, 21.

26. Matthew Grimm, "The New Activism Sets the Agenda," *Adweek's Marketing Week,* Apr. 23, 1990, 12.

27. Lydia Saad, "Most Important Problem," *Gallup Poll Monthly,* Jan. 1993, 31.

28. Eric J. Zanot, "The National Advertising Review Board: Precedents, Premises, and Performance" (Ph.D. diss., University of Illinois, 1977), 62–63. See also G. E. Miracle and T. R. Nevett, *Voluntary Regulation of Advertising: A Comparative Analysis of the United Kingdom and the United States* (Lexington, Mass.: Heath/ Lexington, 1987).

29. J. J. Boddewyn, *Advertising Self-Regulation and Outside Participation: A Multinational Comparison* (New York: Quorum Books, 1988), 296.

30. Ibid.

31. National Advertising Division, *NAD Case Report* (New York: National Advertising Division, Council of Better Business Bureaus, 1992), 1; ibid. (1993), 1; ibid. (1994), 1.

32. Ibid. (1985), 1; ibid. (1986), 1; ibid. (1987), 1; ibid. (1988), 1; ibid. (1989), 1; ibid. (1990), 1; ibid. (1991), 1.

33. Ibid. (1992).

34. Ibid., 1; ibid. (1993), 1; ibid. (1994), 1.

35. Gary M. Armstrong, "An Evaluation of the Children's Advertising Review Unit," *Journal of Public Policy and Marketing* 3 (1984): 39.

36. *Self-Regulatory Guidelines for Children's Advertising,* 4th ed. (New York: Children's Advertising Review Unit, National Advertising Division, Council of Better Business Bureaus, 1993), 1–2.

37. *NAD Case Report* (1994), 118.

38. Ibid. (1993), 103, 104; ibid. (1994), 118.

39. Ilyse J. Vernon, "Citizens to Partake in Cutting Waste," *Congressional Quarterly* 51 (Mar. 6, 1993): 513.

40. Ibid.

41. Regulation of Unfair Advertising no. 3, *Journal of Marketing* 55 (Jan. 1991): 87.

42. Regulation of Unfair Advertising no. 1, *Journal of Marketing* 56 (July 1992): 100.

43. Regulation of Unfair Advertising no. 7, *Journal of Marketing* 56 (July 1992): 102.

44. Regulation of Advertising and Promotional Methods, *Journal of Marketing* 56 (Oct. 1992): 100–101.

45. Regulation of Advertising and Promotional Methods no. 3, *Journal of Marketing* 57 (Jan. 1993): 109.

46. "Deregulation: A Fast Start for the Reagan Strategy," *Business Week*, Mar. 9, 1981, 62.

47. William H. Bolen, *Advertising* (New York: John Wiley and Sons, 1984), 59.

48. *Southwest Sunsites, Inc., Green Valley Acres, Inc., Green Valley Acres, Inc., II, Sidney Gross, and Edwin Kritzler v. Federal Trade Commission,* CCH #67,021 (Ca-9, Apr. 1986; BNA ATRR no. 1260, Apr. 10, 1986), 633, in "Legal Developments in Marketing," *Journal of Marketing* 51, no. 1 (Jan. 1987): 114–15.

49. Cohen, *Advertising*, 608.

50. William L. Wilkie, Dennis McNeill, and Michael B. Mazis, "Marketing's Scarlet Letter: The Theory and Practice of Corrective Advertising," *Journal of Marketing* 48 (Spring 1984): 11–31.

51. Cohen, *Advertising*, 608.

52. *ITT, Continental Baking Co., et al.* (1971), 3, *Trade Req. Re,* par. 19, 539.

53. Boddewyn, *Advertising Self-Regulation*, 298. The in-depth discussion of these issues is also taken from Boddewyn.

54. Ibid., 299.

55. Ibid., 300.

56. Patricia F. Bailey, "When Is an Ad Deceptive?: The Regulation of Advertising at the FTC," *New Trends in Advertising*, Proceedings of the American Advertising Federation's 1983–1984 Law and Public Policy Conferences (Washington, D.C.: American Advertising Federation, 1984), 14.

57. Bolen, *Advertising*, 76. See also T. Barton Carter, March A. Franklin, and Jay B. Wright, *The First Amendment and the Fifth Estate* (Mineola, N.Y.: Foundation Press, 1986), 291.

58. See Eric Zanot, "Unseen but Effective Advertising Regulation: The Clearance Process," *Journal of Advertising* 14, no. 4 (1985): 44–51.

8

Ethical Issues in Advertising

Over the years there have been a great many nasty things said about advertising and advertising people. A sampling:

- After reviewing a number of novels about the advertising business published in the post–World War II period, the historian Stephen Fox concluded: "From these dozen novels came a remarkably consistent picture of the advertising world: false in tone, tense in pace, vacant and self-hating, overheated and oversexed."[1]
- In 1976, the economist Robert L. Heilbroner called advertising "the single most value-destroying activity of business civilization." Reviewing his remarks more than ten years later, he found no reason to recant.[2]
- Richard W. Pollay, whose article we examined in chapter 3, summarized the evaluation of advertising by significant humanities and social sciences scholars: "They see advertising as reinforcing materialism, cynicism, irrationality, selfishness, anxiety, social competitiveness, powerlessness and/or loss of self-respect."[3]
- "The ad world," claims the columnist Ellen Goodman, "says that for every problem you see there is a fix and it's quick. Its woes are, by and large, freezer burn, static cling, hemorrhoids, diarrhea, slipping dentures and morning breath. All thoroughly curable by the end of the spot."[4]
- Or consider this thought by the late Howard Luck Gossage, a member of the Advertising Copywriters Hall of Fame and one of advertising's most penetrating gadflies: "To explain responsibility to advertising people is like trying to convince an eight-year-old that sexual intercourse is more fun than a chocolate ice-cream cone."[5]

The Larger Ethical Climate

Now, it could be contended with considerable force that advertising is hardly alone in the ethics jungle:

- A cover story of *Time* magazine was entitled "Lying (Everybody's Doing It, Honest)."
- David Rankin, editorializing in *Newsweek* under the title "A State of Incivility," offered this telling thought: "We have come to accept as normal broken contracts and broken dates; public display of pornography and profanity and, I fear, even theft."[6]
- The media abound with accounts of the ethical improprieties of congresspersons, sports figures, Hollywood deal makers and, of course, media reporters and entertainers.
- Then there are the everyday volatile concerns of right-to-life, right-to-choose, right-to-death, the homeless, gene splicing, etc., etc.

So advertising can be categorized as being in good (or bad) company on the larger societal ethical scale. This is not a new perspective. In 1927, the advertising pioneer Bruce Barton observed: "If advertising persuades some men to live beyond their means, so does matrimony. If advertising speaks to a thousand in order to influence one, so does the church. If advertising is often garrulous and redundant and tiresome, so is the United States Senate."[7]

The Business Perceives Itself

Rather than taking Barton's we're-no-worse-than-the-other-guy position, the trade organizations that represent the advertising business frequently emphasize what they perceive as advertising's societal responsibility. For example, apart from the now familiar litany of serving the sovereign consumers and lubricating the economy, they point to *"enforced" social responsibility* through:

- A Federal Trade Commission that is more of a midnineties presence after its relative inactivity during the Reagan/Bush years
- A proactive Food and Drug Administration that has become quite assertive about advertisers' health claims dealing with terms such as "light," "low fat," "reduced calories," "natural," and the like
- A downright feisty group of state attorneys general who have attempted (albeit unsuccessfully) to establish national guidelines for airline

and rental car advertising in addition to their often robust activities within individual states

and *"voluntary" social responsibility* through:

- Codes of advertisers, media, agencies, and trade organizations
- A much respected National Advertising Review Board
- The Advertising Council and its more than $1 billion efforts dealing with such causes as crime prevention, arresting high blood pressure, AIDS education, and racial intolerance, among hundreds of others
- The Partnership for a Drug Free America with its $1.5 billion in donated space and time over a three-year period
- The American Association of Advertising Agencies' $25 million effort to combat functional illiteracy
- Virtually daily goodwill efforts on the part of advertisers, agencies, and media for a host of state, regional, and local concerns

The Ethical Battlefield

Why, then, the ongoing conflict? Perhaps in part, as William Leiss and associates observed in their provocative work, *Social Communication in Advertising:* "Because it stands at the intersection of industry, communications, and group interactions, advertising can come under attack from anyone who is upset about any feature of these three domains."[8]

Of course, "industry" (marketing practices), "communications" (the mass media), and "group interactions" (stereotyping) represent fertile fields for ethical encounters; thus advertising's everyday functions and interactions make ethical conflict an ongoing reality.

───── Seven Areas of Inherent Ethical Conflict in Ongoing Advertising Practice

Inevitably, we believe, the individual involved in advertising will encounter areas that seem fraught with moral controversy. They are, simply, part of the implicit or explicit experience of many advertising practitioners.

1. *The advertising business is rationalized predominantly by assumptions at the classical liberal end of the neo-liberal continuum.*

Recall the basic assumptions of self-interest, the individual as a competent decision maker, and the virtue of competition leading ultimately to the good of all through a "natural harmony of self-interests" that are central to a classical liberal orientation and the ensuing ideology of the market system.

Now, if one *accepts* these positions (as practitioners generally do) there will also be an acceptance of:

- Consumer sovereignty
- Advertising as a mirror of our wants and needs, a socially passive force

But if one *questions* these positions (as critics generally do) there will generally be an acceptance of:

- Advertising as sovereign, with the consumer open to manipulation
- Advertising as a shaper of behavior, a reinforcer of some values at the expense of others, a socially influential force

Thus, at a very fundamental philosophical level, practitioners and critics are "seeing" advertising from divergent points on the neo-liberal continuum (see figure 2–1). A clash of what constitutes "ethical" behavior is, then, inevitable.

2. *The advertising message is one-sided communication, with the inherent potential of deception by omission.*

In his important work *The Making of Modern Advertising*, the historian Daniel Pope addressed the issue of the bias of the advertising message: "For advertising to play a large part in market strategy, consumers had to be willing to accept this kind of self-interested persuasion as a tolerable substitute or complement to more objective product information."[9]

Thus, advertising is seen as a trade-off, sacrificing value-free information for a form strong on convenience but laced with persuasion. The ethical mine fields seem apparent.

For example, do we (or should we) learn:

- From a beer or liquor ad that nearly 50 percent of automobile fatalities are linked to alcohol?[10]
- From a shampoo ad that a consumer test using disguised samples indicated that all major hair shampoos would do a fine job of cleaning hair, including a liquid dishwasher detergent that was thrown into the test for comparison?[11]
- From a drug ad in a medical journal that a major 1990 study of 109 full-page ads printed in 10 major medical journals revealed that 92

percent failed to meet at least one rule of the Food and Drug Administration?[12]

- From Camel cigarette advertising that a survey conducted for *Advertising Age* indicated that the "Old Joe" campaign "is highly effective in reaching young people, especially kids under 13?"[13]
- That it's estimated a family can conserve $2,500 a year at the supermarket, without sacrificing nutrition, largely by buying store brands rather than their heavily advertised national counterparts?[14]

Might these and other pieces of information be helpful in the consumer's decision-making process? Arguably, yes. Yet, a consumer seeking information such as this would be far more likely to find it in publications such as *Consumer Reports* or, perhaps, reliable word-of-mouth, rather than advertising.

Of course advertisers will contend that their advertising is a nakedly transparent form of self-interested communication, accepted as such by the public, and that other sources of market information should pursue their own agendas while advertisers pursue theirs. The consumer, they would contend, is well served in such a climate of market communication *pluralism*. Of course critics will argue that advertisers take their responsibilities as reliable communication sources too lightly.

By its nature, advertising is a form of "interested" communication. The ethical underbrush, then, is tangled indeed.

3. *The purpose of all advertising is to cause us to think or act in accordance with the advertiser's intent, whether it be noble or venal.*

The legendary advertising practitioner Theodore MacManus was an eyewitness to what several historians consider the beginnings of the "culture of consumption" in the twenties. His thoughts on advertising's role in setting a consumption agenda are insightful:

> The cigarette has become almost a health food—certainly a weight reducer [as in "Reach for a Lucky Instead of a Sweet"]. The humble cake of soap has risen far above its modest mission of cleansing, and confers the precious bloom of beauty upon whomsoever shall faithfully wash. We are all glowing, and sparkling, and snapping, and tingling with health, by way of the toothbrush, and the razor, and the shaving cream, and the face lotion, and deodorant, and a dozen other brightly packaged gifts of the gods. Advertising has gone amuck in that it has mistaken the surface silliness for the sane solid substance of an averagely decent human nature.[15]

Here, advertising sets the consumption agenda. In chapter 3, we explored similar themes from Potter, Schudson, and Pollay, not only in terms of setting priorities for goods and services high in the individual's agenda, but also indirectly, as we had previously noted through Leiss and colleagues, suggesting interpretations about "interpersonal and family relations, the sense of happiness and contentment, sex roles and stereotyping, the uses of affluence, the fading of older cultural traditions, influences of younger generations, the role of business in society, personal autonomy and persuasion, and many others."[16] Then there are, of course, more *specific* areas of concern about advertising's persuasive power as well:

The Advertising of Alcoholic Beverages

Sports Illustrated has devoted a cover story to the relationship between sports and beer. Among its conclusions: "It is the cause of some ugly social problems, which leads some to wonder just what kind of cultural hypocrisy is going on when Americans relentlessly insist on immersing sport—our most wholesome, most admired, even (sometimes) most heroic institution—in a sea of intoxicating drink."[17]

Not surprisingly, advertising figured prominently in the ensuing discussion, as did television, with reference to the eye-catching statement that American children between the ages of two and eighteen see some ten thousand commercials for beer.[18] (It is interesting to note that the same issue of *Sports Illustrated* contained a full-page Budweiser ad. *Sports Illustrated*'s readers between the ages of eighteen and twenty-four are estimated to be 25.5 percent of its total audience. Doubtless many of those are under twenty-one, the legal drinking age in many states.)

The irreverent *Adbusters* magazine lampooned the highly acclaimed Absolut Vodka advertising with a depiction of a coffin over the headline "Absolute Silence" and followed it with spoof ads with headlines such as "Absolute Cirrhosis," "Absolute Beating," and "Absolute Collision." They editorialized that "the alcohol industry's $2–billion a year disinformation campaign should not be the only voice getting out."[19]

The Advertising of Cigarettes

Many consider it unprincipled that over $2 billion is spent annually advertising and promoting a product that has been called the only legally available product that is *harmful when used as intended*.

The "Old Joe" camel campaign from R. J. Reynolds has, of course, generated enormous controversy both in and out of the business, as well as

Reynolds's aborted attempts to sell Uptown cigarettes to African Americans and Dakota cigarettes to "virile young women." Even an anti-smoking campaign from the Tobacco Institute ("Smoking Should Not Be a Part of Growing Up") has been criticized because "they talk about not smoking because it is an adult choice. In many respects, the ads legitimize smoking."[20]

Of course in addition to beer and cigarettes there are concerns about advertising's persuasive activities on behalf of:

- Birth-control products
- Political candidates
- Lotteries
- Etc.

Thus it seems inevitable that since advertising has a persuasive agenda—like preaching, politics, and numerous other activities of our civilization—it will be accused of unethical practice by those who (1) disagree with the *ends promoted* (e.g., smoking) and/or (2) disagree with advertising as the *means* (e.g., whether it is a proper voice in the discourse).

   4. *Frequently, advertising seeks out the individual instead of the individual seeking it.*

Except for catalogs, classifieds, television shopping channels, the Internet, shopping directories, the food ads in the midweek newspaper, and the like, we are frequently the sought rather than the seekers. Not surprisingly, this raises other ethical questions about advertising in areas such as timing, privacy, and frequency to mention only the most obvious. For example:

- An *Advertising Age* survey of one thousand adults concerning the most disliked television commercials showed a clear winner (or loser)—women's personal hygiene products. Many regarded the information in the ads as potentially useful, but found the context—a television viewing room, often in mixed company—totally unacceptable.[21]
- Halfway through a Chicago White Sox–Seattle Mariners baseball game the fans observed the Energizer Bunny marching from one bullpen to the other by way of the outfield. It was dramatic evidence of an ever growing commercial presence in professional sports.
- The controversial "Channel One" program of ten minutes of news and

two minutes of commercials directed at secondary school audiences continues to come under fire by critics who contend it "force-feeds commercials to a captive audience and has little educational value."[22]

- A Grand Rapids, Michigan, radio station gained both attention and derision by using billboards with pictures of the Pope ("Father Knows Best") and a nun ("Nun Better") in promoting its programming.[23]

- *USA Today* announced a program called "Sky Radio" to reach air travelers ("this coveted captive audience") with a "clutter-free eight [commercial] minutes per hour."[24]

- It is now commonplace to find advertising in and about college football stadiums, where only a decade or less ago such a presence would have been considered unseemly.

- Cinema advertising (the appearance of brand advertising before the main feature in theaters) continues to be a growing presence. It is, we believe, the only major form of advertising not requiring even a grudging consent on the part of the potential viewer.

- Another emerging presence is the appearance of advertising messages before feature films on videotapes. In a classic example, the *Advertising Age* columnist Bob Garfield lamented the presence of a Jeep ad before the award-winning movie *Platoon*. The message, he said, was "War is hell. Buy Chrysler."[25]

The reader is invited to add his or her own examples of advertising's apparently ravenous appetite to "get at us."

Now, it can be contended that some of this potential conflict will subside as market and media fragmentation continue apace. That is, we are more likely to find advertising for golf clubs interesting if we read *Golf* magazine, and messages about low-cost insurance policies may be welcomed by the readers of *Modern Maturity*. Indeed, even television, clearly the lightning rod in this and other areas of advertising/ethical encounters, may find it easier to match viewer interests with appropriate advertising as CATV specialization becomes even more routine, with appropriate selectivity in program (and advertising) content.

Yet, it is clear to all that advertisers will be seeking us perhaps more relentlessly than ever before through the mass media, as well as through increasingly untraditional forms. The ethical signal flags are apparent.

5. *Advertising continues to be a controversial third party in the media-audience relationship.*

In newspapers beginning in the mid- to late nineteenth century, in magazines beginning in the early twentieth century, shortly after the earliest days of radio, and from the outset of the American television system, advertising has been a third party within the traditional publisher-reader and broadcaster-audience relationship. The ensuing trade-offs are the ongoing stuff of pride (advertising helps the media to be available less expensively without possible dependence on government subsidies), as well as controversy. Herewith, some of the more common ethical charges:

That Advertising Can Change the Subject of the Media Coverage Itself

The most obvious case is television, where the availability of advertising dollars for some kinds of programming in some particular time slots has proven a seductive lure. How common it is, for example, for college football and basketball teams to reschedule their starting times for games, almost oblivious to the wishes of the spectators, to accommodate network time preferences. Simply, the selection of television subjects and subsequent timing is frequently determined by the explicit or implicit preferences of advertisers.

That Advertising Can Alter the Content of the Media Coverage

A study in the *New England Journal of Medicine* concluded that "magazines become increasingly reluctant to cover smoking risks as their revenue from cigarette ads rises."[26]

Ms. magazine is now supported solely by revenue from readers. In a essay bidding farewell to the old advertising-carrying format, Gloria Steinem, its founder, wrote: "Goodbye to cigarette ads where poems should be. Goodbye to celebrity covers and too little space. Goodbye to cleaning up language so that *Ms.* advertisers won't be boycotted by the Moral Majority. In fact, goodbye to advertisers and the Moral Majority."[27]

That Advertising Can Affect the Type of Available Media

As Calvin whimsically suggests (figure 8–1), media follow markets, so it seems self-evident that we are more likely to see advertising-supported magazines with titles such as *Self-Indulgent Jogger* and *Young and Possessive* than *Migrant Worker* or *Old and Poor.*

Again, there may be hope in the increasing specialization of the media, albeit to pursue advertisers' markets more efficiently. Thus, specialized magazines, zoned editions of newspapers, CATV, interactive media,

Figure 8-1. CALVIN AND HOBBES © Watterson. Dist. by UNIVERSAL PRESS
SYNDICATE. Reprinted with permission. All rights reserved.

and the like seem destined to arrive at a more satisfactory relationship
between the media, their advertisers, and their audiences than the more
heterogeneous couplings. (As customized media become more routine,
remember as a benchmark the May 1985 issue of *Farm Journal,* which
claimed 8,896 different advertising/editorial mixes in that single issue.[28])

There is, however, offsetting concern with the growing "clutter" in *all*
advertising media. Again, however, the focus falls on television, with the
acceptance of the fifteen-second time slot as a standard advertising buy.
The advertising practitioner Stan Freberg reflected on his experience
watching one commercial "island" in a made-for-television movie on
NBC: "There were only a few 15s. But melding one into the other were a
montage of images for: Volkswagen, Visine, Kellogg's Raisin Squares, Fab,
a movie promo, Reunité, an NBC promo, an 'NBC News Digest,' Salad
Bar pasta, Miller Lite, Toyota, a Phil Donahue promo, and the NBC logo.
Quickly now! The second commercial you saw was . . . what?"[29]

6. *The advertising agency commission system continues to reward agencies for what they buy (media space and/or time) rather than what they
produce (ads).*

Historically, the advertising agency receives a commission (usually 15
percent or less) on the cost of the advertising space and/or time it buys
with the advertiser's money. This venerable system is now somewhat in
decline as a sole form of compensation compared with fee and other
performance-based arrangements, but it still represents a significant force
in the process. The former practitioner Howard Gossage observed: "You

show me a business where one's income is dependent on the amount of money spent rather than the amount of money that comes in and I will show you a business that is doomed, even with the very best of intentions, to mutual distrust and enormous psychological barriers."[30]

It is, for example, hard to imagine an agency recommending that an advertiser *cut* her or his advertising budget and devote the savings to some other aspect of marketing activity—say, beefing up the sales force. In addition, some claim that the value of the advertisement itself is diminished because the best ad and the worst have equal (media-cost) value; however, the counterargument would assert that the "good" ad is likely to be repeated more often, thus benefiting the advertising agency.

7. *Finally, the underlying uncertainty regarding the outcome of the advertising process leaves it wide open for differing interpretations of the same event.*

We will not tax the reader with needless repetition here, but encourage the rereading of premise 3 in the introduction. The longtime advertising observer Ed Buxton noted: "The advertising business is rife . . . with baffling intangibles. Nobody knows for sure how it works in many cases. The ad-making process itself is highly subjective, opinionated—and largely unprovable as to what is a good ad and what is not. Such pervasive uncertainties are breeding grounds for disquietude."[31] The reason, according to a leading researcher, is that "it is often difficult to separate the effect of advertising from numerous other factors that influence purchase. The purchase may result from product quality, previous experience with the product, the proximity of a retail outlet that stocks the products, money or credit availability, the absence of deterring factors, such as the veto by a family member or a cut-rate campaign for a competitive product."[32]

As we discussed in the introduction about "clearing the deadwood," these pervasive uncertainties are breeding grounds for ethical ferment as well. For, given the ambiguity of the process, critics and supporters will "see" different advertising realities.

If, for example, a critic and a supporter are each asked to assess such topics as *advertising to children* and *advertising of cigarettes,* one "reality" could depict a highly principled meshing of the self-interests of sellers and buyers in a strictly voluntary relationship, while *another* "sees" the unprincipled actions of manipulation and exploitation involving a crafty communicator and a hapless, if not helpless, audience.

_____ Perspectives on the Ethical Dimensions of Advertising Practice

At this point some observations seem in order:

1. These seven areas of ethical confrontation are likely to be an ongoing presence for advertising practitioners and critics for the foreseeable future.

2. Some of these areas of concern are simply not high on advertising's ethical agenda. For example, studies by Kim B. Rotzoll and Clifford G. Christians as well as Shelby D. Hunt and Lawrence B. Chonko[33] have revealed that practitioners' primary areas of concern are (1) agency/client/vendor relations and (2) the advertising message.

   At the very least, these don't touch such sensitive areas as advertising as a third party with the media and advertising as the seeker rather than the sought.

3. Therefore, critics will tend to regard advertising practice as _unprincipled_ to the extent that (1) they regard advertising practice in any of these areas as _not_ being based on ethical principles and/or (2) that the ethical principles that the practitioners _do_ choose to invoke to support their decisions are different from those the critics would deem appropriate.

Now, what principles _do_ practitioners bring into play? Based on observation and the findings of research, they would seem to be:

a. _The personal criteria of individuals_ (advertisers, agency people, media personnel) that frequently involve some standards of _fairness_, often based on variations of the "Golden Rule," the "Golden Mean," and so on, as well as such prima facie ideals as "Don't lie," etc.

   Following this reasoning, it is obvious to contend that the advertising business contains many principled _people;_ yet, there is no assurance that these highly individualistic criteria will have an impact on the overall ethical standards and performance of the business.

b. _The level of formal principles_ embodied in a host of codes, guidelines, and federal, state, and local regulations. Some examples:

   • A set of principles by the American Advertising Federation and its predecessor from the early 1900s, with the most recent re-

vision in the 1980s as well as similar standards by the American Association of Advertising Agencies
- The guidelines and codes of dozens of trade associations, ranging from the American Wine Association through the National Swimming Pool Institute
- The gatekeeping activities of the various media, including the standards of individual magazines, newspapers, television and radio stations, as well as the activities of the television networks' commercial clearance offices
- Some normative guidelines in areas such as advertising related to children and women by the National Advertising Review Board (NARB), without question the business's most serious self-regulatory effort

Ethical thinking at this level of formal standards commonly involves the assumption of basic truths that should be applied to all—do this, don't do that, etc.—some very general, some quite specific. Several observations in this critical area:

(1) Historically, advertising business efforts at self-regulation have been spurred by the threat of government regulation, which in turn tends to wax and wane with the political winds and therefore provides an unstable platform for ongoing ethical standards. There was, for example, a relative lull in regulatory activity at the federal level during the conservative Reagan/Bush administrations. As previously noted, some of the resulting vacuum was filled in part by vigorous state activity.

(2) The National Advertising Review Board represents a serious and now institutionalized effort, but it is limited as an ethical force by its predominantly post hoc functions as well as lack of exposure to the general public.

There are several assets to the use of these relatively formal standards for ethical decision making:

- They do provide touchstones for practice, if utilized.
- They provide the business with showpieces to promote their good works and to ward off potential regulation.
- In their development and implementation, there is likely to be at least some thoughtful discussion of ethical principles and their application to everyday practice.

The *limitations,* however, are equally apparent:

- The stipulations of the codes are sometimes too general (e.g., "Advertising shall tell the truth, and shall reveal significant facts, the omission of which would mislead the public"[34]) to be readily transferred to moment-to-moment decision making.
- No matter how well-intentioned, they are often not part of the mind-set of the working practitioner when ethical decision making is not critical. (At a meeting of a chapter of the Public Relations Society of America, for example, one of the authors asked the practitioners if anyone could cite any of the principles of the thoughtful PRSA Code of Professional Standards. None could.)

c. *The level of inherent business ethics.* These ethics are learned from watching the actions of others, hearing them explain decisions, and hearing and reading pronouncements from the trade organizations.

In advertising practice, this ethical system is often expressed in terms of "market forces," loosely based on classical liberal thinking and rationalized in the ethical sphere by the concept of *utilitarianism,* the greatest good for the greatest number based on some notion of cost-benefit analysis. One variation commonly used by advertising's defenders is that advertisers pursuing their self-interests will result in the good of the whole—we are reminded of Adam Smith's often abused but much cited phrase "as if by an invisible hand." Thus, the system is assumed to be self-corrective, so "if they don't like the advertising we do, they won't buy the product and we'll be punished at the cash register." A representative statement is found in the American Association of Advertising Agencies' (AAAA) response to a government inquiry about imposing limits on the number of commercials in children's programming. "The AAAA's position is that advertising self-regulation provides adequate safeguards against advertising abuses; that advertising does not harm children and that, therefore, there is no need to protect them from it; and that if a program has 'too many' commercials, children will stop watching it. In sum, market forces will serve the interest of children by naturally regulating what is broadcast to them."[35] The classical liberal heritage is clear—"market forces" will regulate, "naturally."

Thus, the primary asset of the use of utilitarianism as the working ethic for the advertising business is its use to rationalize the entire market system, of which advertising is a part. And it is, of course, a system that can be quite appropriate as an ethical touchstone when the "greatest good for the greatest number" can be estimated.

But therein, it has been argued, lies a problem in implementing utilitarianism for much day-to-day advertising practice centered on the business's crucial product—the advertisement. For, given the difficulty in determining advertising's "effects," which has been discussed so frequently through this book, there are serious problems in predicting the outcome in most advertising situations.

For example, is it "the greatest good for the greatest number" for more than $2 billion to be spent annually on the advertising of cigarettes? Critics contend that this massive effort encourages people to smoke, while defenders argue that it merely tempts smokers to switch brands. There is virtually *no* "evidence," they claim, indicating that advertising stimulates smoking rather than brand switching. The issue then flounders on the ambiguity of what *is* (or is not) done, rather than what *should* (or should not) be done.

Thus there is a rather discomforting irony, with advertising's predominant ethical system (utilitarianism) often being incompatible with the uncertainty of the outcome of its primary product (ads).

——— A Normative Perspective on Advertising's Ethical Milieu

We again return to the premise that the advertising business will continue to be criticized in the ethical arena for either being unprincipled *or* for utilizing principles seen as inadequate for the task. We have observed that two fundamental ethical systems seem to be found in the business in varying degrees—deontological principles (standards to be held to *regardless of effects*—e.g., "Don't lie") and utilitarianism (*concern with effects*—e.g., the greatest good for the greatest number). As Donald P. Robin and Eric Reidenbach observe:

> Of the two dominant ethical traditions, deontology is favored by many moral philosophers today. Further, deontological reasoning offers many people who are critical of marketing an approach for justifying their

attacks. Utilitarianism, the other major tradition, has been attacked by moral philosophers because it seems to suggest certain untenable outcomes when applied to particular hypothetical situations. Utilitarian arguments are used historically to provide much of the ethical justification for the modern economic systems of capitalistic democracies.[36]

Now, considering what we have learned, we offer several observations for the reader's consideration:

1. Deontological thinking, with a dash of fairness, seems perfectly adequate for agency/client/vendor encounters—e.g., don't lie to suppliers, honor contracts, deal with others as you would like to have them deal with you, etc.

2. But to deal adequately with the full range of ethical quandaries outlined in the previous pages, there may be a need to:

   - Not rely on the *randomness* of individual ethical systems
   - Not rely on the *formalities* of codes (which are often not part of the mind-set of individuals in day-to-day decision making) or the *verities* of the regulatory and self-regulatory winds
   - Not become overly comfortable with *utilitarianism,* to the degree that it is often uncritically assumed in day-to-day practice

At a normative level, then, one could suggest that a serious attempt be made to modify the current ethical climate at the *individual firm* level with a more systematic injection of principles of *fairness* into the system, which would compensate for the abstractness and lack of flexibility in many codes and guidelines and the lack of certainty in predicting utilitarian outcomes.

This would, of course, be a long-term effort and would become a force only if there were enough advertisers, agencies, and media who:

- Recognize advertising's ethical performance as a problem
- See it on the larger scale of areas of inherent ethical encounter described in this chapter
- Want to do something about it

One option could be the establishment, within interested firms, of an *ethical ombud,* who could essentially represent the consumer in the advertising transaction, introducing the arguably missing dimension of fairness in some persistent way.

Why might a firm take such action? Certainly, many would not, but:

- The resulting actions and publicity could prove good business in an increasingly skeptical marketplace.
- Such an action would lend itself to effective public relations among employees, stockholders, government officials, consumer organizations, etc.
- Such a principled action could appeal to a high company official with compatible individual ethics.

There could be at least three principal benefits:

1. Such an action would at least assure a raising of ethical issues that are not always apparent under the easy and frequently unexamined assumptions of market utilitarianism.
2. There could be a raising of consciousness on the part of individuals within the firm with, potentially, greater sensitivity to virtually all the likely areas of ethical confrontation.
3. The ongoing presence of the ethical ombud would assure that the enculturation process of the firm includes ethical thinking. The firm would be in essence saying, to existing and new employees, "We take ethics seriously here."

Summary

Advertising is frequently perceived as being ethically unprincipled by critics and is apparently unappreciated by the public in various polls. Yet practitioners point to their social responsibility through self-regulatory codes and guidelines, as well as their various voluntary good works through the Advertising Council, special task forces to deal with social issues, and so forth. In the face of these seeming contradictions, it is apparent that advertising will continue to confront ethical issues because:

1. The advertising business is rationalized primarily by a classical liberal ethic.
2. The advertising message is one-sided communication with the inherent potential of deception by omission.
3. The purpose of all advertising is to cause us to think or act in accordance with the advertiser's intent.
4. Frequently, advertising seeks out individuals instead of individuals seeking it.

5. Advertising continues to be a controversial third party in the relationship between the media and the audience.

6. The agency commission system continues to reward agencies for what they buy rather than what they produce.

7. That underlying uncertainty of the advertising process leaves it open to differing interpretations of the same event.

Advertising practitioners seem to operate on the ethical level of (1) individual criteria, (2) formal principles embodied in codes, and (3) the workday ethic of utilitarianism. It was proposed that a presence of fairness was needed to overcome the limitations inherent in each of the present levels.

Notes

1. Stephen Fox, *The Mirror Makers* (New York: William Morrow, 1984), 206.

2. Robert L. Heilbroner, "Advertising as Agitprop," *Harpers*, Jan. 1986, 71.

3. Richard W. Pollay, "The Distorted Mirror: Reflections on the Unintended Consequences of Advertising," *Journal of Marketing* 50 (Apr. 1986): 18.

4. Ellen Goodman, syndicated column, *News-Gazette* (Champaign-Urbana, Ill.), Feb. 8, 1992, A-4.

5. Howard Luck Gossage, *Is There Any Hope for Advertising?* ed. Kim Rotzoll, Jarlath Graham, and Barrows Mussey (Urbana: University of Illinois Press, 1986).

6. David Rankin, "A State of Incivility," *Newsweek*, Feb. 8, 1988, 10.

7. Bruce Barton quoted in Fox, *Mirror Makers*, 108.

8. See William Leiss, Stephen Kline, and Sut Ghally, *Social Communication in Advertising: Persons, Products, and Images of Well-Being* (New York: Methuen, 1986), chap. 12.

9. Daniel Pope, *The Making of Modern Advertising* (New York: Basic Books, 1983).

10. "Absolute Silence," *Adbusters*, Summer–Fall 1992, inside cover.

11. "Shampoos," *Consumer Reports*, Sept. 1984, 192.

12. "Drug Ads Aimed at Doctors Misleading, Study Finds," *News-Gazette* (Champaign-Urbana, Ill.), June 1, 1992, A-5.

13. Gary Levin, "Poll Shows Camel Ads Are Effective with Kids," *Advertising Age*, Apr. 27, 1992, 12.

14. "How to Save $2500 a Year in the Supermarket," *Consumer Reports*, Mar. 1988, 156–63.

15. Fox, *Mirror Makers*, 117.

16. Leiss, Kline, and Ghally, *Social Communication*, 3.

17. "Beer: How It Influences the Games We Play and Watch," *Sports Illustrated*, Aug. 8, 1988, 70.

18. Ibid., 78.

19. "Absolute Silence."

20. Fara Warner, "Tobacco Takes Back the Fight," *Adweek's Marketing Week,* Feb. 24, 1992, 16–17.

21. Scott Hume, "'Most Hated' Ads: Feminine Hygiene," *Advertising Age,* July 18, 1988, 3.

22. Scott Donator, "More Turbulence for 'Channel One,'" *Advertising Age,* May 18, 1992, 48.

23. "Radio Station Tunes into Controversy with Boards," *Advertising Age,* Apr. 20, 1992, 17.

24. "Introducing an Unusual New Vehicle for Live News," *Advertising Age,* May 4, 1992, 38–39.

25. Bob Garfield, "Ad Review," *Advertising Age,* Oct. 19, 1987, 32.

26. Ronald K. L. Collins, *Dictating Content* (Washington, D.C.: Center for the Study of Commercialism, 1992), 41.

27. Maria Braden, "Ms. Doesn't Miss the Ads," *Quill,* Jan.–Feb. 1992, 25.

28. "Data Bank Driven Binding," *Marketing Communications* 10 (Mar. 1985), 46.

29. Stan Freberg, "Irtnog Revisited," *Advertising Age,* Aug. 1, 1988, 32.

30. Gossage, *Is There Any Hope?* 9.

31. Ed Buxton, "Fear and Loathing on Agency Row," *Adweek,* Sept. 5, 1983, 34.

32. Jack Haskins and Alice Kendrick, *Successful Advertising Research Methods* (Lincolnwood, Ill.: NTC, 1992), 10.

33. Kim B. Rotzoll and Clifford G. Christians, "Advertising Agency Practitioners' Perceptions of Ethical Decisions," *Journalism Quarterly* 57 (Aug. 1980): 425–31; Shelby D. Hunt and Lawrence B. Chonko, "Ethical Problems of Advertising Agency Executives," *Journal of Advertising* 16, no. 4 (1987): 16–24.

34. American Advertising Federation, "Advertising Principles of American Business," reprinted as "Practitioners' Perceptions" in Clifford C. Christians, Kim B. Rotzoll, and Mark Fackler, *Media Ethics: Cases of Moral Reasoning* (New York: Longman, 1991), 283–84.

35. Patty Siebert, "AAAA Files Kid-Vid Comments with FCC," *The 4A's Washington Newsletter,* Jan. 1988, 2.

36. Donald P. Robin and Eric Reidenbach, "Social Responsibility, Ethics, and Marketing Strategy: Closing the Gap between Concept and Application," *Journal of Marketing* 51 (Jan. 1987): 46.

Afterword

In 1958, a perfectly wonderful book was published called *Madison Avenue, U.S.A.* Among his hundreds of interviews with the leading lights of advertising practice, writer Martin Mayer held a session with J. Walter Thompson's legendary James Webb Young. Mayer recounts: "Early in 1956, *Fortune* magazine sent a girl researcher up to see Jim Young at the Thompson company. . . . 'She wanted to know about all the changes in the advertising business in the last twenty-five years,' Young says. 'When I told her there hadn't been any, she nearly fell off her chair. But it's true.'"[1]

This is a useful perspective to begin this tentative exploration of advertising's future with which we close the book. For it can be contended that advertising's basic institutional forms were in place prior to 1920—i.e., the relationships between advertisers, agencies, and media; the agency commission system; the dependency of the media on advertising revenue; criticism and reform.

This does not, of course, suggest that advertising is immune to a host of variables to which it must react as part of a complex society. For example, entering the nineties, a futurist group at the Leo Burnett agency highlighted four factors that seem particularly likely to affect advertising throughout the decade.[2] Two of the most important:

- Consumer de-massification
- Media fragmentation

Let's examine, and embellish, each.

Consumer De-Massification

"Our society," observes Burnett's director of research, "is no longer made up of a majority of people who fit the 'Cleaver family' (husband, wife, children) description. In fact, Cleaver families [named after the popular fifties television program "Leave It to Beaver"] today account for less than 25% of our total population."[3]

The implications for advertising are, of course, massive. Marketers will find it increasingly difficult to profile homogeneous groups of buyers because "loosely knit clans will become the norm as single parents, confused kids and more oldsters compete for love and support."[4] The emphasis on "oldsters" is particularly telling, as it's estimated that "in the next three decades the number of Americans over 85 is expected to increase fivefold."[5] As one market researcher observed, "We're changing from the melting pot theory to a kind of salad bowl."[6] But, make no mistake about it, there will be advertising-supported media attempting to seek the market segments, whatever their configuration.

Media Fragmentation

Currently, well over half of American homes are linked to cable television systems delivering over fifty channels. Add to this some ten thousand "highly selective" magazine titles,[7] competition for time from VCR watching, a virtual explosion in direct marketing and nontraditional media forms (e.g., supermarket grocery carts equipped with commercial-playing monitors),[8] the increasing commercialization of the Internet, and the combinations of possible advertiser/potential customer interactions are simply enormous.

There are, of course trade-offs here. On the positive side, it may be that a tighter fit for the advertiser/media/potential customer links will result in less irritation with irrelevant advertising messages. For example, Seagram Company has announced it will attempt to run ads "that only go to the portion of the magazine's circulation that reaches drinkers or those likely to drink these brands"[9]—hence, a better "fit" between media readers/viewers/listeners and advertisers.

But on the negative side, there is certainly agreement that there will be *more* advertising, caused primarily by shorter television commercials (e.g., four fifteen-second commercials in a minute rather than two thirty-second messages), but also caused by the expansion to other media forms, many quite intrusive (e.g., ads in the classroom, in restrooms, on prerecorded videotapes, on virtually every available square foot of space in sports arenas, etc.).

There are several other significant variables in advertising's future.

Population Factors

By the turn of the century the much discussed "baby boomers" will be between their midthirties and their early fifties, with predictable effects upon institutions. This is a group much sought after by marketers due to their sheer numbers and overall affluence, and they will clearly continue to influence the subjects and tone of advertising messages.

The population of the United States will continue to diversify, so more advertising attention will be directed toward the consumption potentials of specific groups (e.g., "Advertising trade journals today commonly have new opportunities in the $278 billion market of black consumers or the $141 billion Hispanic market").[10]

It has been estimated that in the relatively near future 75 percent of women may be in the work force, possibly reinforcing the trend toward smaller households, which will lead to expanded efforts by advertisers to reach an increasingly elusive population segment.

Finally it is reasonable to expect the average life span to lengthen as a result of medical advances, better nutritional and exercise habits, and the diffusion of Health Maintenance Organizations (HMOs) promoting preventative medicine and health-care practices.

Technological Changes

Inventions, of course, do not arrive at fixed intervals. Even when the potential is present, a host of economic, political, or cultural factors may keep an innovation from being fully developed. (If much of the futurist literature of the forties were to be believed, we would all be commuting by personal autogyros and living in fully roboticized homes.)

What seems safe at this juncture is to project a twenty-first century strongly infused with computer-assisted technology, affecting virtually every facet of society through "multisensual media, smart roads and robotics."[11] And, as one visionary puts it, "thanks to a telecommunications system that will link phone networks, cable-TV systems, satellite broadcast and multimedia libraries, getting connected to anything or anyone in the most remote parts of the world will be a simple matter."[12] For better or for worse, this also will presumably enable more personalized persuasion appeals—with all of the ethical land mines that suggests.

Regulatory Climate

As we have seen, there have been three relatively clearly defined periods of intense regulatory activity in relation to advertising: the first two decades of the century, the thirties, and the late sixties through the midseventies. As the regulatory hand is lightened, excesses eventually emerge, thus leading to a new cycle of confinement. Certainly, for example, the Reagan administration's laissez-faire economic philosophies supported deregulatory practices. Yet, as history would indicate, there is every reason to expect a future tightening of the reins. In middecade, this seems less likely with a Republican Congress, but the flash points will probably remain special audiences (particularly children) and controversial product categories, particularly cigarettes and alcohol. The potential problems in even more personalized direct marketing efforts are also readily apparent.

Global Imperatives

The notion of Spaceship Earth is apparently gaining credence again with worldwide "green" movements. Yet, the specters of overpopulation, poverty, hunger, and pollution are present for all wishing to look. In a nineties "future poll" for *Time* magazine, a majority of respondents felt that the twenty-first century would have more environmental disasters, poverty, and disease.[13] These visions can give pause to individuals pondering the allocation of planetary resources by market mechanisms that at times seem deadened to the imbalances of the haves and have-nots. The advertising business is not insensitive to these issues (e.g., "green marketing" became a topical subject in the early nineties), and there is much good work done at the advertiser, agency, and media levels (e.g., "Ad Council Targets Racism in Wake of L.A. Rioting").[14] Yet, these offerings are unquestionably secondary in relation to the priorities of consumption. One may pause to realize that there is now more than $2 billion spent advertising and promoting cigarettes in this country and speculate what good might ensue if the same amount was spent to encourage programs meant to lead to *healthy* ends.

Worldview

Certainly, as Idea Systems ⟵⟶ Institutions, it is clear that advertising enjoys full flower as an institution under idea systems encompassing such assumptions about human nature as the positive values of self-interest, competition, and the belief that the private pursuit of profit will ultimately lead to societal gain. To the degree that we can change these ideas, the expectations and tolerations of advertising will change apace.

In many ways, the heart of this issue hinges on perceptions of the individual as a decision maker. For, as we have seen, advertising flourishes in economic systems that allow considerable latitude for individuals to make their own decisions. And as the previously "closed" economies of eastern Europe, the former Soviet Union, and the People's Republic of China move toward greater reliance on market mechanisms, it seems inevitable that advertising will have an increasing presence in these and other economies placing emphasis on individual decision making, rather than central planning, for allocation of resources.

The broadest question, then, is likely to be To what extent can societies through the last decade of this century and beyond continue to allow individual decision making instead of some type of government direction? Topics such as these will put this fundamental ideological question to a test:

Energy

The world has some finite natural energy resources and there is an enormous gap between the use of those limited resources in the have versus the have-not countries. Can we allow individuals to continue to call their own energy shots through their purchases or will elimination, or at least redirection, of opportunities be necessary?

Ecology

Can we survive as a living planet? What price of individual and corporate freedom are we willing to pay to attempt to restore clean seas and waterways, healthy air, drinkable water, nontoxic environments? Again, can we continue to allow corporate individual decision making, even though the end result may be a depletion of our precious ecosystem?

•　•　•

In a very fundamental sense, then, the answers to these and related questions will determine the *presence* of advertising in the remaining years of this century and beyond.

As for its *impact*, that, of course, will continue to be the stuff of debate, due in no small part to differing assumptions about rationality, competition, the proper dimensions of self-interest, the state of the economy, and the proper role of regulation, as developed in chapter 2.

"Increasingly regulated on one side and increasingly scorned or ignored by consumers on the other, advertising has been shooting smaller weapons at a more garrisoned target. Along with most other contemporary institutions, advertising now has trouble finding anybody to believe it."[15]

Thus concluded the historian Stephen Fox in assessing advertising's modern *influence* on society—an influence that, he contended, reached its peak in the twenties in spite of advertising's substantially enhanced *presence* now. Of course we can refer back to Schudson's perspective of "capitalist realism" (chap. 3) and its understanding that advertising does not need to be *believed* in order to selectively reinforce parts of our value system over others.

On reflection, then, a realistic assessment of advertising in society, now or in the foreseeable future, should require at least the following questions:

- What, precisely, is the advertising *issue* under discussion, given due consideration for the tendency to generalize from very specific pieces of the advertising experience?
- What are the essential *assumptions* about human nature, the relationship between the individual and society, etc., that are held by the contending parties?
- Which *set* of assumptions, or which combination, do *you* find most compatible?

For a host of reasons that we hope we've made clear, advertising in contemporary society seems destined to remain ambiguous, structured in many cases by its own internal complexities and by the interests and passions of those observing it.

Daniel G. Boorstin once observed, "If we consider democracy as a set of institutions which aim to make everything available to anybody, it would not be an overstatement to describe advertising as the characteristic rhetoric of democracy."[16] It is our hope that these chapters have provided you with some perspectives, and an array of analytical tools, to come to a clearer understanding of this fascinating rhetoric.

Notes

1. Martin Mayer, *Madison Avenue, U.S.A.* (New York: Harper and Brothers, 1958), 21.
2. *The Burnettwork* 8 (Jan.–Feb. 1990): 8.

3. Ibid.

4. "The Nuclear Family Goes Boom," *Time*, Fall 1992, 42.

5. Ibid.

6. Charles S. Clark, "Advertising under Attack," *CQ Researcher*, Sept. 13, 1991, 662.

7. *The Burnettwork* 8 (Jan.–Feb. 1990): 8.

8. See Thomas McCarroll, "Grocery-Cart Wars," *Time*, Mar. 30, 1992, 49.

9. Gary Levin, "Seagram Runs Selective Ads," *Advertising Age*, Jan. 27, 1992.

10. "Advertising under Attack," 662.

11. "Dream Machines," *Time*, Fall 1992, 34.

12. Ibid., 40.

13. "The Future Poll," *Time*, Fall 1992, 13.

14. "Ad Council Targets Racism in Wake of L.A. Rioting," *Advertising Age*, May 11, 1991, 1.

15. Stephen Fox, *The Mirror Makers* (New York: William Morrow, 1984), 380.

16. Daniel G. Boorstin, "Advertising and American Civilization," in *Advertising and Society*, ed. Yale Brozen (New York: New York University Press, 1974), 11–12.

KIM B. ROTZOLL is the dean of the College of Communications at the Urbana-Champaign campus of the University of Illinois. His other co-authored or co-edited books include *Media Ethics: Cases and Moral Reasoning, Advertising Theory and Practice,* and *Is Advertising Worth Saving?*

JAMES E. HAEFNER is the head of the Department of Advertising at the University of Illinois at Urbana-Champaign, director of the Cummings Center for Advertising Studies, and director of the James Webb Young Fund.

STEVEN R. HALL is a doctoral student in the Institute of Communications Research at the University of Illinois at Urbana-Champaign.

Mar 10/08